Marin Waldorf School Parent Handbook

Waldorf Student Reading List

Waldorf Education
A Family Guide

EDITED BY PAMELA JOHNSON FENNER & KAREN L. RIVERS

ILLUSTRATED BY MARY BETH LUGRIN RAPISARDO

Waldorf Education— A Family Guide

Edited by Pamela Johnson Fenner and Karen L. Rivers

Illustrated by Mary Beth Lugrin Rapisardo

WALDORF EDUCATION —A FAMILY GUIDE, Copyright 1995 by Pamela Johnson Fenner, Michaelmas Press. This edition is an expansion and revision of a work previously published as *The Marin Waldorf School Parent Handbook* published by the school in 1988 and subsequently by Michaelmas Press, © 1989, 1990, 1991, 1992 by Pamela Johnson Fenner.

10 9

Printed in the United States of America

The opinions and statements expressed herein are those of the individual authors. Although the editors have exhaustively researched all sources to ensure the accuracy and completeness of the information contained in this book, we assume no responsibility for errors, inaccuracies, omission, or any inconsistency herein. Every effort has been made to trace owners of copyright material, but in some cases this has not proved possible. The editors would be pleased to know of any corrections.

Published by:
Pamela Johnson Fenner
Michaelmas Press   www.waldorfshop.net/michaelmaspress
PO Box 702
Amesbury, MA 01913-0016 U.S.A.   Telephone: 978-388-7066

ISBN 0-9647832-1-5

To our children —

Liesel Ware Fenner

Gillian Jackson Fenner

Francesca deGomez Fenner

and Cherie´ Rivers

— and to the children of the next millennium

Foreword

It is a crisp October morning as my six year old son gets ready for school. Try as we might, we never seem to get out the door on time, and this makes me crazy. Thank goodness there's no traffic today. I try not to get stressed, but there are so many things that need doing. I plan most of the day before I even get on the freeway.

Twenty minutes later, we're at the school and thankfully on time. Before we walk to Stephen's classroom, I check to see—does he have his lunch? Are his shoes tied? Is his shirt on backwards? Still in a rush, we run down to his kindergarten classroom. Yet as I step in the door, I am suddenly aware of a completely different world. Around me I see warm quieting colors, inviting me in. Stephen is greeted with a loving hug, and sent on his way to join the others in their rich imaginative play. The teacher is already beginning to prepare the bread that will be eaten with lunch today. I find myself wishing I was six years old, too. But most of all, I am so happy that I am able to offer my son the experience of a Waldorf education.

Welcome to *Waldorf Education: A Family Guide*. I cannot tell you how pleased I am that this compendium has made its way into the mainstream. The first of its kind, this book explores the unique world of Waldorf Schools (also known as Steiner Schools). Yes, Waldorf Education is a world of its own. Its history, philosophy, and curriculum are like no other, and within them are the promise of an educational program that understands, loves, and respects the whole child.

To begin, I'd like to highlight the trails of discovery you will find within. Our first stop, "An Overview of Waldorf Education" is an historical one, and a good place to begin. There you will find out the answers to such questions as "Who is Rudolf Steiner?", "What is Anthroposophy?" and "How did Waldorf Education get its start?". You will find that within the answers to these questions lies a rich, deep, and passionate vision to meet the needs of the whole child.

"Moving Through the Grades" describes the nature of each classroom's experience as a child moves from Kindergarten to the Eighth Grade. As you read you will discover the weaving of an amazing tapestry of integrated academic skills, each building on the one before. Morning verses, main lessons, handwork, beeswax, sewing, painting, drama, singing, and instrumental playing are all ways to open a child's awareness, and in this section you find out how teachers help that unfold.

New parents, grandparents, friends, and educators unfamiliar with Waldorf education often have many questions. In the section "What About . . . ?" *A Family Guide* addresses many of the most common concerns. From "Do they teach religion?" to "Will my child have difficulty moving on to high school?" , readers will find reassurance that their child's academic as well as social needs are being met.

As we know, education doesn't start and stop at the door to the classroom. "Family Life and Waldorf Education" offers many suggestions on how parents might bridge school and home life. Thus a parent can further enhance a child's Waldorf experience.

"Celebrations Through the Year" is a cavalcade of the lovely and enriching festivals celebrated by Waldorf schools across the United States. Though not all festivals are celebrated by all schools, each one marks changes in the seasons as well as changes within each of us.

Those who want more information can turn to the comprehensive Appendix of resources at the close of the book. It includes an annotated reading list; Waldorf Education resources and a list of organizations inspired by the work of Rudolf Steiner.

Waldorf Education: A Family Guide provides an incredible framework of the history, pedagogy, and philosophy of the Waldorf Movement. As in any educational paradigm, there may be ideas included that stir things up for the reader. This is good. It is out of this mixing and stirring that new ideas come. So read, question and wonder. But most of all enjoy *Waldorf Education: A Family Guide.*

Denise Torres, Michaelmas 1995

Contents

Foreword .... Denise Torres   viii

An Overview of Waldorf Education

Waldorf Education and the Social Demands of the 1990s .... Joan Almon   3
Learning That Grows With the Learner .... Henry Barnes   8
Rudolf Steiner: A Sketch of his Life .... John Davy   13

Moving Through the Grades

A Special Note to the Reader: Each Waldorf School is Unique .... Pamela Johnson Fenner   21
Life in the Kindergarten .... Deborah Meyer   22
Morning Verse for Grades 1 - 4 .... Rudolf Steiner   24
First Grade .... Barbara Jacquette and Alan Greene   25
Second Grade .... Manette Teitelbaum   27
Third Grade .... Daniel Bittleston   29
Fourth Grade .... Source unknown   31
Morning Verse for Grades 5 - 12 .... Rudolf Steiner   33
Fifth Grade .... East Bay Waldorf School   34
Sixth Grade .... East Bay Waldorf School   36
Seventh Grade .... Chanticleer   38
Eighth Grade .... Lucille Clemm   40
Waldorf High School/Upper School .... Betty K. Staley   42

Understanding the Waldorf Curriculum

Creating a Balance in Thinking, Feeling, and Willing .... René Querido   53
Rhythm in the Kindergarten .... Nancy Foster   55
Knitting and Intellectual Development .... Eugene Schwartz   58
Role of Temperaments in the Life of a Child .... René Querido   60
The Beauty of Color .... Manette Teitelbaum   68
Eurythmy in Education .... Steiner Centre   70
Literacy, Not Just Reading .... Arthur M. Pittis   72
Drama, a Tool for Learning .... Grace Broussard and Richard Lindley   77
Waldorf Education and Science .... Clifford Skoog   79
A Humanist Talks About Waldorf Education .... Joseph Chilton Pearce   82

What About . . . ?

Building a Waldorf School Community .... Robert Schiappacasse   85
Religion and Waldorf Education .... Karen Rivers   89
The Nature of Culture and Multiculturalism in Waldorf Schools .... Jeffrey Kane, Ph.D.   91
Waldorf and Montessori: A Comparison .... Barbara Shell   97
Teaching an Eight-Year Cycle .... Herbert Saperstein   100
"It Was Once So Easy to Say" .... Richard Betz   102
Commentary on Waldorf Graduates .... James Shipman   104

Family Life and Waldorf Education

Home Life .... Sharifa Oppenheimer   109
Bringing Nature Inside: Creating a Seasonal Garden .... Carol Petrash   113
Building a Bridge to Waldorf Fathers .... Jack Petrash   118
Push-Button Entertainment and the Health of the Soul .... Christopher Belski-Sblendorio   121
Who Me — Make a Doll? .... Sherry Pimsler   125
When Your Child Needs Help: To Tutor or Not to Tutor .... Anne Jurika   127
A Birthday Celebration at School .... Pamela Johnson Fenner   129
Thoughts on Children's Parties .... Midge Heath   132
The Unbirthday Party .... Sandra Holland   136
Rhythm During the Summer .... Karen Rivers   138

Celebrations Through the Year

Festivals — Seeds of Renewal .... Philip Wharton   143
Michaelmas .... Karen Rivers   145
All Hallow's Even .... Richard Moeschl   147
Thanksgiving .... Karen Rivers   150
Advent Wreath .... Gertrud Mueller Nelson   152
Advent Garden .... Nancy Foster/Waldorf Kindergarten Association   154
Celebrating Advent in One Classroom .... Anne Jurika   155
Hanukkah: The Festival of Lights .... Karen Rivers   157
A Token of the Victory of the Sun: The Christmas Festival .... Rudolf Steiner   159
Epiphany: Day of the Holy Kings .... Karen Rivers   161
Festivals of Spring .... Lucille Clemm   163
Spiritual Threads of Passover and Easter .... Karen Rivers   165
May Day .... Kathryn Hall   169
Whitsun .... Karen Mortenson   171
St. John's Tide .... Karen Rivers   174

Appendix

Acknowledgements 179
Authors and Sources 181
Recommended Reading 187
Anthroposophical Resources 197
    Waldorf Education Resources 199
    Anthroposophical Society 202
    Biodynamic Agriculture 203
    Curative Work 203
    Medical Practice 204
    Health and Hygiene 204
    Community 205
    For the Elderly 205
    The Arts 205
    Finance and Consultancy 208
    Publishing 208
    Christian Community 210

The need for an effective, truly human education has never been greater than it is today. Our times call out for individuals who can recognize needs and bring right initiatives to the world. To achieve this, children need schools in which childhood is appreciated and allowed to unfold, and where capacities of imagination and intelligence, of courage and fortitude, of practicality and skill are gradually awakened, nurtured, and strengthened.

— The Association of Waldorf Schools of North America

An
Overview
of
Waldorf
Education

Those in the public school reform movement have some important things to learn from what Waldorf educators have been doing for many years. It's an enormously impressive effort toward quality education, and schools would be well advised to familiarize themselves with the basic assumptions that underlie the Waldorf movement.

— Ernest Boyer, President
Carnegie Foundation for the
Advancement of Teaching

Waldorf Education and the Social Demands of the 1990s

JOAN ALMON

If it is impossible to decide which comes first, the chicken or the egg, then it's equally difficult to decide whether social change precedes educational change or vice versa. What is clear at the moment is that the 1990s are full of dramatic change at the social level as well as within education. Whether the change will simply be turbulent and chaotic or whether a sense of direction and transformation will evolve remains to be seen. More and more, American Waldorf education finds itself catapulted out of the quiet backwaters where it has largely resided and into the midst of the central educational and social questions of the decade. At times Waldorf educators feel overwhelmed by the new challenges, but on the whole they are grateful to be able to participate, to be able to bring their insights and experience to an age bursting with possibilities.

Worldwide, the winds of social change began blowing visibly about 1989 and were most evident in the demise of the Berlin Wall, the disintegration of the Iron Curtain, and shortly thereafter the end of apartheid in South Africa. While these countries are working intensely on new social forms, they are also exploring new forms of education. Those who have grown up with the message of totalitarianism permeating their classrooms place a strong value on independence in education. They want an education for their children that allows them to blossom and grow, to shine forth as strong individuals in their adulthood.

Even before the walls of communism crumbled, educators from the East began to look for new approaches to education. As soon as the walls were gone, the Waldorf community was flooded with requests for help in founding schools and training programs. Today, there are Waldorf training programs, courses, or schools in Russia, Hungary, Poland, the Czech Republic, Romania, the former Yugoslavia, and the Baltic lands. Other countries join the list each year. Teachers and parents are making huge sacrifices to found schools that will help children to grow into strong and creative individuals. They have stood at the barricades and seen firsthand the need to stand upright as free and independent human beings while at the same time displaying a strong social concern. They look to Waldorf educators and others for help in creating an education that fosters these qualities.

A similar process is at work in South Africa today. Within the black townships there is tremendous interest in new forms of education that will help strengthen the children to stand as individuals yet be part of a community. The courage with which Waldorf teachers – black and white – are meeting the challenges of uniting our divided society is an inspiration to us all.

Although less outwardly dramatic, recent changes in the United States also point to new possibilities for the future. Here, too, the winds of change are blowing, doors are opening, and people are thinking new thoughts and exploring new possibilities. One sees this strongly in the realm of education. In the late 1980s the United States acknowledged that its education was in crisis. Huge numbers of children were not learning to read and therefore not learning other subjects, either. By third or fourth grade many children showed strong signs of burnout; by adolescence many could not form independent thoughts. Discipline had disintegrated in many schools, and violence in the schools was growing. Drug use and alcoholism, teen pregnancy, and high school drop out – problems that were viewed as nightmares in the 1950s – had become commonplace by the 1980s.

Fortunately many people in the world of education were painfully honest about the problems. They acknowledged that American education had hit rock bottom and needed help to come back to a healthy existence. School systems began to experiment in many directions, and one heard more and more about choice in public education, about site-based management where teachers had much more freedom than before, about school districts where parents were free to create schools they felt would meet their children's needs. At the moment it seems that anything and everything is possible in the world of public education.

In addition, the question of vouchers is being looked at in new ways. Vouchers or tax credits are a way of providing education funds directly to families and letting them choose schools run by the government or run independently, as they see fit. The funds are used as tuition for one or the other. The voucher system gives greater freedom to parents than do choice systems limited to public education. Ten years ago it seemed that vouchers would be of interest only if they were created by middle class and upper class conservatives. Now they are being introduced by people with strong social concerns for all children. A few cities such as Milwaukee now have a voucher program for low-income families.[1]

There is great concern, however, that if the government controls the vouchers, independent schools will be pressured to conform to a uniform picture of education. This would run counter to the present need for more independence and freedom in education. Hence, an even more radical step toward freedom in education has been taken in a number of cities, including Indianapolis (IN) and Albany (NY), and a few other cities where funds for the voucher program are raised from the business community rather than from the government.[2]

Waldorf educators view this latter approach to education, where the funding of schools comes from the economic sphere rather than the government sphere, as having much potential for the future. Already in the spring of 1919 the founder of Waldorf education, Rudolf Steiner, addressed the workers at the Waldorf Astoria Cigarette Factory. He spoke to them of the need for education to be independent of state control in order for it truly to meet the needs of the child. Without such freedom from state control, it is hard to help children grow into strong individuals. The goal of democratic government is to guarantee the equal rights of its citizens, and this equality is an important aspect of life. Equality under the law means treating *everyone* alike. In legal realms that is the ideal, but education strives for a different idea – to recognize the unique individuality of each student and to cultivate it. Although the state has a responsibility to guarantee the equal rights of each child to an education, the education itself is best provided when it is free from the state's concerns.

Now in the United States the idea of business helping to support education is beginning to appear, and this opens many new doors. But even here one must proceed with caution, because it will be tempting to the business community to put their own needs before those of the students. Business interests may want to use education to "train" students for jobs rather than to educate for life, or they may want to use the school as an advertising forum. One sees this tendency strongly in Chris Whittle's Edison Project, through which he hoped to create hundreds of for-profit schools. Because Whittle already sells, to schools, media programs that contain advertisements, it is not hard to imagine how he envisioned making profits in his schools. Nonetheless, the clearer the public is regarding its own ideas on education, the more likely it is to succeed in moving forward with a voucher system. The possible pitfalls should not paralyze us, but simply make us cautious where we place our feet.

Although Waldorf education is primarily concerned with strengthening independent education that can reach out and serve all families, it is also becoming more involved in finding ways to help low-income children who are presently in public schools. As one African American educator said to a group of Waldorf teachers, "The public schools are killing our children. Can't you do anything to help?" The answer is yes, and in that community work is moving forward to found a Waldorf school to serve low-income families. In other communities courses are being offered to interested public school teachers who then take Waldorf ideas back to their own classrooms. In yet other communities Waldorf educators and public educators are working together to create Waldorf schools within the public sector.

One such public Waldorf school began in Milwaukee in September 1991. Going from nursery through fifth grade, it serves 350 children, many of whom live in inner-city neighborhoods. Those who are involved with the school are amazed at how the children are blossoming. Although many of the children had previously developed a dislike for schooling, they now come eagerly to school and express great sadness when vacations begin. They are discovering that learning can be a joy when it is brought in forms appropriate to their ages. In the kindergarten the emphasis is on creative play as well as on artistic activity, movement and music, verses and stories. A foundation is laid for academic study but it is experienced through the creativity and play of the young children. In the elementary grades academic subjects are taught, along with foreign languages, handwork, and *eurythmy*, a movement art developed by Steiner, but all subjects are taught through the arts and speak strongly to the imagination of the students. They are inspired by the timeless stories drawn from fairy tales, legends and myths. Hearing tales from all over the world gives them a context for appreciating their own heritage within the richness of human culture.

Such a school cannot be viewed as a panacea for all of society's problems. Nor was the creation of such a school easy, for it has demanded the utmost from its teachers, many of whom took part in a three-year Waldorf training while teaching. The school also receives much help from experienced Waldorf teachers. Yet it clearly speaks strongly to the children, and its existence is one more indication that the 1990s are radically different from the 1980s, when few would have dreamt of such a program. In that decade not many had heard of Waldorf education although by 1989 there were about 100 schools or kindergartens in North America. The place of Waldorf education then was humorously described by a bumper sticker that read, "Waldorf - the best kept secret in education." How different it is now when the Waldorf Association is flooded with requests for information from public school districts, communities wanting to start Waldorf schools, researchers wanting more information about Waldorf education, and parents seeking places to move so that they can send their children to a Waldorf school.

What is it that parents and educators are seeking today that draws them toward Waldorf education, and toward other forms of holistic and transformative education? They are looking for an education that speaks to all aspects of the child, not just to the head alone. They seek an education that is respectful of all races, ethnic groups, and religions, and finds a place for many cultures in the school curriculum. As adults they seek a school that will respect them and value their own growth and development as well as their children's. Most central, however, is parents' and educators' wish for an education that has a deep respect for the growth of the individual child while at the same time nurturing a healthy social process. They want their children to grow into creative human beings, and they know this takes time.

The deeper we delve into the needs of the 1990s the more Waldorf teachers realize that they cannot work in isolation. They need to be part of the large educational community and welcome opportunities to work with those active in public education, in programs for low-income children, prison work for youth, remedial and curative programs and much more. At the same time, Waldorf educators are deepening their work with one another. Colleagueship has always been a central facet of Waldorf schools, which are faculty-led with an elected faculty chair, rather than being directed by a principal or headmistress.

In meeting the demands of our times, however, we see more clearly than ever the need to work together in a deeper and more conscious manner. Waldorf faculties work together in the carrying of the children, but also in their study of *anthroposophy,* Steiner's overarching philosophy which sheds light on the spiritual nature of the human being. Such study nourishes the soil into which Waldorf education sets its roots. In a healthy Waldorf school, it is not only the children who are growing but the teachers, as well. In addition, more and more parents look to the school as a place for inner renewal and growth.

The modern Waldorf school is challenged to become a healthy community that fosters the growth of all individuals connected with it. Individuals in turn lend their strength to the development of the school, allowing it to serve as a center of renewal for the community around it. The ripples can extend widely, and in this decade fraught with difficulties but filled with possibilities, it is hard to say how far education can go in fostering social renewal. But it is clear that the possibility exists and that it is time to take courage in hand and allow education and society to bring forth the best in each other.

— Revised excerpt from *Holistic Education Review,* December, 1993.

Original article can be obtained from Waldorf Kindergarten Association.

An introduction to Waldorf education

Learning that Grows with the Learner

HENRY BARNES

When children relate what they learn to their own experience, they are interested and alive, and what they learn becomes their own. Waldorf schools are designed to foster this kind of learning.

Waldorf education has its roots in the spiritual-scientific research of the Austrian scientist and thinker Rudolf Steiner (1861-1925). According to Steiner's philosophy, man is a threefold being of spirit, soul, and body whose capacities unfold in three developmental stages on the path to adulthood: early childhood, middle childhood, and adolescence.

In April of 1919, Steiner visited the Waldorf Astoria cigarette factory in Stuttgart, Germany. The German nation, defeated in war, was teetering on the brink of economic, social and political chaos. Steiner spoke to the workers about the need for social renewal, for a new way of organizing society and its political and cultural life.

Emil Molt, the owner of the factory, asked Steiner if he would undertake to establish and lead a school for the children of the employees of the company. Steiner agreed but set four conditions, each of which went against common practice of the day:

- that the school be open to all children;
- that it be co-educational;
- that it be a unified twelve-year school;
- that the teachers, those individuals actually in contact with the children, have primary control of the school, with a minimum interference from the state or from economic sources.

Steiner's conditions were radical for the day, but Molt gladly agreed to them. On September 7, 1919, the Independent Waldorf School (Die Freie Waldorfschule) opened its doors.

Today there are more than 600 Waldorf schools in 32 countries. In North America there are more than 110 schools affiliated with the Association of Waldorf Schools of North America, and one public Waldorf program in Milwaukee, Wisconsin and a handful of charter schools using Waldorf methods. There are also 33 full-time Waldorf teacher training institutes around the world. Of these, four are in the United States and one in Canada.

No two schools are identical; each is administratively independent. Nevertheless, a visitor would recognize many characteristics common to them all.

Early childhood

Infants and young children are entirely given over to their physical surroundings; they absorb the world primarily through their senses and respond in the most active mode of knowing: imitation. Imitation is the power to identify oneself with one's immediate environment through one's active will.

Everything – anger, love, joy, hate, intelligence, stupidity – speaks to the infant through the tone of voice, the physical touch, bodily gesture, light, darkness, color, harmony, and disharmony. These influences are absorbed by the still forming physical organism and affect it for a lifetime.

Those concerned with the young child – parents, caregivers, nursery and kindergarten teacher – have a responsibility to create an environment that is worthy of the child's unquestioning imitation. The environment should offer the child plenty of opportunities for meaningful imitation and for creative play. This supports the child in the central activity of these early years: the development of the physical organism. Drawing the child's energies away from this fundamental task to meet premature intellectual demands robs the child of the health and vitality he or she will need for later life. In the end, it weakens the very powers of judgment and practical intelligence the teacher wants to encourage.

In the nursery-kindergarten children play at cooking; they dress up and become mothers and fathers, kings and magicians; they sing, paint and color. Through songs and poems they learn to enjoy language; they learn to play together; hear stories, see puppet shows, bake bread, make soup, model beeswax, build houses out of boxes, sheets and boards. To become fully engaged in such work is the child's best preparation for life. It builds powers of concentration, interest, and a life-long love of learning.

Middle childhood

When children are ready to leave kindergarten and enter first grade, they are eager to explore the whole world of experience for the second time. Before, they identified with it and imitated it; now, at a more conscious level, they are ready to know it again, by means of the imagination – that extraordinary power of human cognition – that allows us to "see" a picture, "hear" a story, and "divine" meanings within appearances.

During the elementary school years, the educator's task is to transform all that the child needs to know about the world into the language of the imagination, a language that is as accurate and as responsible to reality as intellectual analysis is in the adult. The wealth of an earlier, less intellectual age – folk tales, legends and mythologies, which speak truth in parables and pictures – becomes the teacher's inexhaustible treasure house.

When seen through the lens of the imagination, nature, the world of numbers, mathematics, geometrical form, and the practical work of the world are food and drink to the soul of the child. The four arithmetical operations can, for instance, be introduced as characters in a drama to be acted out with temperamental gusto by first graders.

Whatever speaks to the imagination and is truly felt stirs and activates the feelings and is remembered and learned. The elementary years are the time for educating the "feeling intelligence." It is only after the physiological changes at puberty, which mark the virtual completion of the second great developmental phase, that imaginative learning undergoes a metamorphosis to emerge as the rational, abstract power of the intellect.

Adolescence

Throughout the glorious turbulence of adolescence, the personality celebrates its independence and seeks to explore the world once again in a new way. Within, the young person, the human being to whom the years of education have been directed, is quietly maturing. Eventually, the individual will emerge.

In Steiner's view, this essential being is neither the product of inheritance nor of the environment; it is a manifestation of the spirit. The ground on which it walks and into which it sinks its roots is the intelligence that has ripened out of the matrix of will and feeling into clear, experienced thought. In traditional wisdom, it is this being who "comes of age" around age 21 and is then ready to take up the real task of education – self-education – which distinguishes the adult from the adolescent.

In the classroom

How is Steiner's theory reflected in Waldorf classrooms? The school day begins with a long uninterrupted lesson. One subject is the focus, the class deals with it in-depth each morning for several weeks at a time. This long main lesson – which may well run for two hours – allows the teacher to develop a wide variety of activities around the subject at hand. In the younger grades lively rhythmic activities get the circulation going and bring children together as a group; they recite poems connected with the main lesson, practice tongue twisters to limber up speech, and work with concentration exercises using body movements.

After the day's lesson, which includes review of earlier learning, students record what they learned in their notebooks. Following recess, teachers present shorter "run-through" lessons with a strongly recitational character. Foreign languages are customarily taught from first grade on, and these lend themselves well to these later morning periods. Afternoons are devoted to lessons in which the whole child is active; eurythmy, artistically guided movement to music and speech, handwork, art, or gym, for example. Thus, the day has a rhythm that helps overcome fatigue and enhances balanced learning.

Class teachers continue with a class from one year to the next, ideally, right through elementary school. With rare exceptions these teachers lead the main lesson at the beginning of each day. Other teachers handle special subjects, but the class teachers provide the continuity so often lacking in our disjointed world today.

The class teacher and the children get to know each other very well and it is this teacher who becomes the school's closest link with the parents of that class. When problems arise, the strong child/teacher/parent bond helps all involved work things through instead of handing the problem on to someone else.

This experience of class community is both challenging and deeply rewarding to teachers. Having to prepare new subject matter as their students get older from year to year is a guarantee against going stale. Children begin to see that a human being can strive for a unity of knowledge and experience.

When children reach high school age, the pupil-teacher relationship changes: specialist teachers replace the class teacher.

The ascending spiral of knowledge

The curriculum at a Waldorf school can be seen as an ascending spiral: the long lessons that begin each day; the concentrated blocks of study that focus on one subject for several weeks. Physics, for example, is introduced in the sixth grade and continued each year as a main lesson block until graduation.

As the students mature, they engage themselves at new levels of experience with each subject. It is as though, each year, they come to a window on the ascending spiral that looks out into the world through the lens of a particular subject. Through the main-lesson spiral curriculum, teachers lay the ground for a gradual vertical integration that deepens and widens each subject experience and, at the same time, keeps it moving with the other aspects of knowledge.

All students participate in all basic subjects regardless of their special aptitudes. The purpose of studying a subject is not to make a student into a professional mathematician, historian, or biologist, but to awaken and educate capacities that every human being needs. Naturally, one student is more gifted in math and another in science or history, but the mathematician needs the humanities, and the historian needs math and science.

The choice of a vocation is left to the free decision of the adult, but one's early education should give one a palette of experience from which to choose the particular colors that one's interests, capacities, and life circumstances allow. In a Waldorf high school, older students pursue special projects and elective subjects and activities, but, nevertheless, the goal remains: each subject studied should contribute to the development of a well-balanced individual.

If the ascending spiral of the curriculum offers a vertical integration from year to year, an equally important horizontal integration enables students to engage the full range of their faculties at every stage of development. The arts and practical skills play an essential part in the educational process throughout the grades. They're not considered luxuries but fundamental to human growth and development.

The arts and practical skills

Waldorf teachers believe that the human being is not just a brain – but a being with heart and limbs – a being of will and feeling, as well as of intellect. To ensure that education does not produce one-sided individuals, crippled in emotional health and volition, these less conscious aspects of our human nature must constantly be exercised, nourished, and guided. Here the arts and practical skills make their essential contribution, educating not only heart and hand but, in very real ways, the brain as well.

The sixth grader who, as part of the class study of Roman history, has acted Cassius or Calpurnia, or even Caesar himself, has not only absorbed Shakespeare's immortal language but has learned courage, presence of mind, and what it means to work as a member of a team for a goal greater than the sum of its parts.

The ninth grader who has learned to handle red-hot iron at the forge, or the senior who caps years of modeling exercises by sculpting a full human figure have, in addition to a specific skill, gained self-discipline and the knowledge of artistic form.

Students who have worked throughout their education with color and form; with tone, drama, and speech; with eurythmy as an art of bodily movement; with clay, wood, fiber, metal, charcoal and ink, (and ideally, with soil and plants in a school gardening program), have not only worked creatively to activate, clarify, and strengthen their emotions, but have carried thought and feeling down into the practical exercise of the will.

When the Waldorf curriculum is carried through successfully, the whole human being – head, heart, and hands – has truly been educated.

— Association of Waldorf Schools of North America.

(AWSNA)

*All over the world, there are activities - schools, communities for
the handicapped, farms, hospitals and medical practices, artists
and architects, banks and businesses - whose work acknowledges
a special debt to Rudolf Steiner. His life spanned the last part of
the nineteenth century and the first part of this. But his inspiration
is proving capable of reaching into the end of our century with
enhanced rather than diminished vigor. Who was Rudolf Steiner?
And what is the meaning of his life and work for our time?*

A sketch of his life and work

Rudolf Steiner

JOHN DAVY

Steiner was born in Kraljevec (Lower Austria) in 1861, and died in Dornach, Switzerland in 1925. He thus saw the end of an old era and the birth pangs of a new one. His life echoes the transition intimately. The outer surface of the late nineteenth century gave little hint of the extraordinary events the twentieth century would bring, and a superficial biography of the first part of Steiner's life might not easily foresee the extraordinary activities of his later years. Yet the seeds of the later are to be found in the earlier times.

Outwardly, we see the gifted son of a railway official, growing up in the small peasant villages of Lower Austria. He attends the village schools, and then the modern school in Wiener Neustadt. His father is a freethinker, and sees his son as a railway engineer rather than as a priest (the more usual destination for bright boys from the villages). Steiner takes a degree in mathematics, physics and chemistry and later writes a philosophical thesis for a doctorate.

He supports himself through university and afterwards by tutoring. He is drawn into literary and scholarly work. The famous Goethe scholar, Professor Karl Julius Schroer, who has befriended the young man, arranges for him to edit the scientific works of Goethe for a new complete edition. He participates actively in the rich cultural life of Vienna. Then he is invited to Weimar, to the famous Goethe archive, where he remains for seven years, working further on the scientific writings, as well as collaborating in a complete edition of Schopenhauer. The place is a famous center, visited by the leading lights of Central European culture and Steiner knows many of the major figures of the artistic and cultural life of his time.

In 1894 he publishes *The Philosophy of Freedom*[1] but is disappointed by its reception (we shall return to the significance of this work). Then, as the end of the century approaches, he leaves the settled world of Weimar to edit an avante-garde literary magazine in Berlin. Here he meets playwrights and poets who are seeking, often desperately, for alternatives of various kinds. The city is a focus for many radical groups and movements.

Steiner is invited to lecture at the Berlin Workers' Training School, sponsored by the trade unions and social democrats. Most of the teaching is Marxist, but he insists on a free hand. He gives courses on history and natural science, and practical exercises in public speaking. His appeal is such that he is invited to give a festival address to 7,000 printers at the Berlin circus stadium on the occasion of the Gutenberg jubilee. But his refusal to toe any party line does not endear him to the political activists, and soon after the turn of the century, he is forced to drop this work.

Beginning in 1899, Steiner's life begins to change quite rapidly. Only later does he give a more personal glimpse of his inner struggles, which matured into a far reaching decision during the 1890's.[2] On August 28, 1899 he publishes in his magazine a surprising article about Goethe's mysterious "fairy tale", *The Green Snake and the Beautiful Lily*. The essay is entitled "Goethe's Secret Revelation", and points definitely, if discreetly, to the "occult" significance of this story.

The article attracts the attention of a Count and Countess Brockdorff, who invite Steiner to speak to one of their weekly gatherings. The Brockdorffs are Theosophists. They give Steiner the first opportunity to realize the decision he has come to during the last years of the century, namely to speak openly and directly out of the inner faculties of spiritual perception he has known since childhood and has been quietly nurturing, developing and disciplining ever since.

Quite soon, Steiner is speaking regularly to groups of Theosophists, which upsets and bewilders many of his former friends. There is uproar at a lecture on the medieval scholastics which he delivers to the Giordano Bruno Society. The respectable if often radical scholar, historian, scientist, writer and philosopher is emerging as an "occultist". It is truly shocking to many of those around him. Steiner knows he is running risks of isolation. Only in the fringe culture, the Theosophists at first have an ear for what he now wants to say. Yet he sees around him a culture in decay, and profound crises to come. Much later, he writes:

> In the spiritual domain, a new light upon the evolution of humanity
> was seeking to break through into the knowledge gained during the last
> third of the nineteenth century. But the spiritual sleep caused by the
> materialistic interpretation of these acquisitions in knowledge prevented
> any inkling of this, much less any awareness of it. Thus the very time
> arrived which ought to have developed in a spiritual direction of its
> own nature, but which belied its own nature – the time which began
> actually to bring about the impossibility of life.[3]

Steiner's decision to speak directly of his own spiritual research was not prompted by a desire to set up as a spiritual teacher, to feed curiosity or to revive some form of "ancient wisdom". It was born out of a perception of the needs of the time. As we approach the end of our century, it is perhaps easier to appreciate what Steiner meant by times which "begin to bring about the impossibility of life". This lay behind what he described as "my heartfelt desire to introduce into life the impulses from the world of the spirit... but for this, there was no understanding."[4]

It took him nearly two decades to create a basis for the renewing impulses in daily life which he sought to initiate. At first he worked mainly through lectures to Theosophists and others, and through articles and books. These works remain an extraordinarily rich resource which is still far too little known in the English-speaking world.

Within quite a short period of years, Steiner surveyed with clarity and intimacy the spiritual realities at work in the kingdoms of nature and in the cosmos, the inner nature of the human soul and spirit and their potential for further development, the nature and practice of meditation, the experiences of the soul before birth and after death, the spiritual history and evolution of humanity and the earth, and detailed studies of the workings of reincarnation and karma.

The style is sober and direct throughout, and it often calls for an effort to realize the quite remarkable nature of these communications. For they are not derived from earlier sources, nor was Steiner acting as a spokesman for a spiritual guide. They are fruits of careful spiritual observation and perception – or, as Steiner preferred to call it, "spiritual research" – undertaken in freedom by an individual thoroughly conversant with, and deeply serious about, the integrity of thought and apprehension striven for in natural science.

After seven or eight years, Steiner began to add to his work in "spiritual science" a growing activity in the arts. It is significant and characteristic that he should see the arts as a crucial bridge for translating spiritual science into social and cultural innovation. (We are now vividly aware of what happens when natural science bypasses the human heart and is translated into technology without grace, beauty or compassion). Between 1910 and 1913 he wrote four Mystery Plays, which follow the lives of a group of people through successive incarnations, and include scenes in the soul and spiritual worlds as well as on earth. With his wife, Marie von Sievers, an actress, new approaches to speech and drama were initiated. In this period, too, lie the beginnings of eurythmy, an art of movement which makes visible the inner forms and gestures of language and music.

In 1913 the foundation stone was laid for the first Goetheanum at Dornach in Switzerland. This extraordinary building in wood, with its vast interlocking cupolas, gradually took shape during the years of the First World War, when an international group of volunteers collaborated with local builders and craftsmen to shape the unique carved forms and structures which Steiner designed.

The building stimulated much innovation in the use of form and is now increasingly recognized as a landmark in twentieth century architecture.[5] Yet Steiner was not concerned to build an impressive monument. He regarded architecture as the servant of human life, and designed the Goetheanum to support the developing work of Anthroposophy[6] and particularly the work in drama and eurythmy.

An arsonist caused this building to burn to the ground during the night of December 31, 1922. There survived only the great sculpture of the "The Representative of Humanity" on which Steiner had been working in a neighbourhood workshop with the English sculptress Edith Maryon. Steiner soon designed another building which was completed after his death and now serves as a centre for the world-wide Anthroposophical Society and its School of Spiritual Science. There is a magnificent stage and auditorium, where the Mystery Plays are given regularly as well as Goethe's *Faust* in full, other plays and concerts, and frequent performances of eurythmy.

As the First World War neared its end, Steiner began to find ways to work more widely and deeply for a renewal of life and culture in many spheres. Europe was in ruins, and could have been ready for quite new impulses. Attempts to realize a "threefold social order" as a political and social alternative at that time did not succeed, but the conceptual basis which Steiner developed exists as a seed which is even more relevant for today.

Steiner's social thinking can only be adequately grasped in the context of his view of history, which he saw, in direct contrast to Marx, as shaped fundamentally by inner changes in human consciousness in which higher spiritual beings are actively participating. Just in this century, quite new experiences are awakening in the human soul. (Since Steiner's time this is a good deal more apparent than it was then.) But we cannot expect to build a healthy social order except on the basis of a true and deep insight not only into the material but also into the soul and spiritual nature and needs of human beings as they are today.

These needs are characterized by a powerful tension between the search for community and the experience of individuality. Yet community, in the sense of material interdependence, is the basic fact of economic life and of the world economy in which it is today embedded. But individuality, in the sense of independence of mind and freedom of speech, is essential to every creative endeavour, to all innovation, and to the realization of the human spirit in the arts and sciences. Without spiritual freedom, our culture will wither and die.

Individuality and community, Steiner urged, can only be lifted out of conflict if they are recognized, not as contradictions but as a creative polarity rooted in the essential nature of human beings. Each pole can bear fruit only if it has appropriate social forms. We need forms which ensure freedom for all expressions of spiritual life, and forms which promote brotherhood in economic life. But the health of this polarity depends on a full recognition of a third human need and function, the social relationships between people which concern our feeling for human rights. Here again, Steiner emphasized that we need to develop a distinct realm of social organization to support this sphere, inspired by a concern for equality - not equality of spiritual capacity or material circumstance, but that sense of equality which awakens through recognition of the essential spiritual nature of every human being. In this lies the meaning and source of every person's right also to freedom of spirit and to material sustenance.

These insights were the basis from which Steiner then began to respond to a great variety of requests for new beginnings and practical help in many fields. He was approached by doctors, therapists, farmers, businessmen, academics and scientists, theologians and pastors, and by teachers. From these beginnings have grown the many activities which have survived all the tensions and upheavals of this century, and which continue to spread round the world.

Best known, of course, is the work in Waldorf education and curative education. The former originated in a request from Emil Molt, director of the Waldorf-Astoria cigarette factory, for a school to which his employees could send their children. The homes, schools and village communities for handicapped children and adults are also flourishing.

Biodynamic agriculture originated in a course of lectures at Koberwitz in 1924, held at the request of a group of farmers concerned at the destructive trend of 'scientific' farming. It has made its main impact so far in European countries, but is now attracting rapidly growing interest in many other parts of the world. From Steiner's work with doctors, a medical movement has developed which includes clinics and hospitals and a variety of therapeutic work. From a request by a group of German pastors there arose the Christian Community, a movement of religious renewal. The art of eurythmy, which also serves the educational and therapeutic work, has developed strongly, and there are now a number of eurythmy schools where a full four-year training is given. Other training centers – for teacher training, agriculture, the arts, social work, and general orientation in anthroposophy – have grown up in recent years.

Rudolf Steiner died on March 30, 1925, surrounded by new beginnings. The versatility and creativity which he revealed in his later years are phenomenal by any standards. How did he achieve all this?

The last part of the twentieth century is bringing a growing recognition that we live within a deeper reality which we can call spiritual, to which at present we have direct access only through altered conditions of consciousness. We are also learning to see that these realities were known in the past, described in other images and languages, and were the source of all great religions and spiritual teachings. They have been obscured and forgotten for awhile as our scientific culture devoted itself to the material world revealed by the senses.

Many individuals have glimpses during their lives of spiritual realities. Some recollect a more consistent experience in childhood. A few achieve some form of enduring insight as adults. Rudolf Steiner spoke little of his spiritual life in personal terms, but in his autobiography[7] he indicates that from childhood he was fully conscious of a world of invisible reality within the world of everyday.

His inner struggle for the first forty years of his life was not to achieve spiritual experience, but to unite this fully with the forms of knowledge and insight of our time, and in particular with the language and discipline of natural science. Historically, this can be seen as the special challenge and contribution of Steiner's life and work. He himself saw the scientific age, even in its most materialistic aspects, as an essential phase in the spiritual education of mankind. Only by forgetting the spiritual world for a time and attending to the material world, he said, could there be kindled new and essential faculties, notably an experience of true individual inner freedom.

Steiner indicated that his own capacities to meet, in the most practical way, the life questions and working needs of people from so many walks of life, had their origins in the struggles of his earlier years, when he kept almost complete silence concerning his inner experiences, and gradually learned to grasp and articulate their relationship to the mode of consciousness from which science arises. His book *The Philosophy of Freedom* embodies a first fruit of these struggles – he himself described it as "a biographical account of how one human soul made the difficult ascent to freedom". Studied more intimately, this book contains the basis for a path of knowledge that can lead the soul to discover spiritual experience and reality right into the world of ordinary thought and experience. Along this path, Steiner sought to develop a spiritual science which is a further development of the true spirit of natural science.

This path led him in his thirties to waken to an inner recognition of the "turning point of time" in human spiritual history, brought about by the incarnation of the Being we know as the Christ.[8] He saw that the meaning of this event transcends all differentiations of religion, race or nation, and has consequences for all humanity, of which we are as yet aware only of the beginnings. This also led him to know the new presence and working of the Christ, which has begun just in this century, not in the physical world but in the sphere of invisible life forces of the earth and mankind.[9]

Steiner was therefore not concerned to bring old teachings in new forms, nor to promulgate doctrines of any kind, but to nurture a path of knowledge in freedom, and of love in action, which can meet the deep and pressing needs of our times. These are the ideals, however imperfectly realized, by which those who find in Anthroposophy a continuing inspiration for their lives and work, seek to be guided.

Moving Through the Grades

The teacher must be one who is true in the depths of his being. He must never compromise with untruth, for if he did so we should see how through many channels untruth would find its way into our teaching, especially in the way we present our subjects. Our teaching will only bear the stamp of truth if we are intently striving after truth in ourselves.

— Rudolf Steiner

A special note to the reader
Each Waldorf School is Unique

PAMELA JOHNSON FENNER

As the children move through the grades there are developmental milestones for which there are appropriate curriculum guidelines for the teachers. One strength of the Waldorf approach is that the teachers are free to select the specific age-related material and present it in their own way for that particular group of children. **Thus each class in each Waldorf school is unique and yet universal.**

The following descriptions of the curriculum in each grade, therefore, are general, not definitive and have been edited to reflect the characteristics of the particular grade. The ages and grades of this section reflect those common to most Waldorf schools in the United States. [For the corresponding grades and ages in Waldorf or Steiner schools in Britain, please review the "Authors and Sources" section in the "Appendix".]

Many of the descriptions were originally written for *Chanticleer,* a seasonal publication of the Marin Waldorf School, and for the School's *Parent Handbook.* Others were derived from newsletters and handbooks from other Waldorf communities. They are offered for your inspiration and information.

If you have more questions about the curriculum, please review the sections, "Understanding the Waldorf Curriculum" and "What About …?" and, whenever possible, talk with a Waldorf teacher.

Life in the Kindergarten

DEBORAH MEYER

Have you ever sat down next to a 4 or 5 year old, clapped your hands and said, *"Peas porridge hot, peas porridge cold, peas porridge in the pot, nine days old."*? If you have, you'll notice how quickly they begin to say and do it with you. What is this quality in young children that allows them to spontaneously enter into the world of rhythm and movement? It lies at the very center of a young child's being. It is imitation.

When we look at the first seven years of a child's life, we ask ourselves, "How does a child learn? What is her source of learning?" The young child is most awakened in her will (his limbs); it is through this awakening in the will life that the child has a natural feeling to do and imitate the world around him. How then will what she learns be of benefit in later life?

> The small child exerts unconscious energies never again equaled. He is a being of will and imitation, identifying himself with each gesture, intonation, mood and thought of his environment, and making these his own free activity of creative, imitative play. He is engaged in the great task of shaping and transforming his inheritance to individual and specific use. To divert these formative energies from their task in these early years is to weaken the vitality, undermine the health, and take from the developing child the endurance and strength he will need in adult life. Premature demands upon the intellect, sharp criticism, undue excitement of fantasy – as by television – and over stimulation of the senses combine to rob the child of his native physical resources.[1]

Given this view of the child, the kindergarten teacher knows well that everything in the child's environment is his teacher. Therefore, the teacher's task is to create an environment worthy of the child's unquestioning imitation. The child instinctively places his trust in the world around him, copies it without hesitation and thinks that all that surrounds him is truly good!

It is most important in the early years that the child is led into *doing* things in an enriching environment which brings about healthy growth. His toys, his books, the color of his room and clothing, the nature of his food, the speech he hears, the song he sings are the seeds now planted from which will spring forth in later life reverence for all that surrounds him – a love of learning, and appreciation of art and beauty.

A morning in the kindergarten begins with creative free play. Through this play the child acts out the world around him. Together we become mothers caring for our babies, or birds learning to build a nest. As we put away our toys (each having their own special names), we learn to love and care for our things.

When we light a candle each day, as we sing good morning to the birds and the bees, the flowers and the stones, the child forms a relationship to the world of nature. We learn to bake and paint, go over the rainbow with our crayons and model bright colored beeswax.

Together we learn to work with our hands in useful ways, delighting in the joy and beauty of what we create. Through a feeling of love and warmth, our Kindergarten becomes a little family, a small universe within a larger universe.

— *Chanticleer,* a publication of the Marin Waldorf School

Morning Verse for Grades 1 - 4

The sun with loving light

Makes bright for me each day,

The soul with spirit power

Gives strength unto my limbs,

In sunlight shining clear

I revere, Oh God,

The strength of humankind,

Which Thou so graciously

Has planted in my soul,

That I with all my might,

May love to work and learn.

From thee stream light and strength

To thee rise love and thanks.

Rudolf Steiner

First Grade

BARBARA JACQUETTE AND ALAN GREENE

First Grade is a bridge between the kindergarten and the grades. The loss of the milk (baby) teeth indicates that the children have completed the formation of their physical bodies and are ready to begin to work with their minds. An important task for the teacher is to create a rhythm for the children's school lives to enable them to grow and learn in a healthy way. Towards this end the teacher designs a rhythm not only through the season's festivals, and holidays, but also within each day and within each lesson during the day.

The year begins with the discovery that behind all forms lie two basic principles: the straight and curved line. The children find these shapes in their own bodies, in the classroom and in the world beyond. The straight and curved line are then practiced through walking, drawing in the air and sand, on the blackboard and finally, on paper. These form drawings train motor skills, awaken the children's powers of observation and provide a foundation for the introduction of the alphabet.

Through fairy tales and stories the children are introduced to each letter of the alphabet. In this way the children experience the development of language in a very concrete yet creative way: instead of abstract symbols the letters become actually characters with whom the children have a real relationship. "S" may be a fairy tale snake sinuously slithering through the grass on some secret errand; the "W" may be hiding in the blackboard drawing of waves.

When the children have mastered the sounds and can name and write them, they are ready for their first reading experience. The episodes of a story are illustrated by a series of pictures drawn on the blackboard by the teacher and in notebooks by the children. The class composes short descriptive sentences to accompany each picture. The wording is then copied from the teacher's model. Through these activities the children learn word and sentence structure without conscious effort and have the joy of creating their own illustrated books for reading material.

In a similar way, the children first experience the qualities of numbers before learning addition or subtraction: What is "oneness"? What is there only one of in the world? ("Me!") So the characteristics of one, two, three, etc., are explored in the children's inner experience and in nature. Stones, acorns or other natural objects are used to introduce counting. Children take delight in this, especially when the strong, rhythmic choral-speaking of the numbers is accompanied by stepping and clapping. Through these activities the children befriend themselves with the form and movement of the number element. Only after considerable practical experience in adding, subtracting, multiplying, and dividing are the written symbols for these operations introduced.

Children learn best at this age by entering with love, sympathy and wonder into the world they are studying; the imaginative pictures and stories help to inspire the love and sympathy and wonder they will need for the task. Nature study takes the form of an experience of hearing the world speak, talking of life and its adventures. The child learns the true facts of nature, but always in vivid, dramatic, story form.

First graders enter the world of music through the pentatonic scale. In this scale all the notes have a harmonious sound in any order they are played. Songs are based on seasonal themes: the playing of the pentatonic flute develops finger coordination, concentration and breath control.

Knitting is an indispensable first-grade activity as there exists a close relationship between finger movement, speech and thinking. [See article by Eugene Schwartz.] Some classes may choose to make scarves or perhaps knitted squares to be joined into a blanket.

Painting in the first grade is intended to give the children an experience of working with color rather than attempting to create formed "pictures." The children's feelings for form are encouraged through honey-fragrant beeswax modeling and crayon illustrations. In coloring, the children imitate the teacher's work, attempting to draw whole shapes rather than filling in outlines.

The imitative genius of early childhood makes this an ideal time to learn through hearing and speaking another language (often two languages) chosen for their appropriateness to the time and the school's location. Eurythmy, an art of movement developed by Dr. Steiner, is taught by specially-trained teachers. Exercises affect the children's grade of movement, sensitize hands and fingers, heighten drawing and modeling ability, relieve strain and tension, and stimulate musical, poetic and dramatic senses.

The concentrated nature of the first grade work makes new increased demands on children's energy levels. They may require more rest than before, a more consistent routine at bedtime and more nutritious snacks and meals. Any of these changes are common and should not alarm parents. However, children may exhibit some resistance to changing home routines (e.g., bedtime). Parents may need special encouragement from one another and suggestions to achieve the desired changes which they know will benefit their child.

— Marin Waldorf School Parent Handbook

Second Grade

MANETTE TEITELBAUM

A second grade child is like a butterfly who has just emerged from the hard imprisoning chrysalis and sits upon the leaf waiting expectantly for those glorious new wings to dry and strengthen. He is truly poised for flight.

Rudolf Steiner has described the seven year life cycles and the importance of the moment when the forces working within the child cast off the baby teeth and construct a smile that gleams with permanence and strength. A second grader has this process well underway. He is on the threshold of newly awakening faculties. Energies freed from the process of forming the body now awaken the subjective world of feeling – wonder, pity, joy, tenderness and sorrow. These are the currents of air upon which these new little butterflies will rise, on which they will find their relationship to the world about them.

The first grade was a time of creating wholeness and a sense of rhythm in this new world of the classroom becoming one class, learning and growing together. The land of fairy tale was peopled by a prince, a king, a princess, three brothers, a stepmother, all the aspects of the human community without individual distinction. The children delighted in identifying with each and every one of them.

Second graders retain this love of the archetypal imagery, but as their feelings awaken they are also ready to see the dual aspect of the human nature. Their own feelings of sympathy or antipathy may be unsettling for the adults in their lives, and require us to seek for creative responses.

We do not wish to burden the seven or eight-year-old with responsibility for his strong judgment, so we must seek other ways to show them the foibles of their own animal natures. Literature from every culture provides fables which show man's animal characteristics pitted one against another. The pictures speak of the children's imaginations allowing them to form their own inner pictures so the morals need not be given to them.

A second grader has a ready appreciation for a fox who invites a stork to dine on a low plate from which the stork cannot manage to feed himself, simply to enjoy the other's shortcomings. But to see the stork "pay the fox in his own coin," and invite him to a sumptuous meal served in an impossibly tall vase is to show the child the scale of justice with which Mother Nature balances her affairs.

On the other hand, the second grade child still delights in the mystery of the spiritual world where he still dwells at heart. He sits in rapt attention to legends of those spiritual beings who have the forces of nature in their service. When a snow white doe comes daily to sustain the Holy St. Giles with her milk, no one questions how she came to do this. And when the huntsman gives chase and shoots her, as she places her head in St. Giles lap, not a muscle moves nor an eye remains dry as the Saint removes the arrow from the shoulder of the mystical doe. Thus the second grader, still sustained by the unity he retains with his environment, is an eager participant in all that comes to his attention. He loves to have a choice - to choose a partner, to choose a part, but, as in the story of St. Jerome who is approached by a roaring lion, it is difficult for him to decide whether he wants to play the Holy Jerome or the lion he heals.

In arithmetic, the children carry out more complicated operations with the four processes. Imaginative stories still form the basis of these problems. Through rhythmic counting accompanied by accented clapping and movement of the whole body, they learn to count by twos, threes, fours and fives and can begin learning the multiplication tables.

Grammar is introduced with liveliness and humor by acting out stories in which the children can experience the contrast between doing words, naming words and describing words. Nature study continues with nature walks along with poetry, legends and imaginative descriptions of natural processes. Painting and modeling are continuously integrated in the main lesson subjects.

Crocheting is introduced, and small projects of the children's own creation always exemplify an important principle that handwork products be useful and functional as well as beautiful.

Foreign language, singing and flute lessons continue to be taught as in the first grade with eurythmy leading the children into a more conscious forming of vowels and consonants.

The class teacher who progresses with his pupils from first to second grade can look back on all his pupils' previous learning experiences, build step by step on his own foundation, and can endow his teaching with real unity. Thus, young children, who are very sensitive to readjustments and changes, are given the security of knowing one personality and method intimately and thoroughly.

— *Chanticleer*

Third Grade

DANIEL BITTLESTON

The third grade is often called the turning point of childhood. Every age has its drama, but the eight or nine-year-old is going through a change that is particularly profound; you might hear Waldorf teachers referring to it as the "Crossing point", the "Watershed" or the "Rubicon". What is prescribed in the curriculum for this age? Farming and gardening, the Old Testament, Building and Grammar. Why these?

Do you remember the time before your ninth year? Can you recapture even a hint of the qualitative richness of a home landscape, a certain house, particular relationships? And then, can you remember how things and people began to look 'ordinary'? As a nine-year-old we feel ourselves growing apart from the world. We become separated, independent, and begin to question all that was previously taken for granted. "Are my parents really my parents?" "Why is it called oak?" This questioning is accompanied by a serious stream of interest in everything practical. "How is a house built?" "Where does my food come from?"

Rudolf Steiner describes how the nine-year-old experiences at a spiritual level what the three-year-old experienced when first using the word "I". Before the age of nine, the major part of our being is not incarnated, not yet within us, and therefore lives within everything and everyone we perceive. We feel inwardly related to everything and can identify very fully with almost anything.

Now an experience arises of self as something independent of everything else. This brings the first suffering of loneliness, but also the first conscious joy in solitude. It brings the first capacity to understand death as a reality. Now we may suddenly feel very insecure; our relationship with Nature, with Eternity, with Others, with Ourselves has to be re-established.

Nine-year-old children usually love to go out into Nature in a more methodical and challenging manner than before. They become capable of more sustained physical effort; it is an ideal time to start regular family hikes. They become capable of more sustained interest in an animal or a plant. And this should be encouraged as much as possible; it lays the foundations for active caring about our planet Earth. The Waldorf curriculum gives them practical farming and gardening experience.

If their imaginative powers have not been paralyzed by technological entertainment, eight and nine-year-olds like to say "What if...?" and plunge into spontaneously created fantasies. The Old Testament stories give substantial material on which their imaginations can feed, leading to a wrestling with fundamental moral ideas.

Nine-year-olds form clubs and delight in battles between clear-cut opposites: us and them, heroes and enemy, good and bad. The "Building Block" teaches them about the far-reaching co-operation that is necessary for the achievement of civilization.

The question, "Who am I?" may arise, and this is possibly the most difficult of all. Many of us side-stepped this new awareness through increased external activity or by clinging to established patterns. Those who have not had particularly warm personal relationships, begin at this time to pursue external success with sometimes fanatical determination. These children may become ruthless and inconsiderate in their working and private lives. It is important, therefore, that nine-year-olds achieve a new inner security, new clarity of thought, new techniques for coming to terms with their emotions.

The Waldorf curriculum also provides drama, music, and grammar. Class plays allow the children to experience the great relationships of the Old Testament, and there is always lively relationship with their teachers. Machine-learning at this stage deadens the courage for such lively relationship.

Through round-singing, the student learns that holding your own voice against others is a necessary part of harmony; that a rhythm must be consistent if it is to be a reliable vehicle for melody and harmony. The children also progress in their instrument learning. After two years with the pentatonic flute, the third grade child learns how to play a simple recorder. Although the student may be introduced to stringed and wind instruments as he moves through the middle years, the recorder will continue to be an instrument used throughout the grades.

In the third grade English may become a special subject assigned its share of main lesson periods. Grammar awakens living rational thought, the awareness of a qualitative difference between words that are "naming," those that are "doing," and those that are "describing." In the previous years the teacher may have prepared the ground by writing whatever was to be copied from the board with nouns always in blue, verbs in red and adjectives perhaps in yellow or green.

Now we see why our third graders require more understanding, guidance and companionship from their responsible parents and teachers. In a Waldorf school, they are helped to form new relationships with nature through farming and gardening experience, with eternity through Old Testament experience, with others through building experience, and with themselves through drama, music and grammar.

— *Chanticleer*

Fourth Grade

To understand the fourth grade curriculum and why it is so suited to the nine and ten-year-old, one must first look back to the preceding years of schooling, and especially the curriculum of the third grade. There the children who, up until now, have lived in a certain harmonious relationship to the world, were cast out of Paradise. They were no longer allowed to dwell in the fairy tale realm of the first grade or even to fluctuate back and forth between heaven and earth as in second grade when the stories of saints and fables are told to accompany this duality. They have arrived! Now, how are they going to survive?

Just as the people of the Old Testament challenged and were challenged by their Father God as they learned to survive, to make shelters, and to work the land, so did the third graders challenge their authority as they took up the studies of farming, housing, measurement, and a deepening of those survival skills, reading writing and arithmetic. All along stories of the great men and women of the Hebrew nation were told. There was a feeling of ultimate wisdom and justice; a blanket of trust still could be wrapped around the third grader; there was a reason to all the madness.

Now in the fourth grade, that blanket has been tossed aside and the child feels very much separate from any of the security and comforts that previously were supportive. This is a time to look around and see how one stands in relationship to that which is near and to find security and uprightness through that relationship. Four itself is a sign of stability and strength and balance: the four winds, the four seasons, the four elements. Therein lies a sense of steadiness and completion. It is this sense of four, in the midst of separateness and defiance, that is at the very heart of the fourth grade curriculum.

The fourth grader is at odds with the world. Questions take on a personal twist: "How do you know?". There is an earnestness stemming from a new awareness of just what they are up against in the world. Therefore, every possible opportunity is given to meet these oppositions in quite unexpected ways, ways in which the child can have the experience of crossing and at the same time be led towards a wholesome resolution. In handwork, original designs are made which produce a colorful design that is executed in tiny cross stitches. The result is a beautiful wholeness from many little crossings.

In form drawings Celtic knots are challenging tangles of skill and beauty. The feeling of separateness comes in handy here, otherwise one might get lost in the maze. The theme of separateness is further reflected in the mathematics curriculum with the study of fractions. They are introduced with concrete objects to demonstrate truths before forming mental concepts.

Geography, local history, Norse mythology, grammar, composition writing, and a comparative study of the human being and animals are also introduced. In composition simple narration of the child's own real experiences begins and work in grammar continues.

The fourth grade child is now introduced to a stringed instrument — if not introduced in the previous grade — something delicate and yet powerful that will not answer endless questions nor oblige shortcuts to success. A new discipline and respect is called for in the child. There stands the player, and there the instrument, as separate as anything could be! The music is the bridge. Students may have in-class group lessons with the violin, viola or cello as well as private lessons. Another link is made when the children come together as violinists, violists, cellists and flautists and become an orchestra.

Throughout the year we hear and read stories of heroes. The hero emerges as someone to look up to, emulate, laugh at, respect. There may still be the miraculous feats and yet the human qualities, the emotions, the struggles, and the confrontations are emphasized; the children understand more than anyone else the hero's plight to slay the dragon, to woo the maiden, to succeed in the three tasks. In the stories of the *Kalevala*, an epic myth of Finland, there is yet another kind of hero. It is the song. The world was sung into being by the master singer, Vainamoinen; if there is any change to be made, any duel to be fought, task to be done, there is singing. For example:

> …Vainamoinen began his task. It was work he loved and he sang as he sawed and planed and hammered, songs of strength and swiftness. The boat grew as a song grows, each part of it was a word or phrase, each in a place. As an unlucky or misplaced word spoils a song, in the same way the boat would be marred.

It is written in the Talmud: "Let the lesson you study be like a song." And so we begin and end each day. In addition to our unison singing and rounds from previous years, we now add two-part songs. Now it is no longer a matter of singing the same tune at different times. The children sing the same words at the same time, yet each group of singers must hold their own part and not be swayed by the other group if the song is to work.

The child's newly strengthened individuality now gives him the ability to hold his own in this part-singing as he could not have done successfully before; canons and rounds form a natural bridge to this exciting new skill. He shows his first real delight in harmony and the minor key answers a deep-felt need leading inward in self-discovery. Now, standing as individuals we try to work harmoniously together.

— Chanticleer

Morning Verse for Grades 5 - 12

I look out into the world

Wherein there shines the Sun

Where glimmer all the stars,

Where lie the silent stones

The plants that live and grow

The beasts that feel and move

Where man in soul creates

A dwelling for the spirit.

I look inward to the soul

That lives within my being

The spirit of God is weaving

In sunlight and in soul-life

In heights of world without

In depths of soul within.

Spirit of God to thee

I turn myself in seeking

That strength and grace and skill

For learning and for work

May live and grow in me.

Rudolf Steiner

Fifth Grade

The fifth grader has enhanced her recent gains in consciousness and grown more accustomed to being an isolated self, seeing the world in a new perspective. Yet, like the third grader, she is about to leave another phase of childhood behind her and to cross a new threshold of experience. The curriculum must, therefore, not only continue to build on already established foundations, but introduce certain new elements to prepare her for her next step forward.

History has until now only a pictorial and personal nature and no attempt was made to introduce exact temporal concepts or to proceed in strict sequences. Now, however, history becomes a special main lesson subject, as does geography. History, telling of mankind's deeds and strivings, stirs the child to a more intense experience of her own humanness. Geography does exactly the opposite; it leads her away from herself out into ever wider spaces from the familiar to the unfamiliar. History brings the child to himself: geography brings the child into the world.

Ancient history in the fifth grade starts with the childhood of civilized humanity in ancient India, where human beings were dreamers. The ancient Persian culture that followed the Indian felt the impulse to transform the earth, till the soil, domesticate animals while helping the sun-god conquer the spirit of darkness. The great cultures of Mesopotamia (the Chaldeans, the Hebrews, the Assyrians, and the Babylonians) reveal the origins of written language on clay tablets. The Egyptian civilization of pyramids and pharaohs precedes the civilization of the Greeks with whom ancient history ends.

Every means is used to give the children a vivid impression of these five ancient cultures. They read translations of poetry, study hieroglyphic symbols of the Egyptians, sample arts and crafts of the various ancient peoples, trying their hands at similar creations. History is here an education of the children's feelings rather than of their memory for facts and figures, for it requires inner mobility to enter sympathetically into these ancient states of being so different from our own.

A study of American geography emphasizes contrast. Every consideration of the earth's physical features is linked with a study of the way human life has been lived in the region, the human uses made of natural resources, the industry and produce. As a continuation of their study of the living earth, the fifth graders begin botany, the study of the plant world. After discovering some of the secrets of the plant life found in one's own environment, the child's attention is drawn to vegetation in other parts of the world.

Building on the years of form drawing, freehand geometry is introduced. Fractions and decimals continue to be the chief concern of arithmetic study. Regular choral singing is practiced in the fourth and fifth grades and the students may come together to become an orchestra.

Whenever possible in a Waldorf school, the practical arts include woodworking. In some classes the children begin with carving a mallet to be used for subsequent projects. In handwork, knitting returns as a part, but now the students use four needles as they create socks or mittens. Eurythmy, foreign languages, painting, and sports and games also continue.

Many Waldorf schools host a Greek Pentathlon for the fifth grade students where grace, beauty, form and sportsmanship are lauded along with individual achievements of speed or accuracy.

— Admissions material for the East Bay
Waldorf School, El Sobrante, CA

Sixth Grade

The sixth grade is a firm, intentional step into the outer world. It is an arrival upon this earth. As children approach eleven or twelve, changes begin in their physical bodies. One of the most subtle is a hardening of the bones. Boys and girls are more aware of gravity and weight. With the increasing awareness of their physical bodies the time is right for the study of the physical body of the earth.

Geology turns to the structure of the earth, and proceeds from the study of the flora and fauna of the geological ages to minerals, metals, and finally gems and crystals, leading to the functions of mineral and metallic substances in the human organism. The study of minerals and rocks, mountains and rivers awakens great interest and enthusiasm. Here the students can experience a reflection of their own process and inwardly they are eager to embrace earth life and explore physical existence.

As the world continues to expand in geography, the sixth grade students are introduced to the earth's configuration and contrasts; distribution of oceans, seas, continents and mountain masses; and climate studies. These are applied specifically to North and South American geography. The study of the Earth and its relation to the other bodies of the solar system is introduced through astronomy.

The students are introduced to the basic concepts of physics. As with all subjects in a Waldorf school, the approach is first through art. Acoustics, or sound theory, leads from familiar experiences in tone and speech, such as observing how music is made, to experimentation with sound phenomena of other kinds. The sounds in music and nature lead to experiments by which they discover harmonies of relationship made by subdivisions in strings. From these experiments the children proceed to problems of tone conduction and then back to the human organism. They discover that they, too, have a musical instrument within them, the larynx.

Optical studies begin, like acoustics, with familiar experiences in the realm of beauty. Study of color in the world begins with the sun, giver of light. Each color is studied for its own special attributes and then observed in relation to other colors. Experiments with artificial light and shadow in the classroom lead to rainbow and prism, then experiments to determine laws of light refraction. In all these studies the principles underlying the various light and color phenomena are arrived at as end products generalized from concrete experiences rather than stated theoretically before the experiments are made.

Sixth grade history follows the transition from ancient to modern history. Because the 11-year-old herself is involved in such a transition, she begins to move from poetic consciousness to a search for truth in the form of scientific concepts. The child is now able to grasp history as temporal sequence of cause and effect relationships. The students study the decline of Greece, the rise and fall of Rome, and the effects of these two great cultures on European civilization up through the Middle Ages. The Roman epoch epitomizes in an historical sense what the children are experiencing in their bodies. Of all ancient peoples the Romans most strongly dominated their physical world. All their accomplishments – cities, roads, aqueducts, the Roman army and their conquest of the Western world – match a feeling of omnipotence that the sixth grader has: "I can do anything!" Yet equally important for the children is the example of how the excesses of the Roman period led to the fall of the Empire and the Dark Ages, which were illuminated by the new religion of Christianity.

Mathematics continues to exercise the disciplines learned in previous classes and then moves on to the study of percentage and ratio, the relationships between things. Sixth grade geometry is an ideal place to bring all the years of circle movement, eurythmy and form drawing into exact constructions, using compass, rulers, and right angles. These forms can be treated with all the visual artistry that has been so much a part of the curriculum in drawing and painting. Now, however, there is the discipline of precision and the use of tools. Whereas geometric shapes have in the prior grades been drawn freehand as artistic exercises, families of geometric figures are constructed and studied in the sixth grade for the numerical laws they embody. These designs are now done with the utmost accuracy.

Shadows, landscapes, and color contrasts are taken up in painting. Handwork relates to form and structure as the children design and create a gusseted stuffed animal. They continue to develop their skills with tools in wood carving, creating objects that serve the human or animal world.

Singing focuses on two and three-part choruses, songs of the minstrels and middle ages, and recorders in descant, alto and tenor voices. Eurythmy expands to include simple tone eurythmy whereby students learn gestures which correspond to musical forms. A greater depth is sought in this art form with geometrical forms and transformations. English continues with more emphasis on reading, writing and grammar. Foreign language continues with reading of simple texts, humorous stories and free translation.

Sixth grade is the gateway to pre-adolescence and idealism. In their studies of Rome the children are grounded so that through their physical awareness they can begin to discover what "I" means for them. In the Middle Ages they begin to venture out toward the unknown to find what, in the world, they are asked to address. The stories of the Grail offer an introduction to their quest in life. In summary, this year is both an ending and a beginning.

— Admissions material for the East Bay
Waldorf School, El Sobrante, CA

Seventh Grade

Michelangelo died at eighty-nine, leaving an unfinished sculpture and a drawing near where he was found. The drawing was actually a caricature of himself as an old man. Next to the sketch were the words, "Still learning." On his deathbed, Leonardo de Vinci was asked how he felt. He replied, "A day well spent makes it sweet to sleep. A life well used makes it sweet to die."

As the seventh grade children enter puberty, they are also adventuring across a basic threshold experience on their way to selfhood. Can they enter this dark unknown territory carrying a flaming torch to allow discovery as they wander and probe? Can they spend their time productively bearing in mind others behind them also need their light? If their spirit of inquiry and creativity in a social context can be fostered in puberty, they will surely find it *sweet* to enter adulthood. If it isn't fostered, they may stumble endlessly in the darkness, burdened by excess baggage of self-centeredness, criticism and chaotic emotions. To help them cross this threshold, we present a rich panorama designed to take them out to civilizations and people who share their mood of soul, as well as lead them to a closer look at each one's own environment and inner being.

Two subjects addressing these areas are English and History. The history block of the Renaissance and Reformation really begins modern times with a dauntless quest into the unknown that is also akin to the seventh graders' soul mood. Allegiance to traditional authority no longer holds sway. Individualism overcomes feudalism, as personified by Joan of Arc. Human capacities are limitless as epitomized by Leonardo Da Vinci. And as with the true spirit of the Renaissance, the only boundaries acknowledged, are boundaries to be crossed. The teacher must be like Pope Julius II was to Michelangelo – he must present a continuing challenge worthy of the artist's efforts. The student realizes the individual not only can make a difference, but can create a new world if one's conviction is strong enough. As this historical period was an age of doubt which followed the unquestioning faith of the Middle Ages, so too the adolescent needs to find things out for him or herself.

Doubt and resistance of authority mark a giant step toward self-recreation and individual thinking. Birth in the Renaissance parallels birth in a student's thinking, feeling and willing.

World geography, which now runs parallel to the history units, takes up the theme of adventurous exploration and covers the whole globe. The children's knowledge of astronomy is called upon to further their understanding of climate, tides, and other influences on cultural and economic life of the peoples of the earth.

Mechanics begins in physics with the lever principle as found in the human arm. From their experimentation the children learn the basic mechanical concepts and their application in the machinery of ancient and modern times. Inorganic chemistry is introduced as a study of the combustion process. From the beautiful legend of the bringing of fire to earth by Prometheus to a study of combustion in the human organism in the digestive processes, fire can be observed externally in the breaking down of substances by oxidation. Physiology is introduced as the study of life processes in man; blood circulation, respiration, reproduction, and nutrition in connection with digestion, health and hygiene.

Mathematics introduces algebra, including negative numbers, venturing into mathematical thinking that has no relation to physical perceptions. This makes real demands on the child's imaginative powers. Square and cube root and ratio are introduced. Geometrical perspective and black and white drawing are continued in more complex forms.

The English block of "Wish, Wonder, and Surprise" involves creative writing and literature, but is also designed to bring consciousness, balance and refinement to the adolescent's emotional life. Students come to see how personal a 'wish' is, how it comes from deep within and goes toward the outer world. 'Wonder' comes from a meeting between one's inner and outer world, and 'surprise' really originates outside and impresses itself on the individual. It becomes evident that a variety of styles can be employed to convey specific feelings accurately. Bringing consciousness here can also bring confidence and a sense of liberation.

Music includes acappella singing, motets, madrigals, ballads and Renaissance music and individual and group instrumental work. Eurythmy explores poems with contrast, wonder and surprise; ballads with quick dramatic movement, drama and tragedy. In handwork the children sew hand puppets or slippers and learn embroidery. Carving and clay modeling continue.

Through this journey, it is most essential that the child has a close friend as well as adults who are enthusiastically saying "yes" to the world. Service projects can be strongly affirmative at this time. Beneath growing layers of negativism, the child must say "yes" to him or herself. This means courage when there's a tendency to withdrawal. But as one historian noted, "If Columbus had turned back, no one would have blamed him, but no one would have heard of him, either."

— *Chanticleer*

Eighth Grade

LUCILLE CLEMM

The task of elementary education is to give children an understanding of humanity and the world they live in, to offer them knowledge so rich and warm as to engage their hearts and wills as well as their minds. Such an understanding is the basis of all real learning in later years. With the completion of the eighth grade the children should have a well-rounded general picture of human life and universe. This last year of elementary school should not only bring all previous experiences to a new peak, but enable the children to enter fully and potently into the life of their own time.

History is an intensive study of the industrial revolution to the modern day, focusing as well on the outstanding individuals such as Lincoln, Jefferson, Edison in American history and great figures such as Ghandi, Albert Schweitzer, Martin Luther King and others from the 20th century. Geography takes up the same theme, showing the role played by every part of the earth in modern industrial civilization. A comprehensive picture is given of the relation of mineral resources and plant and animal life to the life of human beings in various regions of the world (world economic geography).

Physics lessons complement these historical and geographical surveys. The practical uses made of man's new knowledge of all the physical sciences are thoroughly explored. In addition to further studies in acoustics, thermodynamics, mechanics, climate, electricity and magnetism, the children are now introduced to hydraulics, aerodynamics, and meteorology and ecology. Chemistry is also considered in relation to industry. Organic chemistry is studied for the role it plays in the building of organic substance. Fats, sugars, proteins and starches are identified.

Mathematics also emphasizes the practical applications of arithmetic, algebra and geometry. Demonstrations in plane and solid geometry lead to problems in the measurement of surfaces and volume. The study of graphs is introduced. Man is again the subject of nature study through physiology of the human organism, observed from the standpoint of form and movement, (skeleton, muscular systems, and the senses).

Literature focuses on the theme of human freedom in the short story, letters and Shakespearean drama. Foreign language continues. Music takes up Elizabethan music, American music, symphonic form; eurythmy complements other studies with exploration of poems with contrasting moods.

Painting concerns itself for the first time with studies of highlights and shadows in portraits and landscapes. Machine sewing, darning, artistic hand-sewing projects, soapstone carving, and carpentry devoted to big projects requiring real skill and imagination culminate eight years of handwork.

— *Chanticleer*

Waldorf High School Upper School

BETTY K. STALEY

When the youngsters finish the eighth grade they pass over the threshold into the high school. Here many of the same subjects are taught but in a completely different way. In the lower grades the teaching was through feelings, through dramatic stories, through imagery. Subjects are [now] grasped through presentation, discussion, reflection and thinking, but the artistic is not forgotten. Teachers continue to deepen their artistic approach – to approach their lessons as an artist, to listen.

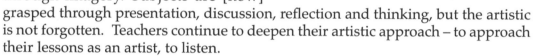

Rather than teachers relying on standard textbooks (although some may be used) they choose material that particularly relates to the students in the class. They describe biographies and events, create assignments that allow the student to explore the subjects in various mediums, and make evaluations based on the special nature of the ninth, tenth, eleventh, or twelfth graders. (Fourth, fifth, lower and upper sixth year in U.K.). Instead of a class teacher to shepherd the class through the years, there is a community of specialists who teach the students out of their expertise. One or two faculty members act as class advisors or sponsors over their four high school years.

The high school curriculum

The Waldorf high school curriculum is based on the understanding that each subject has a special place in the life of the student. For example, through science the adolescent learns to observe natural and mechanical processes. Through foreign languages the teenager learns to enter the thinking of another culture and to be able to communicate. In the study of mathematics the student experiences the wonder of form and pattern in number and nature. Through art the students develop inner sensitivity to living processes, through crafts they learn to bring an aesthetic sense to the practical world. In music the students develop an individual sense of tone and have a social experience of sharing musical works.

The subjects become the stuff of the world through which is woven an integrated view of the universe. In Waldorf education each child is seen as gifted, worthy of the enrichment from all subjects in the curriculum. It is only in the last two years of high school where some subjects will be electives.

The concept of the main lesson continues from the lower school into the high school, but the content and the form are different. After the main lesson time is over, the rest of the day includes a wide range of subjects such as mathematics, foreign language, English skills, literature, choir, orchestra, art and craft, eurythmy and physical education. An attempt is made to work out the daily schedule so that the subjects that require the most alertness are placed in the morning.

The special nature of each high school year

...The curriculum is related to each year of the high school and to the psychological development of the students. Just as children in the lower school experienced the recapitulation of cultures in their development, a similar parallel exists in the high school. There is a key experience related to each stage of adolescence.

Ninth Grade

Ninth graders have left the second seven-year phase behind, and as happens in most life phases, the first year of a new phase carries with it something of the old. Eighth graders have arrived in modern times, they have become contemporaries with others of their age. As they come into the ninth grade there is a strong feeling of the present. They want to be citizens of the modern world, but as of yet they do not have much understanding of it. They are fascinated with power and strength. The curriculum is woven around these themes. For example, both in physics and in history power and energy are addressed – in physics through mechanics and in history through the study of modern times following the American and French Revolutions.

At the same time ninth graders are focused on the physical body and physical world around them. They are trying to understand *what* things are all about. In the course *History Through Art* the student learns the way art was expressed visually from the Ancient world through the seventeenth century. (Art, science and religion were united in the ancient world and this was reflected in the art of most ancient cultures, including Egypt. Most Egyptian art was created from the gods and was not seen by the ordinary person. In Greek art we see the perfect balance of heaven and earth. The gods were portrayed as ideal men, their bodies based on the golden section, viewed as the temple of the gods. Gracefulness, movement, balance and harmony lived in Greek art.)

Art of the Roman, Early Christian periods, the Middle Ages, and the Renaissance are studied. The students draw and paint, using the great masters as their teachers. Seeing and discussing the different standards of beauty over the ages helps ninth graders see that the present standard is not the only one. They learn that they are capable of producing beauty and they gain confidence in their drawing ability.

Rudolf Steiner felt very strongly that ninth graders should study history through art as a way of refining the crude emotions and distorted inner imagery they carry around with them. He said that such a study would go right down into their physical body and have a harmonizing effect.

In biology, the ninth graders study the structure of the physical body, while in geography they study the physical body of the earth – the continents, the mountains, volcanoes, earthquakes and so on. They also study chemistry and foreign languages.

It is wonderful to see ninth graders working with wood, clay, drawing and calligraphy. Some ninth graders are trying to make an impact on everything around them. They have trouble being quiet and concentrating, and for them the arts provide a challenge. They have to learn to respect the medium and to work with it, to give themselves up to the process. Other ninth graders are still very hesitant, afraid to step out and make a mistake. For them the arts provide an opportunity to connect with the material. Instead of exposing themselves by talking, they can talk with their hands.

Tenth Grade

Tenth graders have come to the next step in maturity. Feeling fairly comfortable in themselves they become interested in process, in development, in metamorphosis. How do things happen, how do governments form, how did the Word come into being? Whereas the ninth grader needed stability, the tenth grader responds to that which is in motion.

In geography they study the fluids, water currents and water power. In biology they study the fluids of the body, circulation, the endocrine system and reproduction. In chemistry they study organic processes of fermentation and distillation and so on. In physics the world of mechanics is studied. The idea of finding out how things work is very important in the tenth-grade year, and Rudolf Steiner was especially keen that the teachers develop what he called the practical lessons which would include surveying, first aid, typing or shorthand, technical crafts such as weaving and drawing.

In history the tenth graders now go back to the ancient world and see how rivers and climate affected ancient settlements; they trace the evolution of societies from ancient India to the Hellenistic period in Greece.

The study of Greece is of particular importance. It was during the time of ancient Greece that philosophers became conscious of the act of thinking. When the myths of the gods and goddesses, heroes and heroines no longer satisfied the early philosophers' questions, they turned to the world of phenomena and questioned what was the primal "stuff" from which the universe was made. This formed the basis of modern science. Socrates was put on trial for corrupting the youth of Athens because he questioned traditions and sought to find the meaning of the true, the good and the beautiful. His student, Plato, introduced the analogy of the cave – the imagination of spiritual reality and earthly illusion. Finally, it was Plato's student, Aristotle, who opened the gates of modern thinking with his emphasis on categorizing knowledge and seeking the laws of nature, drama, politics and of thinking itself.

The tenth grader is experiencing many of the same changes. Out of the previous image-like thinking, pure concepts begin to be formed and grasped. Working with Greek ideas helps youngsters to bring form and order into their thinking as well as balance, movement and grace, that so imbued Greek sculpture and architecture.

In literature they study the Word – in the epic, lyric and dramatic poetry of the Iliad or Odyssey, of Greek drama and of the Old Testament.

Many other subjects are included in the tenth-grade year, and of course each school has its own special courses. For example, many schools in the United States include American literature that is appropriate to each grade. For example, in my classes I introduced 19th century American authors such as Hawthorne, Emerson, Alcott, Thoreau, Fuller and Whitman, and English writers such as Blake, Wordsworth, Coleridge, Byron, Keats and Shelley.

In the tenth grade we enjoy their language, their imagery and their exciting lives. Two years later we will look at Emerson and Thoreau again, but in an analytical way as we trace the clarity and meaning of their thoughts.

Eleventh Grade

Most eleventh-graders have gone through or are going through a very important change – the sixteen/seventeen year change. The mysterious inward journey of the soul is mirrored in the curriculum through the question "Why?" In the eleventh grade religious questions are addressed in the study of the Roman Empire, the birth of Christianity, the development of Judaism and Islam, the development of the Roman Catholic church and the Reformation. Just as the Renaissance personalities questioned traditional authority and asked "Why?", so do the eleventh grade adolescents. It gives them satisfaction and insight to see that the questions they ask are the questions of their age. It is exciting to know that to challenge the accepted customs is valuable and necessary for the development of civilization.

Seventh graders respond strongly to the Renaissance because they are experiencing rebellion towards the physical authorities in their lives, but sixteen/seventeen-year-olds experience rebellion in their souls. For example, the doubt mirrored in the reformation is not doubt of whether the authorities have vested power – more a seventh grade concern – but existential doubts such as whether there exists the soul, the spirit, God and eternity.

The emotional or soul life of the adolescent is going through a profound development during this time, and one of the courses taught is History through Music. One major aspect of music through the ages has been an expression of the meeting between the soul and the divine. Listening to music of the different historical periods and coming to appreciate and understand it helps the youngster develop an inner listening. Just as history through art in the ninth grade fed their craving for imaginative visual images, and history through poetry helped the tenth grader relate to language, history through music in the eleventh grade feeds their craving for tone.

In literature the study of *Parsifal* on its most apparent level mirrors the inner journey from foolish young knight to the Grail knight, from naiveté to mature wisdom. There is great wisdom embedded in this story. The study of Shakespeare reveals to the eleventh grader the insight into the modern condition in characters such as Hamlet. Shakespeare's genius opens doors to many soul questions.

The world of the heavens is studied in astronomy, and the sub–earthly power of electricity and magnetism is studied in physics.

The eleventh grade is a turning-point in the adolescent's Waldorf experience. Out of the richness of the courses teenagers are placed in touch with their inner resources and higher selves.

Twelfth Grade

The theme of the twelfth grade is freedom. The main question asked is "Who?" "Who is behind this doctrine?" "Who is working through that personality?" "Who is really speaking?" Through these questions young people confront questions of destiny, of good and evil, of meaning. Twelfth graders analyze and synthesize thoughts. They can look at an issue from many points of view, finding the common elements and the central issues. The Waldorf teachers bring example after example for the students to examine and think about.

Some examples from the literature studies are the great works of the nineteenth century Russians, Germans, and Americans. By reading Dostoyevsky's *The Brothers Karamazov* the student comes to understand how a Russian deals with the deep questions of life. In Melville's *Moby Dick* there is the struggle of the American soul with evil and in Goethe's *Faust* the German approach. In each of these studies an understanding of the particular culture is aroused, but more than that is the realization that the issues addressed are universal. The greatness of these writers is that they have soared beyond their nationality and have given to humanity an artistic expression of questions facing human beings everywhere.

Twelfth graders grapple with the issues of their times. Before they leave school they step into the present. Their teachers examine with them the issues of the day, problems of economics, politics, social issues, nuclear chemistry, modern art, debates over evolution and so on.

The *History Through Art* course of the twelfth grade is the study of architecture in which the students examine the expression of thought in physical form. What is the gesture of an Egyptian pyramid, a Gothic temple, an Art Deco bank, or of a high-tech office building?

Everything twelfth graders study is done by the young Ego penetrating the world – reflecting, shaping thoughts, discussing, sharing. In mathematics the young adults have passed into the abstract world of trigonometry and calculus, in English classes they work with *precis* and research, synthesizing viewpoints, and analyzing a theme. In their foreign language study they delve into literature, exploring similar themes to their English literature studies – the battle between good and evil and the nature of freedom.

The twelfth graders can reach way back in their education into the imaginative first-grade world of the fairy tale and bring the powerful shaping forces into creative writing. They experience the sweep of history through thousands of years and see patterns and threads working in human life from the kindergarten children they pass every day to their teachers who are quickly becoming contemporaries. They are able to understand the paradoxes of life without losing sight of the ideals. Their eyes are on a distant shore while they prepare to leave their school-home and bid their school mates and teachers good-bye.

— *Between Form and Freedom: A practical guide to the teenage years*

One Example of a Waldorf High School Curriculum

The following is only a list, not a full description, from the Sacramento Waldorf School, Fair Oaks, California. If you are interested in this or any other Waldorf school, please write directly to that school for complete information about their curriculum.

Ninth Grade

English:	Literature (tragedy-comedy, mythology, the novel), English skills, grammar, composition, vocabulary, speech
Foreign Languages:	German & Spanish (accelerated levels)
Mathematics:	Algebra I, pre-algebra, probability
Science:	Chemistry (organic), physics (thermodynamics, transportation and communication technology), geology, biology (anatomy)
U. S. History:	Early American history and government
World History:	Revolutions and history through art
Music:	Performing choir, beginning instruments, performing orchestra
Arts/Crafts:	Light and dark drawing, woodworking, drama, mechanics, calligraphy, clay, eurythmy, baskets

Physical education

Tenth Grade

English:	Literature (*The Iliad, Old Testament,* Romantic poetry, 19th century American authors), term paper, grammar, composition, vocabulary, speech
Foreign Languages:	German & Spanish (accelerated levels)
Mathematics:	Geometry, surveying, trigonometry
Science:	Chemistry, physics (mechanics), biology (physiology), physical geography, meteorology
U. S. History:	The period 1798 through 1914
World History:	Ancient history, Greece, the Far East
Music:	Performing choir, beginning instruments, performing orchestra
Arts/Crafts:	Sculpture, drama, block printing, pottery, eurythmy, drawing, weaving, painting.

Physical education, word processing, health, and First Aid

Eleventh Grade

English:	Literature (survey of early English literature from *Beowulf* through Chaucer), Shakespeare, Dante, *Parsifal*, *Brave New World*, *New Testament*, grammar, composition, vocabulary
Foreign Languages:	German & Spanish
Mathematics:	Advanced algebra, problem solving, projective geometry, computer science
Science:	Chemistry, physics (electricity, magnetism and digital electronics), biology (cellular biology, botany, biology lab), astronomy
U. S. History:	World War I to the present
World History:	Rome, The Middle Ages, The Renaissance, music history
Music:	Performing choir, performing orchestra, beginning instruments
Arts/Crafts:	Bookbinding, clay, life drawing, drama, woodcarving, eurythmy, wood working, painting

Physical education, computer education

Twelfth Grade

English:	Literature (Russian literature, Emerson, Goethe's *Faust*, contemporary novels), review of English skills, word usage, vocabulary, creative writing, independent literature, honors program
Foreign Languages:	German & Spanish
Mathematics:	Trigonometry, analytic geometry, business math, advanced math topics
Science:	Chemistry, physics (optics, color theory and quantum physics), computer science, biology (zoology, evolution)
U. S. History:	Development of 19th and 20th century economic theory from the rise of mercantilism to the present
World History:	Architecture, modern art, Third World nations, symptomatology
Music:	Performing choir, beginning instruments, performing orchestra, honors program
Arts/Crafts:	Bookbinding, clay, drama, wood working, eurythmy, painting independent study, textiles, honors program, stone carving, graphics, drafting and architectural drawing

Physical education, computer education.

Physical education is required. There are regular field trips for theater productions and other cultural events and for site studies in geography, history and the natural sciences. Students also have an opportunity to participate in musical productions every two years and community career work experiences.

Understanding the Waldorf Curriculum

All understanding begins in wonder!

— Johann Wolfgang von Goethe

Creating a Balance of Thinking, Feeling, and Willing

RENÉ QUERIDO

The Three-Fold Concept of Man as a whole person, fully developed in willing (doing), feeling, and thinking is maintained throughout the curriculum. Children experience the world differently from adults. The child is not a miniature adult who grows bigger; differences in the child's experience of the world can be illustrated by how memory functions at different stages.

In the early years from birth to age seven visual memory dominates. As the child matures from ages seven to fourteen, his feelings emerge in strong combination with story memory.

Emphasis in the middle years (Grades 1-8) of the Waldorf curriculum is appropriately placed on the feeling-filled experience of knowledge.

Finally, with adolescence from age 14 to 21 comes the "ah-ha" of ideas, thoughts and concepts through logical insight.

The fundamental capacities of the child are developed through the balance of subjects.

Geography

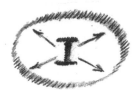

…introduced first in Grade 4, develops the capacity to see the world first from where one stands and moves out into the world to include family, then community, to the world as a whole.

History

…applies to the opposite capacity to see how the larger story applies to oneself. Fairy stories, legends, and Old Testament stories in the first three grades, Norse myths in Grade 4 and Indian and Persian stories and Greek gods and heroes in Grade 5 bring the child gradually into history as a record of mortal man, with ancient history culminating in modern man by Grade 8.

Science

…or the capacity to see the physical world from the "inside out" begins with nature stories in Grades 1 and 2 and moves closer to the earth in Grade 3 with studies of farming and the caring, responsible, grateful farmer. The sequence continues with animals (4th), plants (5th), minerals (6th) and acoustics, optics and astronomy (7th), and Human kingdom (8th).

Mathematics

…which develops a capacity to build one step at a time, begins with the introduction of all four processes in Grade 1 and develops further using whole numbers until Grade 4. Then, fractions and percentages are introduced, building to algebra and geometry by Grade 7.

English

…builds the capacity to convey meaning (with the meaning always being larger than the means to express it - words and sentences). The child reads first what "I" wrote. Writing comes first, and the active, creative process is always emphasized.

— Notes of a lecture for Waldorf parents

Rhythm in the Kindergarten

NANCY FOSTER

When I was a parent new to Waldorf Education, I wondered why my sons' nursery and kindergarten teachers spoke of "the rhythm of the day." "Why don't they just say 'schedule'?" I wondered. Gradually, I became used to hearing this term.

As a musician, I was certainly acquainted with the concept of rhythm, but it was not until I became a Waldorf kindergarten teacher myself that I began to understand the importance of the concept – and the experience – of rhythm in the kindergarten. As years have passed, I have been amazed at the depth to which rhythm permeates the life of the kindergarten and the experience of the teachers and children on a daily, weekly, and yearly basis.

The extent to which the children become imbued with the day's rhythm was graphically illustrated by an experience in our kindergarten some years ago. The parents had joined us, first thing in the morning, for our Harvest Festival, and as part of the Festival we shared a snack with them – the harvest loaf we had baked. In due course we said good-bye to the parents and continued with the morning.

When planning the day, I had reasoned that we would not need to have our usual snack time, following circle, since we would already have eaten. Thus, after playtime, clean-up, and a short circle, I said to the children sitting quietly on the rug, "And now let's get our coats; it is outdoor time." The children got up – and went straight to the snack tables and sat down! There was clearly nothing to be done but to gather together quickly the remnants of our harvest loaf and have snack after all!

How *does* "rhythm" differ from "schedule"?

A schedule is a list of planned events with times assigned to each. These events need have no relation to each other aside from following a prescribed sequence. There is a definite end to one activity and a beginning of the next (as in some schools when a bell signals the change of classes). Rhythm, on the other hand, implies a flowing quality of movement from one activity into another; the movement and sequence are not arbitrary, but are governed by the internal quality of the activities themselves. I was interested to note the descriptions of rhythm given in one dictionary:

1) any kind of movement characterized by the regular recurrence of strong and weak elements, e.g., the rhythm of the tides;

2) denotes the regular patterned flow, the ebb and rise, of sounds and movement in speech, music, writing, dance, and other physical activities and in natural phenomena, e.g., the rhythm of the heart.

These are beautiful descriptions of rhythm in the kindergarten. Another image of the kindergarten rhythm is that of breathing, with its contraction and expansion. This image may be applied to the kindergarten morning on different levels. On the level of group dynamics, in-breathing may occur when everyone comes together in one activity such as circle time or story time; out-breathing may take place during times when children find their own pace of activity, such as creative play or outdoor time. From the perspective of an individual child, however, in-and out-breathing may have a different aspect. For example, during creative play, a child may be totally absorbed in creating a fishing boat; this kind of concentration is surely an in-breathing. Or, during story time, which for the group is a time of contraction, a child who is truly dreaming into the story is probably experiencing an out-breathing on the soul- level.

An analogy which I find particularly helpful in characterizing the kindergarten rhythm is that of a gently rolling landscape. But whatever image one chooses, a characteristic of the image will be that there are no abrupt stops and starts, no tidal waves which come crashing out of control, or precipices over which one may fall. Rather, there is a regular rise and fall, expansion and contraction.

One day an experienced Waldorf teacher from abroad was visiting my classroom. In the midst of creative play, there occurred, as sometimes happens, a moment when the noise in the room gradually stilled almost to a silence and, then after a brief breath of balance, gradually returned to its previous level as play continued. Afterwards my guest asked if I had noticed the quiet moment.

"Yes," I said, "why does that happen?"

"Rhythm!" she replied.

In this example one sees that smaller rhythms occur within larger ones, just as in a fairy tale there are invariably moments of humor or, perhaps, a little rhyme, which create small out breaths, or as in circle time there are rhythms of contraction and expansion.

There is no one "correct" rhythm of the day. Each teacher must find the rhythm which works best for the particular situation; this may depend in part on the length of the kindergarten morning and the age of the children. In our three-hour mixed age group, the morning begins with creative play for an hour or hour and a quarter. During this time the children may take part in the special activity of the day.

Toward the end of this period my assistant begins to help each child have a turn in the bathroom while I begin, with the children's help, to tidy up the room. When all is in order and the room made beautiful once again, the children lie on the rug while I do some handwork and sing to them until everyone has finished in the bathroom. Following this short rest, we begin our circle as I sing "Let us form a ring..." and the children join me in beginning to move around. After circle, which lasts ten to twenty minutes, depending on the group of children in a given year, we go to the snack table and then outdoors. The morning comes to a close with story and our good-bye song. This daily rhythm occurs within the week's rhythm, which in turn takes place within the still larger rhythm of the year, with its contraction into midwinter and expansion into midsummer.

The experience of these rhythms brings for both children and adults a healing much needed in today's busy world. How frequently a visiting parent or other guest will comment that sitting in the kindergarten for a morning is truly therapeutic! We can all sense that moving in harmony with the rhythm of the heart or of the tides – the images used in the dictionary – would have a calming effect.

The regular recurrence of the daily rhythm, in which one element flows smoothly into the next, is indeed calming, and offers the children a sense of security through which their forces of will, expressed in their play, can be strengthened and their imagination take shape in the environment. The form provided by the rhythm allows the children to live in dream-consciousness, in which they can unself-consciously and wholeheartedly participate in the day's experiences.

When the rhythm of the school day is supported by a strong, nurturing rhythm at home, the child is able to experience these early years of life in the most healthy, harmonious way possible.

— Peridot

Knitting and
Intellectual Development

EUGENE SCHWARTZ

Out of an in-born understanding and psychological insight, many ancient peoples connected weaving, braiding and knot-tying with intellect and wisdom. Isis, the female goddess of Egypt who exemplified wisdom, became known on earth after she taught a princess and her ladies-in-waiting to braid their hair. Athena, who was born out of the head of Zeus and ruled over the world of thoughts, was also the patron of weaving. The preponderance of braid-like and woven strands in temple paintings and ritual sites in New Mexico, northern and southern Africa, Peru and central Asia confirm the link between the weaving/braiding activity and humanity's aspirations to the very highest inner activities.

In the Middle Ages, a third mode arose to take its place alongside weaving and braiding. Although the origins of knitting are obscure, old woodcuts and medieval illuminations place its ascendance in Europe at about the same time that the game of chess and the mathematical approach of algebra became known to westerners.It is significant that the most intellectual of games and the most thought-out approach to numerical problems accompanied the development of knitting. It was as though a new degree of adeptness in the hand had to go side by side with newly discovered capacities in the head.

Recent neurological research tends to confirm that mobility and dexterity in the fine motor muscles, especially in the hand, may stimulate cellular development in the brain, and so strengthen the physical instrument of thinking. Work done over the past seventy years in hundreds of schools using the Waldorf method worldwide, in which first graders learn to knit before learning to write or manipulate numbers, has also proven successful in this regard.

What occurs when a child sets about to knit? Needles are held in both hands, with each hand assigned its respective activity; laterality is immediately established, as well as the eye's control over the hand. The right needle must enter a fairly tightly-wound loop of yarn on the left needle, weave through it and pull it away, in the process tying a knot. Only a steady controlled hand can accomplish such a feat, so the power of concentration is aroused – indeed, there is no other activity performed by seven or eight year-olds that can evoke such a degree of attentiveness as knitting. This training in concentration will go far in supporting problem-solving abilities in later years.

To knit properly, the child must count the number of stitches and the number of rows. By using different colors and different lengths of row(as in a pattern of a little animal with legs) the teacher encourages not only attentiveness to number, but also flexibility in thinking. As children learn more arithmetic, teachers can devise patterns that call, for example, for two rows of blue, four rows of yellow, six rows of red, eight rows of blue, etc., reinforcing numerical skills in a challenging, yet enjoyable manner.

Lastly, we cannot underestimate the self-esteem and joy that arise in the child as the result of having made something practical and beautiful – something which has arisen as the result of a skill that has been learned. In an age when children are too often passive consumers, who, as Oscar Wilde once said, "know the price of everything and the value of nothing," learning to knit can be a powerful way of bringing meaning into a child's life.

The Role of Temperament in Understanding the Child

RENÉ QUERIDO

The child's world is full of wonder and creativity – it is a world that cannot be analyzed and mechanized. Although very practical, Waldorf education is also concerned with the inner life of the child. Every child is different, even those who share the same parents and the same environment. One cannot explain a child's nature in strictly biological terms. Each child is unique.

This becomes more clear when we delve into what the child actually is. He or she brings a unique spirit incarnated in a body, belonging to a family, with a father and mother who receive and guide this child's life on earth. The child's hereditary characteristics interact with the stimuli he receives from his surroundings. The temperament is the meeting of the spiritual aspect of oneself, which one refers to as "I", and the contributions of the father and mother. The temperament is the result of the blending of these two streams, the spirit and heredity.

Once you begin to live with the concept of spirit and heredity, you start to notice the change in mood throughout the cycle of the seasons. This change of mood can be expressed in different ways: the blazing heat of summer, the decay and dying of fall, ice and snow of winter, or the joy of spring. We try to express these moods with the color circle. Blue is the winter, an icy cold watery mood. At the first pulse of spring, many shades of green appear. The summer mood is red, suggesting the strength and heat of the sun. As the summer passes, we retreat inward, and nature around us slows and appears to be dying. We begin to feel as if we have lost something – much has died, and we don't know exactly where life will reappear.

Children's moods are associated with the seasons. Some children are summer children – not because they were born in the summer, but because their gestures and characteristics show an affinity with summer. Some children are fiery like the summer, others watery like the winter; some are earthbound like the fall, while some are light and airy like the spring. If we look at children between the ages of five and fourteen, we will notice that temperament is really predominant. Before that, temperament is less overt. During the elementary school years, temperament is really crucial and, for the teacher, it provides a means of relating not only to the individual child, but also to the whole class.

Each temperament responds to the world differently because each person sees the world from a different perspective. The child of autumn [melancholic], for example, grows tall very quickly, he walks with his head bent and he shuffles, and when there is a game with many children he thinks, *"Well, I'm going to watch that. Aren't they funny people, playing with that ball? The ball goes this way and that way...."* This child is already thinking about the meaning of life. He tries to understand all the things that are happening around him, he broods a great deal, and he likes to be a spectator and let the world go by. If you suggest a party, he says, *"Oh no, I don't like parties. I'd rather be off by myself and work on my models. I'm closing my door."* About the age of twelve, he puts on his door a sign that says *"Abandon hope, all ye who enter here. This is the gateway to hell."* He wants to be on his own. He wants to plumb the very depths of existence.

Melancholics ask awkward questions of their teachers. If such a child senses that the teacher is not interested in his quest for the meaning of life, he becomes very disillusioned. He thinks, *"This teacher is not interested in my deeper questions. In that case, I will keep things to myself."* Thirty or forty years later he will remember that particular second or third grade class when he asked a question and his teacher responded, *"Oh, don't be foolish!"* To this day, he still suffers from it. I'm exaggerating a bit, but if we get into the mood of a melancholic child, we see that his mood is intimately connected with his soul. The melancholic child is extremely perceptive and wants to plumb the deepest aspects of things. He wants to understand, he is tremendously interested in grammar and meaning, in structure, in knowing why.

The opposite is true of the spring child [sanguine]. This child is light-hearted, fleet-footed, smiling and delightful. Such a child learns quickly, will be tremendously enthusiastic and the next day when you ask, *"Catherine, what did we do yesterday?"* she'll say, *"I can't remember, but it was so much fun!"* The children of spring are as bright as the sunshine on a spring morning and they love flowers, butterflies, and insects. The feet of such children hardly ever touch the ground. They run along and the heels of their shoes are never worn even if the rest of the shoe has holes in it, because they are always on tiptoe. They have a wonderful fleetness in life.

The sanguine child can be difficult too. For example, if you go to your friends' house unannounced, your friend's daughter Sarah, a lovely sanguine child, might say, *"Mama and Papa are not here because they are at the hospital visiting Aunt Mort. She had a terrible fall. But do come in, I'll make you a cup of tea."* While you wait for Sarah's parents to return, she tells you the family history, disclosing all the details you don't feel you should be privy to. Sarah is, of course, delighted, and she is a charming child, but Mommy and Daddy may not be equally pleased when they hear what she has revealed.

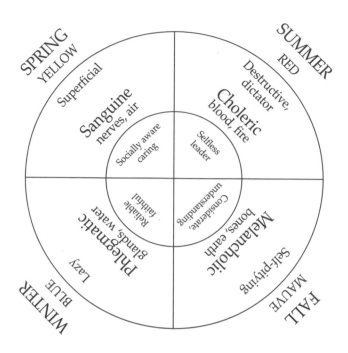

The four temperaments and the corresponding seasons, elements and colors.

Faced with the same circumstances, William, who is the melancholic child, would probably spend the afternoon by himself, and if you came to the door he might not even open it. He would reason, *"These strangers might be friends of my parents, but they're not my friends."* So the door remains closed, and if you're standing outside, you might feel a little cheated and wonder what is happening, what this is all about.

When the children of the summer [choleric] come home you *know* they are home – they slam the door and yell, *"Hello!"* as they stomp inside. There is no doubt about it. If they are stormy, it is quite obvious in their attitudes, and if something terrific happened, you will be sure to hear about it. *"I've climbed a tree and knocked nails in wood today"* is a typical phrase from the choleric child.

Choleric children should have a huge garden to play in, trees to climb, things to build. If you haven't time to spend with them, choleric children can be difficult. They seem to become increasingly energetic just as your reserves run low.

Or you might be a melancholic father wanting to read your newspaper while your demanding choleric boy is asking, *"What are we going to do tomorrow? What are we going to do on the weekend? How many mountains are we going to climb?"* You might respond, *"I just want to stay home, I had a very exhausting week."*

Choleric children require a different kind of care than sanguine children. The choleric children of summer are of the element of fire; the children of spring are of air; the melancholic child is more like the earthbound autumn and feels the seriousness of things. The choleric child is always looking towards the future, *"What are we going to do tomorrow?"* and the melancholic child says, *"We're going on a holiday? It won't be as good as the holiday we had three years ago. That was really wonderful. Do you really want to go on this holiday? It's really too painful, it just won't be as good."* The melancholic child is very concerned with the past, with remembering, and sometimes holds grudges because things get so deeply imprinted.

The choleric child is of the fiery forces and likes to barrel through things. He or she usually has a somewhat stocky build. The melancholic child has more neck, more length of this body, and has more difficulty coming down into his limbs; his hands and feet are such a long way away, it is difficult to penetrate them. But the choleric child communicates with tremendous warmth and is oriented toward the future.

The sanguine is more concerned with the here and now. *"If I am happy now, then everything is all right; if not, then I weep or I laugh."* The sanguine child can change his mood very quickly, which can be a strain on those around him. The sanguine child lives in the present and is involved in what immediately surrounds him. He is concerned more with the influences around him than he is with his own mood. If things are going well in school, then the sanguine child is pleased. If things are not going so well in the class, then the sanguine child can be extremely unhappy.

The children of winter [phlegmatic] are very much connected with the watery element. Children of the winter are comfort-loving: *"We have a fire, and we needn't do anything. Outside the snow is falling. There are snowflakes, more snowflakes, and more snowflakes. It's so nice and warm. Let's eat."* So you eat, you're warm and comfortable, and it's snowing outside. *"Why don't we knit?"* The child knits and knits and knits and goes on knitting. The scarf is getting about six feet long, and you have to say to Johnny, *"Don't you think this scarf is long enough?"* If you didn't stop him, it would be eight or ten feet long. *"Don't you think a scarf of eight or ten feet is a bit too long for old Granddad?"* *"Well, perhaps,"* he might answer, *"then I'll start another one!"* Such children love repetition, and they love to feel content and warm. *"How about some work?"* you might ask. *"Work?"* They are hard to move, but don't be fooled. Still waters run deep. At times, such children can act in the most surprising way because they've been quiet for so long. Suddenly, something happens like a storm. But overall, they possess a wonderful placid feeling, an evenness of being.

These children are faithful and loyal. Like all the temperaments, the phlegmatics have a positive and negative side. Just as the choleric can be destructive, the phlegmatic can be lazy, the melancholic interested in himself, and the sanguine superficial.

We don't ever want to change a child's temperament, we only want to harmonize the extremes. This point is often misunderstood. We want the phlegmatic child to somehow get on with it. The combination of a choleric father and a phlegmatic daughter can cause problems. The father wants his daughter, who is slow, kind, peaceful, and calm, to do more. This is the worst approach with phlegmatics, because they can become very obstinate. They will do even less than before. The parent will ask, *"What is the matter with him? He always flies off the handle. Why does he do that?"* And the child thinks, *"I'm going to do less than ever before. I've eaten. I've slept. I'm sitting very comfortably here by the fire, so I'm just not going to respond."* When this occurs, you have real problems.

The idea is not to transform the child, but to ennoble the temperament. How can we ennoble the melancholic, so that the melancholic is not excessively egocentric? If we bring the melancholic child more to the center, then we find a child who is very keen on research. The melancholic child is willing to look at things in depth and work toward a goal. The key to understanding the melancholics is to get them to realize more of their abilities. If the best is brought out, the melancholic will not abandon a particular problem.

So a melancholic can move from egocentricity to involvement, research, reliability, and sacrifice. The phlegmatic child may be inclined toward laziness; he does a lot of sitting and loves to eat potatoes and pasta so that it is difficult for him to move and remain alert. But when you overcome this tendency and have encouraged the positive aspects of his temperament, you will have a faithful child.

The sanguine is a little like a rough diamond – he may appear superficial, but behind his superficiality is a tremendous interest in the world. If this sanguinity is rightly engaged between the ages of six and fourteen, it will become a positive attribute. The sanguine child is a model of sociability.

Let me give you an example. Sarah was a child in the school where I taught in England. In the morning on the way to school, she would run up to me saying, *"Have you got the candles for John? It's his birthday. Do you know so and so is in the hospital? Have you heard...?"* By the time I walked into the classroom, I had all the news. I always made a point of thanking Sarah. She became pivotal in the social activities of the class. When there was a party or outing, Sarah would know exactly what was happening and how to organize it. The sanguine child has an organizational gift that is not always apparent. What may seem superficial and scatterbrained may actually be an asset socially.

When the choleric child is negative, he is very negative, because he flies into tempers and becomes destructive. When his anger erupts, his family trembles. When Richard is in the classroom, something tremendous is happening. Or, if Richard is absent from school, the whole class is a little different that day. The choleric child can be a thorn in the teacher's side. You often wonder how to deal with them and sometimes you think, *"You're really going to get it now."* But cholerics are always looking for a fight, and its important not to add fuel to their fire.

The way to approach the cholerics is to befriend them. If you are going on an outing, or planning a play, take your cholerics aside and say, *"We are going to do something very challenging. It's extremely difficult. I don't know whether you can manage it."* Remember, if it's easy, cholerics will be uninterested. After you have challenged them, you can solicit their help – which they will readily give. If your cholerics are not with you, you will have tyrants instead of selfless leaders and bullies instead of cohorts.

By now you begin to see the importance of working with the temperaments instead of fighting against them. You must always arrange activities to coincide with the temperaments of the children in your class. In my classroom, I like to have my cholerics on my right. I like to have my sanguines on my left near the door, so if they get too rowdy, I can say something like, *"My goodness, I've run out of chalk, would you go to the office and get some?"* They run out and by the time they're run back, they've missed a tremendous portion of the lesson, and they're captivated because they've missed something.

I put my melancholics in the dark part of the room near the blackboard, where they can watch the funny chap in the front of the room *"What is he doing? Does he really know that? The Encyclopedia Britannica knows a lot more."* And I put the phlegmatics in the back of the room near the window. When an ambulance comes screeching by, the phlegmatics say, *"We know what that is."* And they stay put – even if your sanguines are lined up along the windows.

I became aware of the differences of temperaments in a very dramatic way. I had a large class of over thirty fifth or sixth grade children. We had a little ritual for the art block; some children handed out the paper, while others dipped in the water and put it on the boards and sponged it. Some children gave out the brushes and paint. Everything was going pretty well. A large bucket of water stood in the middle of the room and an empty bucket stood next to it. The idea was to paint in silence and to exchange dirty water with clean water whenever it was necessary. One Friday, there was an accident, and a huge bucket of water got kicked over. There was an enormous amount of water, and it went all over everything. What did the melancholics do? They got up and stood in it. The sanguines were immediately standing on their chairs and shouting, "Ooh – what is that?" The cholerics rushed out after mops and buckets. What did the phlegmatics do? You may not believe it, but they sat in their chairs and lifted their legs up above the water. I got the best lesson in my life.

This story has a sequel. I didn't think the cholerics and sanguines would be able to coordinate cleaning up the water, so I took them outside in the courtyard and played a game with them. I asked the phlegmatics to clean up the mess and they did. It took them twenty minutes, but they cleaned up thoroughly. They have a wonderfully practical quality. The melancholics stood around for a while and then joined the game; they felt more comfortable playing than cleaning up. The variety of responses to this common situation was really enlightening.

Let me give you another example. If you put on a play, you should cast the characters according to the temperaments of your students. You might, for example, ask your cholerics to play Julius Caesar, and you might cast your sanguines as messengers, since they would enjoy running in and out with the news. The melancholics love philosophical roles. They might ask, *"Why was Julius Caesar murdered on the Ides of March? What were the pros and cons?"* The phlegmatics, on the other hand, like parts where they can sit and think, removed from the central action of the play. In the time of the Roman Empire, the news didn't travel fast. In distant lands, such as Britain, the news took months to arrive. The phlegmatics are ideal for playing characters who await the news in faraway countries.

If you fit your roles to the temperaments of your children, you will assign the comic parts to the melancholics, since they are the best comedians in the world. Charlie Chaplin and Marcel Marceau are two good examples. Your sanguines just can't carry it, whereas the melancholics, being good spectators and imitators, have all the gestures and mannerisms down pat. As a result, they make excellent comics.

The temperaments should also be considered while teaching history, geography, and the sciences. In arithmetic, for example the phlegmatic child enjoys the constant activity of adding numbers. Subtraction or taking away appeals to the melancholic. Multiplication is a sanguine activity, and division is a choleric activity. In the third grade, you can utilize stories that combine the four operations, so that the children will identify with their favorite operation and yet learn to appreciate the other operations as well.

In an orchestra, children of different temperaments enjoy playing different instruments. Cholerics like drums, the sanguines like violins and oboes, and melancholics like bassoons and cellos. The phlegmatics like the instruments that don't have to be tuned or fussed with, such as the piano. It's ready whenever they are inclined to play it.

In the Waldorf schools, children begin their musical education with recorders. Then they learn and practice on individual instruments and eventually play in small orchestras in elementary school and high school. We also ask the parents for their opinion on which instrument they think is appropriate for their children. Our main objective is to make music a pleasant experience for the children. By consulting the parents, we begin to have a greater understanding of the children's temperament at home.

No temperament is discrete; they all blend into one another. In the color circle, you can see how this blending occurs. It is a mistake to say a child is only choleric, melancholic or sanguine, or phlegmatic. [Emphasis by the editors.] Yet there is usually a preponderance of one temperament or another. And if you recognize this preponderance and ennoble it, then you will bring a greater harmony into the life of the child. If one temperament predominates in the child, say if he is choleric, then something melancholic should be encouraged in the child to restrain him and make him more introspective. But usually the choleric child is also partially sanguine and exhibits some of the liveliness of that temperament. On the other hand, the melancholic child retains something of that fiery aspect, as well as part of the watery aspect of the phlegmatic. It is rare to find a child with totally contrasting temperaments. a choleric-phlegmatic or a melancholic-sanguine.

When we think about the four temperaments, we should remember that all children are fundamentally sanguine. Sanguinity is the temperament of childhood. All children are filled with wonder and a desire to explore the world. Just as cholerics tend to look toward the future and melancholics look back at the past, sanguines enjoy the present outside themselves and phlegmatics like to contemplate the present in an introspective way – *"I've eaten well, I've slept well, and it is so cozy here."*

In teaching any subject, we try to harmonize these different shades and colors. In the classroom, the melancholic children suddenly begin to notice that all the children respond differently, and they begin to recognize alternative ways of responding to situations. The sanguines notice that melancholics always have profound questions, and then they think, *"Well, I don't have any profound questions, I'm happy. But – I've never thought of that, what if…"* In the class empathy begins to develop. The melancholics notice how active the sanguine children are, and they are amazed at their energy. A complementary activity begins to happen in the class. In those six or seven years, the children learn to recognize other temperaments and prepare to become individuals.

We have all seen teenagers enter a period when they feel they can't go on with their rough temperaments. They feel they've got to do something with themselves. With the help of a skilled classroom teacher, their temperaments can be acknowledged and harmonized. That is why Rudolf Steiner told the early teachers of Waldorf schools that they were going to be like plumbers in the dark. Steiner emphasized that teachers should develop a sense of how these temperaments function in varying situations.

If, as a teacher and parent, you can conceive of these four temperaments, you will develop a new awareness of the world. You will be then able to look at the world through a temperament that is not your own. That is the point with this color circle: if you live in the blue and have no concept of the yellow green, then you are impoverished. As parents and teachers, we have a tremendous opportunity to look at the world in a refreshing way. Then, not by criticism, but by taking temperament into account, we can lead the child to harmonize different characteristics. In the later grades, we discuss this approach with the children, so that they can leave school with an appreciation of temperaments. This is a new step in the psychology of understanding the soul and the individuality of the child at each stage of development.

— *Creativity in Education,* originally presented as a lecture

The Beauty of Color

MANETTE TEITELBAUM

The realm of color is a realm where our feelings play – where we experience the mystery, the drama of light and dark played on the stage of matter. The actors, the colors, each have something to tell. Although they speak to each heart in its own way, they also speak the language of the heavens to those who listen well.

In his lectures, Rudolf Steiner speaks about each of the arts and how each is received and experienced by a different aspect of our nature. Music relates to the realm of spirit and man's Ego, and penetrates deeply into our will-nature. Modeling, on the other hand, is a shaping of space and a metamorphosis of form which molds our thinking processes.

Painting comes alive in the realm of the soul. Through color our feelings find expression and order. The bright light of the soul dips into the darkness of the physical body and a breathing, rhythmic relationship begins. This breathing can be seen in the larger cycles of night and day, life and death, where the soul moves in and out like our own breath. Color is to our soul, with its inward and outward movement, as the breath is to our body. Blue recedes into the depth pulling us into the outer-world – we exhale; where red leaps forward and presses in upon us, an in breathing. In a sense the eye itself breathes in a color and breathes forth a color response which we can experience by looking at a patch of bright red, for example, and, then closing our eyes to see that we have formed green. Color has been called the "breath of the living soul."

In each of the arts we have an immediate and individual response to the characters that play before us – the notes, the forms, the colors. Colors evoke vivid personal feelings in us and young children readily express their reactions to different colors. The child's soul shines brightly in his inner world and he is quick to find the colors which portray his inner landscape. Every child loves color and becomes immersed in the feelings that a color calls forth within him. We often see how a child is free with his colors and is not bound by representation of the natural world as adults may be. If we can lift ourselves away from this bondage, that of our likes and dislikes, and our personal reactions to color, we can discover that red is more than warm, blue more than cool in the scheme of life.

Imagine that colors are like people, having much more to themselves than meets the eye at first glance. Though each has its own nature, its activity in the world, each color also bespeaks of the greater harmony, the grander struggle between light and dark that exists in the eternal nature of the world. Therefore, when we work with pure color, if we apply discipline to our efforts, we can open the doors to a new way of bringing balance, harmony and health into our feeling life. We can begin to use color in a conscious way.

There is so much to be gained from the skillful and conscious use of color in our lives and in the lives of the children. Color can be used to help the young child cope with his own nature. The color of his room, his blankets, and curtains call forth an inner response as he awakens each day. For a child of melancholic temperament, a peaceful blue will bring forth a playful orange in his soul. For an energetic child a pale warm red will calm his activity by activating a placid green within.

As teachers, we seek to help the children gain balance and soul-strength through painting. For a child to take up a brush and dip it into a beautiful watery blue, to watch the color flow on to his clean white page, and then to see what change takes place when shining yellow disturbs this quietude – here is a lesson in the laws that govern the soul. How will blue respond to the entrance of the enlivening rays of yellow? Can the child harmonize these elements? This he can learn to do with gentle guidance and experience with the colors, and as he learns to find a harmonious relationship to the colors externally, his inner world will find the sense of order that governs the feelings in his soul. The child's natural love of color needs nurturing and protection in this beautiful God-filled universe that has become such an empty place in this materialistic age.

— *Chanticleer*

A Painting Verse

The sunlight shines into each day

And sends the dark of night away

It brings the colors to my eyes

The bright green earth, the deep blue skies.

The yellow sun, the red, red rose

That in the gentle garden grows.

And from within my loving heart

The light always conquers dark

So on my paper let it be

Sunlight and water - joyfully.

Author unknown

Watching a eurythmy performance is mesmerizing. It's as if a delicate golden thread were winding its bright way through the performers as they inscribe a beautiful, harmonious pattern of movement in the 'soul space' of the stage. The thread is alive and on fire, and the eurythmists move in reverence to it, always aware of the subtle creative force beyond their individual selves. The weaving hands, borealic veils, and solemn gestures spun out on the words of the bard carry me into a contemplative space. I imagine this must be how we 'spoke' before incarnation, when with bodies of light we expressed ourselves with our whole being in movement.

— Richard Leviton

Eurythmy in Education

The center of Steiner education lies in the life of feeling. To acquire ideas without any experience enlivening them, to move without feeling for the movement – this, in Steiner's view, is not true education. But when he spoke of the need for feeling he did not mean *personal* feelings, into which feeling often degenerates, and which has given rise to the idea of art as self-expression. He meant the objective feeling, which links man to the world, to the divine, to his fellow men.

Feeling, however, expresses itself in rhythm, as even the physical form of man reveals. The man of thought has his center in the head, enclosed, motionless, centripetal. The man of feeling rests on the central middle system of heart and lungs, where movement, because it is rhythmical, never tires, and where there is a constant interplay between center and periphery. It is through rhythm that a balance and harmony is established between the two poles of human experience – the consciousness of the head and the will activity of the limbs. In establishing this harmony rhythm frees the forces of the head – the intellectual forces – from their tendency to harden in abstraction, and brings order into the impulses of will, only too liable to explode in wild activity.

All educational exercises in eurythmy have, therefore, a rhythmical character. But starting from the center they work into two directions, the experience of movement in space and the experience of knowledge in the mind.

A child only gradually wins the freedom of space and there are many exercises in eurythmy to foster the process at different stages of his development – from simple clapping and walking in different rhythms to group exercises with copper rods which require considerable skill and exact timing. A number of exercises are specially designed as social education, to make the children aware of each other.

All learning – especially the learning of children – should bring about new distinctions of experience, and there are hardly any such distinctions which eurythmy does not meet and enhance. To give one example, when children learn grammar, it may be at one age to come to terms with past, present and future, at another to feel the difference between active and passive, at another to realize the function of verb, noun and adjective. Eurythmy meets all these fine distinctions with appropriate movement and gesture, so that the grammar lessons enter the domain of the whole man, a form of knowledge enshrined in the old phrase "to know it in your bones"– so different from merely knowing it in the head.

Or, again, before they study the laws of geometrical forms, the children gain a vital experience of them in movement – walking and running in squares, circles, lemniscates, pentagons, pentagrams, etc., It is a kind of golden rule in Steiner Schools that learning begins with movement, and in this respect eurythmy can be the handmaid and interpreter of very many subjects in the curriculum.

Naturally eurythmy also plays its part in relation to those subjects where it would most obviously be expected, in poetry and in music. The tremendous difference between the Mediterranean hexameter and the Northern alliterative meter, the distinction in feeling between poems based on an iambic or trochaic meter, the impact of close or open rhymes, the various stanza forms, the subtleties of free verse, all these find varying expression in the movements of eurythmy. Similarly in music, the inner response to four time or three time, the relation of melody to the fundamental beat, major and minor moods, the interweaving of the several parts in polyphonic music, are carried into the activity of the limbs.

It is here that educational eurythmy touches most closely the sphere of artistic eurythmy, in which sounds in poetry or intervals in music are expressed in definite gestures corresponding to their inner nature, gestures not stereotyped, but capable of an infinite variety of modification. Such gestures constitute a training in the apprehension of the subtle qualities of sounds and rhythms in poetry, keys and intervals in music. The children meet these gestures in various ways at different ages of their development, from simple imitation in the nursery class to a conscious realization of their fitness in the older classes. To perform a fairy tale, or a poem, or a piece of music in eurythmy is also a part of education. Or, if a play contains elemental beings, as in Shakespeare's *Tempest* or Milton's *Comus*, these characters may be performed in eurythmy while the rest is acted dramatically.

Eurythmy began early in this century, as the dance world was undergoing a tremendous artistic revolution, when a prospective dance student asked Rudolf Steiner whether a new impulse could be brought to the existing arts of movement. In answer, Steiner developed the basic principles of eurythmy in collaboration with the actress Marie von Sivers. During the past seventy years these extensive indications have been developed and applied – artistically as a performing art, in education as part of the curriculum in all Waldorf schools and curatively in a special therapeutic form.

— The Steiner Centre, London

Literacy, Not Just Reading

ARTHUR M. PITTIS

To appreciate fully how and when reading is taught in Waldorf Schools, one must first understand the purpose of the entire curriculum. Rudolf Steiner hoped that Waldorf schools would serve as centers for the reawakening of spiritual life. The curriculum and pedagogy would serve as practical tools for this task by directly countering the hardening and narrowing forces of material-ism in modern life. One of the focuses of this work was to develop in children faculties of imaginative thinking capable of inspiring them in their adult lives to morally purposeful deeds. Waldorf education was seen as no less than a seed for the future.

No one would think of giving a child one pair of rugged steel shoes which must last a lifetime. The difficulties of such short sightedness are immediately apparent. But as a society we think nothing of giving our children ready-made concepts and, without much reflection, expect them to go forth with these bits of information and meet life. But true knowledge springs from understanding, and understanding grows out of experience. Experience, understanding and knowledge change through life; just like a child's foot, they grow. A shoe which is flexible and supports one's foot as one travels down the hard paths of life is a good one, and when it is worn out one tosses it aside, regretfully but appreciative of the service given. A shoe, on the other hand, which can never be outgrown, worn out or cast aside will only maim and cripple its wearer. Materialistic, informational education is such a shoe; instead of the foot, it cripples thinking and thinking's ability to engage one's feelings so they can inspire one's will.

The goal of the Waldorf approach to the language arts, of which the teaching of reading is only one integral part, is to inspire in every child a love for the powers of language. In Waldorf education the introduction of reading grows out of the child's own experience of living language. Reading like all the traditional academic subjects is not taught in the Waldorf kindergarten. If a child teaches herself how to read at this time, fine and good; no attempt should be made to actively suppress or develop this skill. What we are seeing in such children is a loving imitation of an adult activity. During these early years the healthiest thing a child can do is experience the natural substances of the world while developing, side by side, a deep and reverent love for nature and fellow human beings. Activity is primary, both the activity of the child herself, and adult activity worthy of devoted imitation. Singing, role playing, running, skipping, building up and tearing things down, doing simple but essential domestic tasks, and learning to get along socially with the other children are the child's most important jobs at this age. Later on, in the elementary school, there will be time enough for academics.

Like standing, walking and speaking, children learn to read at their own pace. While children can be rushed into reading earlier than they would normally master this skill, it is always at a cost, either emotionally, physiologically or academically. One of the saddest signs that children are being rushed in reading prematurely are the escalating numbers of reading difficulties among children of normal ability and intelligence in the early elementary grades. (Television and electronic entertainment bear no small share of this responsibility.) Children who would have learned to read perfectly well in an unhurried and stress-free environment now carry a deep resentment towards and fear of reading. It is a sad commentary on our society that the political forces driving American education continue to fail to observe the harmful effects of their programs on children and the future well being of learning and society in general.

In Waldorf education there are no rigid, time-specific goals for reading or any other subject towards which a class will be driven, and before which individuals will be sacrificed if they do not achieve quickly enough. Rather a class teacher works broadly and flexibly with the materials to be learned and the differing temperaments, maturational rates and abilities of the children in a class. The goal is not test-oriented skill levels but rather an environment in which the picture forming faculties of imagination are nourished and learning becomes a living force within each child.

When a teacher gives imaginative pictures to a class each individual in the class can then transform these pictures into personal experiences which will form the foundation for a healthy and inspired relationship to knowledge. An education founded on imagination, as opposed to one that is a product of "bits" of information, permits children to develop flexibility in their conceptual lives. Education which is full of life and life's pictures is healthy education and acts as a seed for the future, both for the individual and human cultural and social life as a whole.

Now back to reading and how it is taught. In the first grade the picture making quality of Waldorf education is clearly visible in the introductory work with the letters. The first lessons in reading grow out of the archetypal moral images of the fairy tales. Say a tale has a magical snake. After the teacher has reviewed the story with the class, they draw pictures of the snake. In the course of drawing, the undulating gesture of the snake emerges. The teacher then shows the children how the sound of the snake can be found in its picture image as well as the initial letter of its word. The letter 's' thereby emerges. In a similar manner other pictographic relations between the archetypal sounds of the consonants and their modern representations are developed. The work of the eurythmist who creates parallel images of language in the archetypal gestures of speech eurythmy supports and deepens the class teacher's work. Not every consonant needs to be presented in this way; imaginative images are a very economical way of educating, and the child himself will be able to develop additional imaginations of his own. Once all the letters have been presented – the consonants through images of the external world and the vowels through inner soul gestures – the teaching of writing begins.

Writing is slightly more important than reading in that writing is active while reading is passive. Historically, people had to write before they could read, and Waldorf education tries to follow the development of human consciousness as faithfully as possible. So the Waldorf reading curriculum is actually a writing curriculum, and the ability to read emerges out of the activity of writing. One of the most important experiences for a child is the realization that the markings on a page suddenly make sense and that she can now read. By having the children copy their teacher's compositions into beautifully made lesson books, Waldorf education prepares children for this experience, thereby establishing a much more intimate relation with reading than otherwise possible.

Taught through writing, reading starts with the imaginative presentation of letters, moves onto the copying of simple sentences and, in turn, whole stories. Parallel to these imaginative experiences phonics and sight word skills are developed as essential tools for decoding. It is important to emphasize that in first grade the pedagogical intent is to build deep and strong foundations, capable of supporting the very demanding language arts curriculum of later grades.

Throughout first grade the child is given a rich experience of language through the daily use of poetry and story telling. Poetry trains a sense for language's beauty while developing memory. The fairy tales present profound archetypal soul images while developing a sense for narration. The teacher's own compositions, copied from the board by the children, are designed to address the particular needs of that class. As in the better primers (the Dolch series in particular), the language and syntax are controlled, and specific phonetic patterns are emphasized; but most importantly, the composition is alive and was created for that particular class and moment in time. No text book can ever achieve this degree of relevancy. The children receive this type of writing as they would a handmade versus a store bought gift.

The very good question is often asked – how does the Waldorf approach challenge the children who enter first grade already knowing how to read? What will such children learn; won't they be bored? All depends on how open parents are to the goals of Waldorf education. If a child experiences doubt or hostility towards their school from a parent the child will naturally and rightly assume the attitudes of that parent, and the work of even the finest teacher will be of no benefit. But if parents want a child's power of imagination to be nourished and cultivated, if they have faith that not learning to read as quickly as a neighbor or relative expects is fine, then even the most academically advanced child will retain the openness necessary to enjoy and benefit from the Waldorf approach. All children are nourished by imaginative activities; they resonate in a child's soul and impart a purpose and flexibility to life which quantitative, informational based curricula are incapable of giving.

In second grade reading instruction more closely resembles conventional methods of phonetic and sight vocabulary instruction. Second grade is also the time when the majority of children discover that they know how to read. This discovery takes place in the most wonderful manner. Each day during a writing block the class teacher reads from that day's writing assignment. The class "reads" along, following the teacher's voice. One by one the individual children come to the wonderful realization that the teacher's voice is no longer needed, that the reading can be done alone. The child lowers her eyes to her own book, looks upon the writing from a previous day and realizes she can read her own hand. One of life's great threshold's has been crossed.

In third grade the students read from "real" (printed) books as well as their own lesson books. The use of readers may happen as early as second grade, and this decision is left to the discretion of the teacher. But by third grade it is an integral part of the reading program. Third grade is also the time when the students begin to write out most of the lesson book stories in their own words. This independent work was first introduced in second grade, but now it becomes a focal point of the language arts curriculum. Using the class teacher's presentations as starting points each individual student explores his or her own individual voice. Some students write copiously, some cautiously, and others eloquently. The important thing is that each is drawing up to the level of consciousness all they have experienced of narration, character and description in the earlier grades.

In fourth grade and up very little of the teacher's writing is copied into the student's books. Only in cases where very concise information or stylistic examples are needed should the writings be anyone's other than the students' themselves. By now reading is a regular part of each individual's day. Students should be reading at home on a daily basis, and book reports, oral and written, can be continually in process for sharing with the class. Parallel to and supportive of the work with composition and literature is the study of grammar. Work with the modern languages also reinforces and deepens the students' understanding of their mother tongue. By the beginning of middle school children in a Waldorf school have a strong sense for living language and excellent foundations upon which to explore its forms, as well as find their own voices in the succeeding years.

A word about children with learning difficulties in regard to language skills is important. In any class there are increasing numbers of children who experience difficulties with language greater than simple maturational slowness. The reasons for this occurrence can be found in many places, ranging from the destructive influences of television, to physiological and psychological handicaps. There are no easy answers for dealing with these children, but the three essential ingredients in any approach must be patience, compassion and hard work, by both the student, teacher and parents. Worrying about, pampering and procrastinating with these children do them no good. From kindergarten on teachers and parents need to objectively observe their children and watch for signs of any type of learning disability. Many types of screening tools exist to assist us in our evaluations. Evaluation of these diagnostic results can sometimes prove problematic, and it must always be remembered that, while a child certainly needs to learn basic skills, over-reliance on information based remediation without attention to curative work on a constitutional level does little to address the fundamental problem.

The imaginative and artistic work of Waldorf education is not a luxury suitable only for seemingly normal children, just like an enlivening cultural life is not only for the economically privileged. If teachers and family can understand each other and work together to give a child supplemental help when needed, all the gifts of Waldorf education can be experienced by the child. If no such understanding can be reached, then just like in the cases of an academically precocious child, the school/family relationship will not work.

All learning in Waldorf schools strives to imbue the child with a deep appreciation for and love of knowledge. Out of experience develops understanding, and out of understanding develops thought. Through imaginative experiences the language arts curriculum, like all the other subjects, assists each child to develop visions and thoughts capable of inspiring strength, faith and courage needed for meeting what comes to us out of the future. We rebel as human beings against being programmed like machines. Inflexible information deadens us. We feel, if not understand, that our future and, thereby, our freedom is being stolen. Waldorf education, on the other hand, stands in opposition to such materialistic education. It is able to do so because at its very core is a spiritual image of the human being which recognizes the evolutionary implications of all our deeds, even something as remote as how we learned to read.

> — This article first appeared in *Leading Forth* in 1988 and was republished in the Garden City Waldorf School's Alumni newsletter in 1994.

Drama, a Tool for Learning

GRACE BROUSSARD AND RICHARD LINDLEY

Most of us in the parent generation grew up with the idea that drama is a form of entertainment. The play itself might be very sad, even tragic, but the act of going to the theater was one of those things we did at night or on the weekend when we were not engaged in our "serious" work.

From its earliest beginning, nonetheless, the essential meaning of drama lay in its power to transform human experiences and emotions. The early Greeks who watched *Oedipus Rex* were not just observing Oedipus' "hubris" from the other side of an invisible screen. It was their own "hubris" on the stage, embodied in Oedipus, and when Oedipus sacrificed his ego and transformed his pride into wisdom, the audience came away transformed as well. Even today, when we say that a play or a film "moves" us, we mean that we came away from it a somewhat different person.

If drama has a transforming power for adults, it has a forming power in children. Children are not yet fully themselves, and the experience of drama shapes their character and informs their soul in a more direct way. As adults, we constantly need to change or rediscover ourselves, but children need to come into themselves for the first time, and drama is a wonderful way for them to experience the potential of their own soul. There are a number of ways that drama acts to heighten their awareness.

Drama involves the actors directly in another point of view. The student who acts a character discovers that character's situation and feelings, and in turn this experience allows the student to see his or her own self from the perspective of the other. Dramatizing a story brings it to life in a way that simple reading or hearing it can never bring about. The distance between the reader and the character shrinks as the actor steps into the character's shoes. While telling or hearing a story involves our thought, drama engages the whole body and brings the story into feeling and will. Particularly during the lower school years, when children have not yet fully found their own feelings and emotions, drama gives them an opportunity to explore the feelings of others and thus learn to express and control their own burgeoning feeling life. In a sense, the characters "give" their feelings to the actors.

Learning a part and going on stage with it, in other words, "taking action" or "acting", also serves as a laboratory drama for the will. The students exert their own will as they play the characters and thus win awareness and control of their own behavior. On the one hand, existing feelings can be expressed in a controlled, safe context. On the other hand, new ways of feeling can be "tried on" in an emotionally protected way. Children can explore new ways of relating to one another without seeming or feeling insincere.

The teacher or director has an opportunity to guide children in their experiences of strong feelings and problematic behavior through the dilemmas of the characters and this guidance can take place without relying on intellectual attention or direct analysis. Abstract ideas and principles can speak to the student indirectly through concrete experience. This concrete experience takes the subject matter of the play into the body and feelings of the child. The hands and heart thus support the head, and the three aspects of the child are woven together in one experience that brings strength and learning.

Drama thus achieves one of the essential goals of Waldorf education; to integrate thinking, feeling, and willing. This is why in a Waldorf school, drama is not something to be approached through a set of books, nor is it something done only in special interest clubs by a few students. Drama is for the whole class as a part of the curriculum because few other activities address the various aspects of the child's character so globally or in such an engaging way.

The task of working on a play together also contributes to the social dynamic of the class. Completion of the performance leads to a shared experience of pride in accomplishment, an experience that strengthens the bond among the students of the class. "The drama" becomes an especially beneficial social experiment for the class when, as is the case in a Waldorf setting, the dramatic subject mirrors the developmental stage of the class.

Every child moves and speaks, however small the part, in a Waldorf school play. The drama engages each and every child as an individual soul and as a social being. In some measure, each performance works to bring the child toward full awareness of who he or she is, and to give awareness and control that will eventually allow the child to take charge of his or her own destiny in life, a destiny that is as particular and unpredictable, and yet as universal, as the destinies of the heroes and heroines, the gods and goddesses of the ongoing human drama.

— *The Lively Oak*, the Austin, TX
Waldorf School community newsletter

Waldorf Education and Science

CLIFFORD SKOOG

Waldorf education holds that development has a meaning which cuts across different time scales and different kinds of being. The mythical and religious content of the earliest grades bring the child to the same wellsprings from which humanity began its great journey into awareness. Myth and religion are the parents of Art and Science, delivered of them by that dubious midwife, Philosophy. Today Art and Science eclipse and usurp their elders, as if they were themselves characters in a Greek myth or tragedy. They have empowered us to stuff our world with Facts and Artifacts at rates whose increase may well prove pathological.

What we can make and what we can know are taken more and more as the only evidence for what we are. This journey, regardless of the risk, is not optional; we are thrown on our own resources, and both the artist and the scientist, in different ways, come to meet nature as their equal. For both it is a matter of confidence in their faculties and a relentless tension between imagination and reality. Science has shown again and again that imagination gives us the keys to reality, but matching them to the locks never stops being challenging. The physicist Richard Feynman critiqued a colleague's idea with: "That is a crazy idea, but I don't think it's crazy enough to be true."

For children, as for humankind, Science means different things at different ages. And, as always, it is a Waldorf teacher's vocation to discern the potentialities belonging to the child's own interests and enthusiasms and draw them toward investments that will send them strongly where they are going. Natural History places us in a living world and awakens a positive awareness of senses which were made by and for that world. Mechanics explores a doing which our ideas can take complete possession of. Nutrition and Hygiene begin to explore the peculiar way the body belongs on the one hand to oneself and on the other to processes that are impersonal or public or woven into a fabric shared more deeply than anything we can name.

For teachers, Science is about the kinds of challenges that forge a sense of reality out of conflicting inclinations: conceptual intoxication versus sober observation, for instance, or what seems true to one person versus what seems true to someone else. Measure was an idea central to Greek thought, but it was left to Shakespeare to frame the special human importance of "Measure For Measure". Was our faith in yesterday's Science misplaced? How much can we rely on what they are telling us today?

Children in a Waldorf school should be able to experience Science as a journey which gives them confidence in their own measures of things; and, here is the nub of it, in their own sense of evidence wrought from challenges which have had meaning for them. It isn't having the answers that counts, nor even having the questions, but having a sense that one's own experience pertains to both the questions and the answers in a way that unfolds as evidence.

In addition to a comprehensive emphasis on participatory observation and experimentation, the science curriculum in Waldorf schools follow two of the most basic guidelines of Waldorf education:

1. Ordering the kinds of learning most relevant for development, most suited to the kinds of questions and involvement children will be able to call their own.

In the later grades, a Waldorf teacher is called to find approaches to science that answer both the developmental challenges of pre-adolescence and the scientific competencies necessary for subsequent schooling. Science and mathematics teaching in Waldorf schools function as prologues to the demands made by higher education for intensely abstract learning. That capacity naturally gains strength with adolescence.

Before then, many aspects of Waldorf education cultivate competency for abstraction even through arts, music, movement, and games. When the time comes, a Waldorf educated child will typically be able to draw a powerful sense for the abstract from elements of many of the creative skills in which they have become proficient. At the same time, responsible science education in the middle school may have to take account of where science appears to be heading, and what kind of inspirations will serve to maintain interest in science over the long run. From this perspective, what appears important is a sense for the purpose of science: a quest for truth and for the improvement and protection of humanity.

The Waldorf schools typically guide participation in ecologically oriented projects in order to awaken and sharpen an idealism which will consolidate the motivations fueling a career of abstract learning. Our objective is that students be strongly interested and excited by science, have the personal resources to succeed in learning what will show itself as worth learning, and have the confidence and originality to distinguish what is worth learning from what is not. The specialized languages, rapid change, and institutionalization of contemporary science in fact require that students be always able to renew their own motivations when encountering it, be more able to learn new science than contain old science, and be able to distinguish the science that extends human understanding from that which merely proliferates as an academic business.

2. Working from the whole to the part.

In science, where the criteria of comprehension hinges on the ability to apply conceptual abstractions, we feel that it is on the basis of encountering phenomenal wholes that a sense for the kinds of abstractions which are most relevant emerges. One way to emphasize wholeness is to insure that engagement with the subject begins from sense and feeling as well as abstract thought. In biology, organisms and their life-cycles and the ecology in which they participate are given attention before organ systems, cells, and molecular biology: until there is a feeling for LIFE, the instrument readings by which life's components are analyzed invite reductionisms which are neither accurate nor pedagogically nourishing.

Likewise in physics, we find it important that warmth is felt, sound is heard, and light allows us to see: should these phenomenal fundamentals be neglected, the mystery of nature – the awe which has motivated the scientists to which we owe most – becomes nothing more than moving magnitudes and magnitudes of motion. Thus the geometries of soap bubbles can become a more effective introduction to the principle of least action than a mathematical account of Newton's apple.

In science, wholeness is found not only in the phenomena it treats, but also in its own story. Waldorf education is profoundly humanistic but this does not mean it underemphasizes science. As Gregory Bateson often remarked, one can turn a science into a humanity by teaching its history. Waldorf education finds wholeness in science by showing science's own development, and by telling stories of its discoveries and discoverers. By the time science becomes a focal part of the Waldorf curriculum, Waldorf students are already connoisseurs of storytelling: they have experienced dramatic shifts over the years in the kinds of stories that are brought to them and are ready, when new kinds of stories are brought, to unfold new ways to approach learning.

In science they encounter stories where learning and discovery are center stage in such a way that the truths and errors belonging to individual experience come to be sharply defined, and the questions hiding behind every answer are themselves shown to make history. The individual discoveries of science are by this demonstrated to be only part of the truth of their subject. Should a Waldorf teacher, for example, choose to introduce the Linnean taxonomy or the Periodic Table of the elements, (s)he might be careful to show how the sciences and times of which they were part needed to approach things by means of classifications – and how the "truth" of such an approach could also be soon seen as holding back and slowing down what would be the next important understandings of their subjects.

— *Marin Waldorf School Parent Handbook*

A Humanist Talks About Waldorf Education

JOSEPH CHILTON PEARCE

I used to think Waldorf education the most undamaging education, but then the more I looked into it, I found it the most beneficial system we have. People ask, "What will happen to my child in the world if he doesn't learn to read and write very early?"

The issue is that the child's greatest strength for survival in a world of madness is to be whole, sane and in touch with the heart. The beauty of the Waldorf school is that it keeps children intact until they are ready to move out into the world as whole individuals.

Major studies have recently dealt with the "disappearance of childhood" in America. Among many things that the Waldorf system does, it nurtures, protects and develops the intelligence of the true child. What is it that Waldorf education aims to do? We are helping to bring out the best in each child, rather than molding children to a particular perspective of society. As Rudolf Steiner put it:

> One should not ask, 'What does a person need to know and be able to do for the existing social order?' but rather, 'What gifts does a person possess and how may these be developed?'. Then it will be possible to bring to society new forces from each succeeding generation. Then the social order will always be alive with that which fully developed individuals bring with them into life, rather than that each succeeding generation be made to conform to an existing social organization.

— *Marin Waldorf School Parent Handbook*

What about ....?

Children should not cull the fruits of reflection and observation early, but expand in the sun and let thoughts come to them. They should not through books antidate their actual experiences.

— Margaret Fuller Ossoli

Building a Waldorf Community

ROBERT SCHIAPPACASSE

From one point of view, parents are the founders of Waldorf schools all over the globe. It is the parents who put their faith and their money into the teachers who would realize the goals of Waldorf education on behalf of their children. We can ask: to what degree are parents called, like Waldorf teachers, to the co-creation of Waldorf schools? Do schools acknowledge sufficiently that the origin, unfolding and success of the Waldorf school movement is equally in the hands of parents? Can we recognize that parents too are "called" into Waldorf communities and that the Waldorf schools can only exist effectively when parents answer that "call"? That their answer to that call may lead not only their child, but their talents, expertise and insight into the life of the school? Parents are, among other things, a protective membrane around the school organism. Through parents the school has a place in the large civic community.

"Parent education" is a worthy and important activity that the teachers can use to create a deeper understanding of the values and intentions of Waldorf education. But the board, teachers and administration also need to be educated by the parents: what they bring into our midst can be no less vital to the unfolding destiny of the school.

In every Waldorf community recognized or unrecognized examples abound of parents making Waldorf education possible. Parents' social will, in large and small ways, enables the school to grow – in the legal, civic, political, social and economic realities where it would take root. Some parents become involved in the parent council, committees or the board, while others remain on the periphery, contributing independently.

All parents who support Waldorf education are "visionaries" in our contemporary culture. Perhaps a better description for them, as a Shining Mountain parent once shared with me, would be "patrons" – patrons of the "art of education". It is my experience that the parents recognize the creative abilities and intentions of the teachers. They gather together in groups called "classes" to support the work of the teachers of their children. Without their patronage, the "art of education" would not be funded, and our teachers would be starving artists.

Parents can be very demanding patrons indeed! They often have very high expectations and they often identify problems in the work-in-progress, which is very annoying to the artist. Teachers tell them, "Come back in a few weeks, and you'll see how it will develop." And when things don't seem to be developing, they ask difficult questions and their concerns point to developments that are problematic, even aspects of the school that are painful to face. Who would not admit that much which is problematic in our schools is identified and confronted because of the perception of the parents? Parents are indeed, among other things, a significant organ of perception within and around our schools. To overlook their views of matters that concern the school is to misuse a vital resource. They have important perceptions to share on almost every aspect of the school's life – students, classes, the effectiveness of the teachers, the college, administration and board. To undervalue parent input in the organization of our schools, to fail to support this significant dialogue in the community in explicit ways, is to undermine the very fabric of our lives.

Can our Waldorf schools be true partnerships between the faculty, board and parents? What stands in the way? Dialogue with a person is easier than dialogue with an "organization". Unless parents are willing to "get to know the school" through becoming active, there will be many opportunities for misunderstanding. Overworked teachers, administration and board, combined with insufficient resources of time and money, don't allow for many frills. More meetings to this end can be defeating. What's the solution? Encouraging parents to become part of the solution through volunteering time, energy and support to areas where the school *needs* support. Conversely, the board and the college need to actively support a strong and vigorous parent association or parent council through a clearly mandated role in the school *and* through *their own* activate participation in such a parent group.

In a young school, it is apparent that the school actually consists of one-to-one interpersonal relationships. As a school grows, it becomes more and more difficult for it not to be perceived as an organization. Remembering that organizations are the sum total of relationships between the participants, we can ask: "*How can we keep the form of the school, its organization, transparent to the relationships that are at every moment creating and sustaining it?*" We need to be clear as a school evolves that each constituency maintains, out of itself and in association with the others, its vital sphere of activity. The various bodies need to encourage, support and *thank* each other. *Gratitude is the best medicine for the illnesses of our community life. We must never be too busy to find ways to give and receive gratitude.*

When one lives in a community, one senses more and more what it means to live on the threshold of the spiritual world. What does this mean, to live on the threshold? It means to experience every more consciously that we are being "seen". We are being seen by the spiritual world, by our colleagues, and more and more, thereby, we see ourselves in a new light. We come to know ourselves as like the others, wrestling with our shortcomings and with our insufficiencies, trying to live up to ideals that are just beyond our grasp. This is the self-knowledge we need to be able to work effectively with students, parents and our colleagues. Without this sober self-knowledge, we are not yet cognizant that our communities only exist because we are carrying others and being carried by others. We carry others on our back and we are carried on the backs of others, more and less. As well, the spiritual world works with our working together, more and less. To this "more and less" we owe the existence of our schools and the communities of families and friends that surround and enable them.

With the challenge we face at this critical time in our school movement, it is time to share, as parents, teachers and board members, how the inner life can support the healthy development of our communities. Rudolf Steiner has given us a verse for cultivating the healthy social life:

The healthy social life is found

When, in the mirror of each human soul

The whole community finds its reflection

And when, in the community,

The virtue of each one is living.

We can use this verse as a touchstone for the intention of our lives as adults in community. This verse comes alive when it is joined to an inner meditative activity where we learn to "picture the others we work with in community". Rudolf Steiner points to such a community building technique in the book, *The Challenge of the Times*:

> Precisely in the social life of humanity must the principle come into existence: 'Thou shalt make for thyself an image of thy fellowman'. But then, when we form a picture of our fellow man, we enrich our own soul-life; then do we bestow a treasure upon our own inner soul-life with each human acquaintance. Then we do not any longer so live that A lives there, B there, C there, but A, B and C live in D; A, B and D live in C; C, D and E live in A; etc., We gain the capacity to have other human beings live in us… When we form a picture of the other person, which is implanted as a treasure in our soul, then we carry within the realm of our soul-life something from him just as in the case of a bodily brother we carry around something through the common blood.

Teachers meditate in this way on their students. If we could come to know this spiritual activity in the midst of our fast-paced lives, a new leaven could come into our lives together as adults: teachers to parents, parents to teachers, teachers to teachers. This inner picturing of the other can serve to strengthen our communities, creating an atmosphere of warmth and appreciation that will support the uniqueness of each individual in our school community. Active meditative picturing can weave fresh forces of understanding and recognition between soul and soul.

I am not suggesting that this will make our lives or our work on behalf of the students easier or less challenging: this is not our goal. Our goal is to find ways to work with the help of the spiritual world so that our efforts will be fruitful in the life of each student. To learn to interest the spiritual world in our work with each other as adults supports the work of the teacher with the children.

Our movement is flowering at this significant time, as we approach the end of the century. And we can see that flowering is not an end in itself. "Bees" are attracted to our Waldorf school "flowers": public school bees, focus school bees, charter schools bees. We are probably not ready, but our flowering carries with it a cultural deed. It has been noticed, and will change the lives of our schools and communities. It will bring new challenges and activity. How well have we integrated our schools in the larger community? Are we too cloistered? Are we known? Are we valued? Have we valued sufficiently our brothers and sisters in private education? Have we become a school that contributes to and benefits the larger community in which we live? The more we are able to integrate parents, inwardly and outwardly, into the life of our schools, the more our schools will have the warmth, life and light, as well as the strength, to grow in a healthy way into the next century.

> — Excerpts from a lecture presented at a conference on "Administration in Waldorf Schools" sponsored by AWSNA and Sunbridge College, 1995

Religion and Waldorf Education

KAREN RIVERS

The word "religion" is derived from the Latin word *re-lig-io* which means to "re-unite". It is an expression of the universal human quest for meaning, for our source and our destiny. Throughout human history, people from all cultures have asked "Who am I?" "What am I doing here?" "What does it mean to be human?"

We share questions about creation, good and evil, and what exists beyond the starry cosmos and unknown dark matter. These soul questions live deeply within all humanity. Through different periods of history, great men and women have shed light on these universal questions. They have offered their wisdom to help each individual answer them, to re-unite with the cosmic origin and the oneness of all existence.

In our school [Marin Waldorf School], we seek to imbue all our lessons with questions of universal implication. We seek to explore mythology, literature, history, science and art in a way that evokes discussions or pondering about these universal questions. We wish our students to live in an atmosphere that is permeated with (not devoid of) the quest for self-knowledge, for the exploration of life's deepest mysteries. How is this done?

The Waldorf curriculum is designed to create the appropriate relationship between a child and these immense questions. Through art, a child builds a relationship with beauty, and in studying science, one seeks an understanding of truth. Out of beauty and truth develop a sense of morality and reverence for life which leads to profound questions of existence.

Through the study of history our students journey through ancient civilizations, studying the Old Testament, Norse Mythology, Ancient India, Persia, Sumaria, Egypt, Greece, and Rome. They enter the Middle Ages and the Renaissance with burning questions of morality which grow out of their earlier exploration. By the time students reach eighth grade, they have lived with many noble images, many fallen heroes and many searching questions about the nature of humankind and our universe. These questions of great magnitude fill a child with the desire to explore the outer and inner realms of his/her life.

In Waldorf schools throughout the world, we aim to celebrate the cycles of life, to address the essence of these soul questions as they speak to us through nature in the rhythm of the year and the festivals that have evolved through time. We all long to feel the joy and meaning of life through the recognition and celebration of cornerstone events. The seasons mark the turning points of the year and each season has festivals around the world which express the inner wisdom of its nature. Because we live in a primarily Judeo-Christian culture, we emphasize those festivals at our school. Waldorf schools in Israel feature Jewish festivals; Waldorf schools in Japan feature Buddhist festivals; in India, Hindu festivals.

Waldorf schools are founded on the philosophy of Anthroposophy, the wisdom of humanity. Anthroposophy, offered to us by Rudolf Steiner, explores the evolution of human consciousness. Each historic epoch offers a significant contribution to the journey of humanity from ancient times to the unknown future. Each prophet carried a message for his time and we seek to understand our age through the looking glass of the past. Neither Anthroposophy nor religion are taught in our school. They are the foundation under the building which supports and defines the structure.

We seek to educate our students in love and immerse them in the world of great literature, art and science. We strive to awaken within them the longing to "Know Thyself." We wish to send them forth into the world in freedom to explore and discover their own beliefs and destinies in the service of humankind. On this journey, each one finds meaning, joy and reverence for life, creating a new union with his or her spiritual essence.

— *Marin Waldorf School Parent Handbook*

The Nature of Culture and Multiculturalism in Waldorf Schools

JEFFREY KANE, PH.D.

The concept of multiculturalism in Waldorf secondary schools is complex. Almost every direct approach to the issue raises questions related to the broad philosophical ideas and ideals that underlie Waldorf education. We need perhaps to go beyond the immediate questions regarding the curriculum and what goes on in the classroom and first define what we mean by culture.

What is culture? The question is not abstract, but is a very practical and pressing one, and one that requires a good deal of consideration. When we think of integrating different cultures in the classroom, we usually assume that culture can be identified with particular family patterns, customs, beliefs, etc., We fail though to take into account the multiple cultures that affect each of us. For example, when I use the name "Madonna" in a fifth grade classroom, you can imagine that the children do not always think of a virginal young woman with a babe in her arms. What images arise when I use the name "Michelangelo" in that classroom? He is not generally known as a sculptor but as a mutant turtle. Each of us assimilates concepts about ourselves through television, schools, children in the neighborhood, books, and parents, to name a few. Much of what we learn is different from cultural source to cultural source. There are, obviously, layers and layers of culture within each of us that have given shape and form to who we are.

Among our present cultural influences is a technology that affects children in particular in a most profound way. The average American child sees about six thousand hours of television before he or she enters the first grade. That's about twenty percent of his or her waking life. What kind of experience does that child have of others, of his or her own self, and of his or her own body? What happens when you don't move your body for twenty percent of your waking life, especially when you are a young child? How does your ability to "flick off" what you don't like affect your capacity to resolve conflict, to compromise, or simply to concern yourself with others? This technology has also helped to create what might be called "McCulture." Television carries numerous programs and events all over the globe. Its effects are not limited to geographically-based cultures. Its power transcends space and its influence on cultural patterns is both as ever-present and as seemingly innocuous as the television set. Here we are discussing but one layer of culture.

Most of us also partake of a culture which is informed by our religious heritage. We are Jews, Christians, Moslems, Buddhists, etc., Each religious heritage brings with it a certain basic understanding of who you are, and what the world is, and what, perhaps, your given destiny is. You also have a national heritage, a racial heritage, a familial heritage, and a community heritage. Each of these brings a profound cultural legacy and a profound cultural influence to every individual. We are all multicultural.

There are also explicit and implicit aspects of each culture, which can be demonstrated with a map, for example. If you look at the map of the world that was used in most American classrooms a decade or two ago, it shows you what the oceans look like, what the land masses look like, and what their relative positions are. But there is an implicit aspect of culture here, an unspoken cultural message. In the center of the map is the United States. The former Soviet Union, though, is cut in half, is relegated to the edges of the world. The map is not only telling you where things are, it is also telling you which things are more important than others by putting certain things in the middle and certain things on the periphery. I guarantee that if you had gone to the Soviet Union in the 1970's, you never would have seen such a map. You would have seen the United States split in half and the Soviet Union as one. Cartographers have begun to recognize the inherent biases in maps. They have started to create maps that, for example, relate to prime meridian rather than to political realities. The world map I have described and which influenced many of us in elementary school is relatively difficult to find today.

Could we turn the map upside down? Would it still be correct if we turned it upside down? North would be on the bottom! Is that correct? Certainly. Why must north be "up?" There is an explicit message that comes through the map, and there is an implicit message about how to relate to the world, how to orient yourself in the world. And each book that you read, each story that you hear, each painting that you study has an implicit message as well as one that is explicit. Culture always reveals itself in two ways: in a manner that is direct and conscious, and in one that is unspoken and invisible. This second way culture manifests is invisible because it is rooted in our own assumptions – our unconscious patterns of value, belief, and action.

What does it mean to have unconscious dispositions rooted in you? Consider how two of my children learned to experience their bodies in space and in movement. When my son Gabriel was quite young, I would toss him into the air, go out for a cup of coffee, and return to catch him. But, unconsciously, I didn't do this with my daughter, Emily. I held her close and protected her. We throw our sons into the air and hold our daughters close. Gabriel and Emily learned to experience their bodies differently.

Similarly, we acquire dispositions about ourselves in the way we learn to celebrate birth, cope with death, arrange our diets, live in our families, and conceptualize what it is to be a child or to be an older person. These things are addressed by our culture even if they are not explicitly addressed. We are each shaped by many cultures, and we are shaped by implicit cultural messages as well as by the explicit cultural messages we get from reading particular literature or history or critiques of art.

Now, one of the problems we often face in a Waldorf school is that the cultures that shape us often do not conform with the philosophy undergirding Waldorf education. To better understand the foundations of Rudolf Steiner's approach to the world (and to education), consider Plato's allegory of the cave, which he uses in *The Republic*, and which he meant as an analogy for the human condition. Plato describes an individual chained in a cave, his back to the mouth of the cave. On the cave wall before him he sees, and takes for reality, the shadows of the real world outside the cave.

What we know to be the physical world is only a shadow. We are shackled by our senses. There is a spiritual dimension to reality which does not necessarily conform to the laws by which the physical world is governed. The laws governing the spiritual world are not understood in the same way that we understand the material world. We have to transform ourselves inwardly, somehow, in order to be able to see or comprehend them. We have to be able to see the spiritual world reflected in the physical world.

Waldorf education helps us do just that. When you look at flowers as a small child, when you begin to draw flowers in sixth or seventh grade, when you study botany in eleventh grade, and you see the growth and movement of a plant, you begin to look through the physical world to see the forces actually giving form and shape to the physical world. These are spiritual forces.

When you begin to look at the world in this way, you incorporate a cultural assumption that is not widely accepted, at least not in the United States. As a result, Waldorf students experience a different culture than do students raised watching television, working frequently on computers, or studying detached abstractions in the early grades. Waldorf students often have a rich experience of art, music, myth, and story. Even mathematics and science are approached with imagination, mystery, and aesthetic sensibility in a Waldorf school. Waldorf education provides cultural foundations not widely accepted in larger American society. These foundations, I believe, give you an insight into yourself and into the world, an insight that is truly unique. This in turn gives you the strength and courage you need to live in a world which is appealingly materialistic.

In a similar way let us explore how we understand knowledge and learning. In school, you are most often taught that when you learn something, you learn it in a rational way, in a logical way. You learn it so that you can reason from it and you can reason to it. You understand how one idea fits into another idea in a logical way. You learn to be rational. And you think of knowledge as a very rational outgrowth of experience. But some other cultures do not necessarily believe that you can understand the world best through logic, through observation, or through scientific analysis. There are cultures which suggest that you can perceive things more reverently, more deeply, almost as a dream. One of these is the Hasidic culture.

There's a story about a Rabbi who would only put his glasses on when he wanted to stop seeing. When he looked at the world with his glasses on, he saw the physical world. When he took his glasses off, he wasn't deceived into believing he was seeing reality.

In the Bible there is a story in which three men come to Abraham, and Abraham gets a calf to slaughter for dinner. What he did when he went to get the calf is not found in the Bible, but there is a story about it in the "Midrash" tradition. This tradition is concerned with the meaning that is in the spaces around the letters. When we write a letter in English or in Hebrew, we think of it as a black form on a white background. But we can think of a letter in a reverse way, as a space surrounding the letter. And it is with this space with the meaning found there that the Midrash is concerned. It is concerned with what is left out of the Bible, with the meaning to be found in the spaces.

According to the Midrash, Abraham goes to get a calf to slaughter. He chases the calf into a cave and in the cave he sees the bodies of Adam and Eve. And then, deep in the cave, Abraham sees a pinhole of light that comes from the Garden of Eden. As we read, we wonder, how on earth could someone write a story about Abraham seeing the bodies of Adam and Eve, seeing light from the Garden of Eden, when there is nothing of that sort in the Bible? It's just not there. Well, according to the Midrash tradition, that story comes out of the dream consciousness between the letters. There is a dream consciousness there just as there is a dream consciousness for us between our days of wakefulness.

This dreamlike consciousness offers unique insights into different aspects of the human psyche and of human evolution. So when we begin to look at the Jewish tradition, we find that the world can be understood through understanding the dreams, rather than through understanding the written word alone. If that sounds bizarre to you, think about psychoanalysis. Think about Freud; think about Jung. They said that if you analyze your dreams you can begin to understand different elements or aspects of your own psyche, aspects that would not otherwise be readily available to you or understood by you. The Midrash tradition tries to explain humanity not through logic, not through reason, but by providing dream stories that might have the same understanding, the same accuracy in the history of humanity that your own personal dreams have in providing insight into yourself.

This dream-like consciousness is found in all great mythology. When in Waldorf schools you study Norse or Greek mythology, that same dreamlike consciousness is brought forth. Logic does not teach you about yourself. The mythologies of the world do this, and they are generally not understood by your waking consciousness.

Where does this leave us? What I've been saying is that we are all the products of multiple cultures, and that these cultures affect us consciously and unconsciously. There are conscious methods of understanding. The unconscious methods are about who you are, what the world is, how the world is to be known, what it is to live as a human being. Those are all fundamental assumptions and beliefs that you are taught through your culture, through your multiple cultures. What I've done by way of illustration with the Midrash tradition is to suggest that your concept of what it is to know the world may be very lopsided. Some people know the world rationally. Some people know the world through the intellect. But there are entire cultures that say that the best way to understand the world is not through the intellect but through the imagination. And the imagination will perceive not the physical events, the shadows in Plato's cave, but will perceive the spiritual events and will understand the spiritual realities, which include, in the end, you and me.

Those are my basic points, but I'd like to address one last issue. I would argue that teachers should bring stories, myths, histories, ideas, insights and religions from each culture, from Africa, from Asia, from South America, from Europe, from all over the world into their teaching. They should do so to the extent that these resources reveal some aspect of our humanity, an aspect of our humanity that teachers believe is ready to be revealed to students at their particular stage of development. Each culture is like a light, not a full spectrum of light, but a limited spectrum of light. And each culture reveals a different aspect of ourselves and of humanity.

Each teacher has to ask, "What aspect or aspects of their humanity are my students ready to explore?" And he might find that it is an aspect that is best expressed by African literature, or by Middle Eastern history, or by Buddhist religious beliefs. Each culture presents a limited spectrum, and the teacher's job is to determine what spectrum to bring to the students so that they may observe their own humanity in a new way.

If Waldorf education is successful, the student receives a full spectrum of light, a full, rounded perspective of herself or himself as a human being. And strangely, that's actually quite frightening, to get a picture of yourself "beyond culture." If you can begin to free yourself from the limitation of a one-culture perspective, what might happen to you? Truths might be revealed to you as they were to Moses on Mount Sinai. Moses heard the voice of God, and it was not a particular cultural voice, it was direct dialogue between a human being and a high spiritual being.

Similarly, if we learn to transcend the limitations of culture, we begin to think of ourselves as "I am," not as "I am black," or "I am white," or "I am Jewish," or "I am female." And the "I am" is what Moses heard. If we hear the "I am" we will experience the Ten Commandments not with "thou" beginning each but with "I"; hence, "I shall not kill." Martin Buber asks us to think of the Ten Commandments not as words written on stone by the finger of God a long time ago, but to think of them as spoken words, spoken right now, spoken in the first person. Why shall I not kill? I shall not kill because I recognize myself as a full human being, and I recognize the responsibilities of my own humanity.

If we've been educated well, and if we take the gifts of each culture, we can then transcend the limitations of each culture. We become members of a new culture, a culture of free human beings. This is what Waldorf education strives toward and prepares you for: to walk as a whole, responsible, free human being.

Excerpts from a talk given to an audience of Waldorf high school students, gathered for a weekend conference on multicultural and gender issues. organized by the students of the Garden City Waldorf School, NY.

— Renewal, A Journal for Waldorf Education

Waldorf and Montessori: A Comparison

BARBARA SHELL

This comparison of certain aspects of Waldorf and Montessori educational philosophy is based on my personal experience as an educator for nearly 30 years (Waldorf and public school teaching), personal observations in Montessori schools, and workshops with Montessori teachers.

I would, however, preface my remarks by stressing that there can be much difference from one classroom to another in any philosophy due to the style and interpretation of the individual teacher. However, in the main, there are several areas of contrast between Waldorf and Montessori. In both philosophies the young child is viewed with great respect and reverence. I will look at the following areas: play and imagination, social development, toys, and structure and order.

In Waldorf philosophy, play is viewed as the work of the young child and the magic of fantasy, so alive in the young child, is an integral part of how the teacher works with the child. The teacher incorporates storytelling and imagination into the curriculum.

In Montessori there is a feeling that because young children have difficulty distinguishing between reality and fantasy, imaginative work should be postponed until the child is firmly grounded in reality. The tasks and activities the children do are reality oriented. Montessori said that it is a mistake for children to amuse themselves with toys, that children are not really interested in toys for long without the real intellectual interest of associating them with sizes and numbers.

In Waldorf, we feel that it is essential to realize the value of toys to help children to re-enact experiences from life as they actually happen. The less finished and the more suggestive a toy may be, the greater its educational value for it really enlivens the imaginative life of the child. So toys in the Waldorf kindergarten may be rounds of wood cut from birch logs, seashells, lengths of colored silk or cotton for costuming or house building, soft cloth dolls with a minimum of detail in faces of clothing, etc., allowing for open-ended imaginative play.

In Montessori early exposure to reading and mathematics is through manipulatives. Each manipulative material has a step-by-step procedure for being used and focused toward a specific learning concept. For example, math counting rods are not to be transformed into castle walls. The Montessori classroom is set up as an open classroom with prepared activities where children work at an individual pace. Much of the work the young child does is on individual learning tasks done separately; each child will work independently on a small rug doing a different task from the other children with the teacher, a facilitator, to intervene only if the child requests help. Socialization takes place in not bothering other children working, in helping a young child learn to do a new task, or in waiting one's turn if the child wants an activity already in use.

The Waldorf philosophy stresses that the child gradually learns to be a social being and that the development of the young child in the social realm is as important as anything else we do. The teacher has the role of orchestrating how this happens through modeling good social behavior with children, through joining together in movement activities, singing or games to develop group consciousness and by helping children humanistically work through disagreements.

Madame Montessori described the classroom as a place where children are free to move about the classroom at will, where the day is not divided between work periods and rest or play periods. The children are divided into mixed age groups; i.e., 3-6, 6-9, and 9-12 year olds. The children are free to choose their own activities in the classroom and work at an individual pace. This protection of the child's choice is a key element in the Montessori approch. Little emphasis is put on the arts. Art and music programs are dependent on the teachers' ability and interest.

In contrast, Waldorf sees the child thriving in a rhythmical atmosphere – knowing what he can count on from day to day and week to week. There are times for coming together and working as a whole group and times for playing individually or with friends; time for directed activity like crafts or baking or painting and times for creative play like acting out a story, doing finger games or watching a puppet show. The teacher takes advantage of their activity by observing the children at play and plans group activities which will harmonize and balance these impressions he or she receives from observation.

The teacher works with the seasonal themes of the year. A balancing of the impulses from nature is woven through the artistic activities using stories, song, and verses to enliven and capture the children's interest and imaginations.

A child longs for rhythm and order in his world. Both Waldorf and Montessori recognize this, but interpret it in quite different ways: both feel the physical setting needs an underlying order to help the child feel secure. The Montessori classroom has an emphasis on reality to free a child from his fantasies, where the Waldorf classroom enhances the child's world of fantasy and imagination using nature materials; crystals, shells, logs, as well as hand-made toys, gnomes, soft dolls, carved wooden animals.

According to Joseph Chilton Pearce, in his book *Magical Child:*

> Filling in the conceptual gap with imaginary material, ignoring all dissimilarities is the essence of child play. The great rule is: play is on the surface and the work takes play beneath. The child's mind plays on the basic conceptual brain set without altering it. Play reality, like adult reality is neither world nor mind-brain; it is the world plus mind-brain. The child's intelligence becomes invested in his imagined transformation of self and world. And these are singularly compelling. His awareness locks into fantasy; reality becomes that play. For the child, the time is always now; the place, here; the action, me. He has no capacity to entertain adult notions of fantasy world and real world. He knows only one world, and that is the very real one in which and with which he plays. His is not playing at life. Play *is* life.

As Jean Piaget expressed it:

> [For the child] play cannot be opposed to reality, because in both cases belief is arbitrary and pretty much destitute of logical reasons. Play is a reality which the child is disposed to believe in when by himself, just as reality is a game at which he is willing to play with the adults and anyone else who believes in it… thus we have to say of the child's play that it constitutes an autonomous reality, but with the understanding that the 'true' reality to which it is opposed is considerably less 'true' for the child than for us.

Montessori sees the child as having an absorbent mind ready to soak up knowledge and experience like a sponge. Just keep supplying him with ever more challenging intellectual tasks from an early age and you will end up with an educated child.

No early thrust into intellectualism is found in Waldorf, but a keeping alive and nourishing of the child's healthy imagination and creative thinking powers. The child has it all within himself and it unfolds slowly like petals of a maturing flower as the child moves from one developmental stage to the next.

In a Waldorf kindergarten we do not aim to achieve premature "flowers of learning", much as these "flowers" might find appreciation. We rather forego such immediate satisfactions and focus our attentions upon the child's ultimate good and upon the protection of his childhood. We are looking toward a healthy, well-rounded adult in the future.

Being a teacher is a form of desire, a lightning flash.

— Rumi

Teaching an Eight-Year Cycle

HERBERT SAPERSTEIN

I believe it was a turn-of-the-century play that ended with the line, "That's all there is; there isn't any more". To finish an eight year cycle teaching a group of children is a lot like that. The play is over. Of course a play is over rather more quickly – make up is needed to denote the passing of theater time, while I clearly don't need it. If anything, I might prefer make-up to *disguise* the passing of time! "What is it like to complete an 8-year cycle", friends ask. It is almost embarrassing to say that the main feeling I had was as simple and mundane as "Yes, I really accomplished something." However, this sense of accomplishment is more complex than usual because it hasn't come merely from completing a task (and mind you, a pleasurable one), but from knowing that that's *not* all there is, that the children carry forward experiences that I hope will enrich their own lives and the lives of others.

Already I find myself wondering what so-and-so will be doing in ten years or in twenty and selfishly hoping that I will be around to see, and that they will indeed come back to show off their new clothes. It is this strong sense of future that colors my feelings of past. Within a few months after graduation, parents began to call with news of my former students, obviously knowing my innermost feelings.

Teaching is, or certainly can be, one of the most fulfilling occupations in the world. However hard you may work, there is always something received that keeps you going, that wordless something emanating from those children. This is obvious in the early grades and not so obvious in the middle school years.

As I reflect back, I realize very clearly that from the standpoint of student, teacher and parent, there is in the earliest years a sort of romantic glow surrounding the picture. The child still retains a certain amount of innocence and Waldorf schools are good at nurturing this. With the family, the neighborhood, the church or synagogue no longer the stable force that they once were, the class teacher becomes quite a force in the child's life – someone to rely on, someone who will be there every day, a rock in a watery world. The teacher is there long enough to really gain insight into each child's world and to take action to help when help is needed.

It should also be recognized that this whole process is just as helpful to the teacher as it is to the child, for the chances for inner growth are many and unavoidable. With the pressure of the culture and of parents (even Waldorf parents!) innocence turns to experience perhaps earlier than it should. A girl's first menstruation in 1830 was at the age of 17-1/2; today it begins around the age of 12. This is probably due in part to diet, in part to the speed of the whole culture including the treatment of children as if they were responsible adults. Of course, one might also point out the irony that these adolescents *remain* adolescents for ever so much longer than in years past.

A teacher can never do too much parent education in these early years. We all talk incessantly about the media – and rightly so – but perhaps not enough attention is given to parents giving their children unending choices and continual explanations for why they should or shouldn't do this or that. Eventually the children won't do anything without an argument. They are in effect taught to challenge adults, for adults don't know any more than they do! This is all done unknowingly, of course, in the name of democracy or teaching the child to make his or her own decisions. It is hard for parents to see that the normally difficult middle school years will only be made more difficult by what one might call an upbringing without boundaries. This laxness, when combined with the subtle and not so subtle pressures presented by TV and movies, can overwhelm what the Waldorf teacher is trying to accomplish.

This is a time when children normally distance themselves from both teachers and parents, but they still need our guidance. Will they be open to it? It is a time when parents and teachers need to work together and when the tendency to fracture is at its greatest. It is important for parents to know that the community that has been established can have enormous benefits, if only we can see them and take advantage of them.

I have seen that the curriculum serves the students at all ages, perfectly reflecting their stage of development. Problems inevitably arise as the children reach puberty. They now enter what may metaphorically be called a dark forest. This is the point when a community of friends is most needed. I was rather lucky that my class came through this period in an incredibly cohesive way. The history of the class as a unit more often than not will bring on this closeness as the students now are able to reflect and to look forward ever so slightly. This history of togetherness serves the students as Ariadne's thread served Theseus in his successful attempt to slay the minotaur and then make his way out of the labyrinth to safety. The early years can be relatively easy, but sustaining the initial enthusiasm is a true test. Our task is one of having the will to persevere "through thick and through thin". The fruits of our collaboration ripen at a later time. Patience.

It Was Once so Easy to Say

RICHARD BETZ

Soft, rolling waves
inquisitive, passionate, sensitive
purple, indigo, blue

bold, autumnal fires
playful, fanciful, loving
yellow, orange, red

innocent spring in sunlight
and moonlight
crescent moons in starlight
and bluelight
childlike
life like
what we hope was right
snow white
elf like
blue, silver green life
like life
all its own

a call rippling through the rain-soaked grasses
strong as a gale-song, the heart of man is trapped,
captive is Tam Lin, the man, in the fairies' land...
heart of woman hears the call, hears the fall of the heart of man,
on she comes to save the knight, to save the light within
that shines as strong as a gale-song
as strong as a gale-song within

song
word
paint
step
thread
stone
stage
a tool in the hand
a mind lit by fires
a heart lit by love

you have grown so
and it was once so easy to say, I love you,
or have I just grown afraid over all the years...
millions of miniature rainbows shimmering in the morning dew-light
dry and vanish ere the sun has lifted above the trees...
the grace and poise of an ocean wave lifts my soul
for just a moment
and even closing my eyes cannot extend for long the life
of that one special wave about to fall
in upon itself and dissolve...

yes,
you are special
and the moment is slipping,
slipping through my fingers like so many grains of sand
falling away and then
rushing back to the sea with the retreating tide...

yes, you are such a moment
sunset-red caught in granite
and clouds of indigo-night.

Composed for his 8th grade students
Marin Waldorf School
Christmas, 1992

Commentary on Waldorf Graduates

JAMES SHIPMAN

What I like about the Waldorf School is, quite simply, its graduates. As a high school teacher at Marin Academy, [San Rafael, California], I have seen a number of the students who come from your program [Marin Waldorf School, California] and I can say that in all cases they have been remarkable, bright, energetic and involved.

One of my duties is to teach *World Civilizations* to incoming ninth graders, so I tend to be one of the first people who encounters a Waldorf graduate. My course is not like the standard *History of Western Civilization* course, but rather requires the student to investigate the deeper aspects of the world's cultures. For example, we are not so much interested in the chronology of Chinese emperors and the dynasties to which they belonged; instead we want to explore and understand the principles of Taoism and Confucianism and how these underlying philosophies helped to shape the Chinese culture. We aren't so much interested in memorizing name and dates as we are in understanding what motivates people, and why they make the choices that they do.

I find the Marin Waldorf graduates to be entirely willing to undertake this sort of investigation. They are eager to learn. They do not complain when I assign, for example, a passage from the *Bhagavad Gita* and then ask them what they think. Indeed, that is what I find most remarkable about Waldorf kids: they have been taught to think; thinking is an "okay" activity for them to engage in. I think they intrinsically understand the difference between thinking about an issue and merely memorizing "the right answer" for the test.

Waldorf students are not simply bookworms, however. In fact one could find Waldorf kids completely involved in the theater, the arts, music and sports here at Marin Academy. What I see here is an integration of the faculties – mental, emotional, physical and spiritual – which, when coupled with the overtones of personality, unite to form unique individuals.

Marin Waldorf students to me are interesting people. They can converse intelligently on almost any issue, because they have been taught to examine. They can be enormously sympathetic to almost anyone's plight because they have been taught to tolerate. They can gracefully dance or score a goal because they have been taught to move. They can circulate among the various groups on campus and engage in a variety of activities because they have been taught to harmonize.

We used to use the world "holistic" or "whole person" to describe the kind of person I have outlined above. Whatever the term used, it is apparent to me that the Marin Waldorf School consciously turns out calm, centered and confident students. For my part, I deeply appreciate the school's efforts, because based on their work, I get to enjoy those students who come to Marin Academy. It is with humility that I note that Waldorf students allow me and my colleagues to influence them. It is as if somewhere in their early years of schooling they somehow got the idea that learning is a lifelong enterprise.

— The Marin Waldorf School Parent Handbook

Reprinted in *The Results of Waldorf Education*

Family
Life
and
Waldorf
Education

No matter what our family situation or lifestyle, we as parents are our children's first teachers. By understanding how children develop and some things we can do to help their balanced and healthy growth — physically, mentally, emotionally and spiritually — we will not only help our children, but also increase our own enjoyment and growth as parents.

— Rahima Baldwin,
You Are Your Child's First Teacher

Home Life

SHARIFA OPPENHEIMER

Much has been said to Waldorf parents about the fundamental necessity of rhythm in a child. In fact the daily rhythms, songs, and verses from school familiar to our children can, with a little effort, become a part of our family lives as well.

Waking a Child

Waking up is something each of us does every day. Perhaps though, we adults have forgotten the thousands of mornings we woke up as children. Our eyes flew open, scanning the walls, and ceilings for telltale shadows forecasting rain or shine.

Early morning can be a hectic and cranky time with parents trying to prepare each child's choice breakfast or coaxing one more spoon of oatmeal into someone's mouth. ALLOW ENOUGH TIME is the cardinal rule for mornings! If this means waking up thirty minutes earlier, then do it! It will also mean going to bed thirty minutes earlier, but everyone will be ready after such an early morning.

Is getting dressed difficult for your child? One way to simplify conflicts which may arise, is to throw away, or give away, *all* clothing which either you or your child do not like. Then whatever is left has everyone's approval.

The Breakfast Battle (who wants what today) can successfully be won by leaving choice or chance out of the matter entirely. In the Kindergarten our snacks rotate on daily basis – therefore, Monday is oatmeal day; Tuesday is bread day; Wednesday is fruit and nut day; and so on. Always in the first few weeks I hear many comments such as " I don't like oatmeal," or "Do I *have* to eat the bread?" My reply is always the same, "We'll just put your food in front of you as we do for everyone." Often by the end of the year I will overhear this snack-time comment: "Remember when I used to HATE the honey bread? "At home you can rotate breakfasts. Choose five different breakfasts which have a wide appeal, so if your four year old hates eggs, she can at least have the toast (and not come to school hungry) or if oatmeal makes one of your children's stomach turn, serve yogurt with it.

How about the following scheme: Egg Day (with toast), Oatmeal Day (with yogurt), Cereal day, Fruit Day (with toast) and Bagel (or Muffin) Day. These are all quick school-day meals which are healthy and widely liked. Save French toast, pancakes and waffles for weekends when you have more preparation time. Here, too, are simple meal blessings which, when used regularly, can add an element of ritual to your busy morning meal.

Blessing on the blossom,
Blessing on the root,
Blessing on the leaf and stem.
Blessing on the fruit. Amen

Mother Earth, Mother Earth,
Take thy seed and give it birth,
Father Sun, Gleam and glow,
Until the root begins to grow,
Sister Rain, sister Rain
Shed thy tear to swell thy grain.

Let breakfast time be a time of previewing everyone's day, telling your nursery school child what snack will be served that day, and reminding your grade-schooler of her music lesson after school. Sound too good to be true? Only our adult perseverance can begin to change a stressful, anxiety-ridden time of day into — Yes! – a pleasure.

Daily Work

The child soon enters the kindergarten and sees the teacher busy at the "daily work." Each classroom varies, but usually we are baking, sewing, or cooking. Children love to join in these homey activities, but all too often at home they are shooed away because, in fact, we adults do get less work done when small fingers are needing help. There are precious few years when our child joyfully joins in an activity simply because Mommy or Daddy is doing it.

At home as you go about your chores, invite your small ones to join it! Any activity can be accompanied by "this is the way we...make our bed...wash the dishes, etc.," sung to the tune of *Here we go Round the Mulberry Bush.*

Poems, Rhymes, Tongue Twisters

Some circle time material for nursery age children is taken from Mother Goose rhymes. You can augment this at home by taking your three or four year old on your lap and simply saying the rhymes with her. Notice, this is not *reading* the rhymes to her, but rather looking in her eyes, clapping gentle rhythms and saying these rhythmic exercises with her. At this age, dramatization is not appropriate.

We can keep our voice calm and clear. In this way, the simple rhythms alone will delight your child.

A six-year-old may begin to enjoy such word play as turning meanings backward, discovering subtle nuances of definition, beginning to understand puns, simple riddles, and real jokes. You can join in this wonderful exploration of language by saying tongue twisters with your child. Say them slowly enough so she can really hear the words. Speed comes later. This is a hilarious way to share a warm moment and to show your child the flexibility of the human tongue and mind.

Story Telling

The importance of fairy stories cannot be emphasized enough. They have been recognized as a tool for teaching since the first story was recited round the fire, ages gone by. It is recommended that we stay away from "modernized" versions of these stories. Often, essential elements have been left out, or the plot changed to suit a modern editor's needs. Folk tales tend to be geared to the grade school child's needs.

Bedtime is the perfect time for a fairy story. These simple tales pose the hero or heroine in a difficult life situation, and then show how, through perseverance, honesty and compassion major obstacles can be overcome. At bedtime your child may be unconsciously working on one of his own major obstacles. The fairy tale will model for him and reinforce his own ability to meet the challenge of life with perseverance, honesty and compassion. This allows your child to drift to sleep with clear, simple images which can work their way into his dream-life and, in fact, into his physical organism.

Another category of indispensable childhood tales is the "made up" story which you create for your own child. For the younger child, any story in which you can recount the homely happening of life amidst the cycles of seasons, is appropriate. In "The Grandpa Story," a lengthy story I made up for my sons when they were young, the boys grew pumpkins for Halloween. Grandpa taught them to build an Indian teepee for Thanksgiving and days and weeks were spent playing in the snow. Grandma started little seeds indoors with them just about the same time we started seeds in the kindergarten. So you can see, this kind of story can go on forever, just as the seasons do. Your child will ask for it again and again.

Telling your children a story which you have made up "on the spot" for them is a gift which they will carry through a lifetime.

Bedtime

As with mornings, the cardinal rule for bedtime is ALLOW ENOUGH TIME! Observe what your child's natural patterns are and plan for them. If your child only needs a prayer and a peck on the forehead after he's in bed, then you can afford a longer story. If your child needs to review the day with you in his own child-like way, then choose a short story, or start earlier.

I find in the classroom many, many children come to me tired each morning. I cannot state too emphatically, children need lots of sleep! If an adult needs eight hours of sleep, then a young child, who is in fact working much harder all day long, needs half again that much! Often a ten-hour night for your child can be supplemented by a two hour nap in the afternoon. Your child needs much more energy at school than he does at home; plan for this. If your child has to be awakened in the mornings or is drowsy all during breakfast, *she needs more sleep!* You can make bedtime earlier by five-minute increments each night or every other night. Generally a 7:30 bedtime is recommended for a kindergarten or nursery age child.

Lighting a candle at bedtime holds a special fascination for every child. Although a child may have free access to the other elements (water, air, earth) it is rare that he has access to fire. Of course safety must come first, but in our desire to make a safe world for our small one, do we deprive him of this primal element? The ancient alchemists posed that the universe was made of these four elements, and hence humans contain all these elements within themselves.

From time immemorial we have huddled around fires, taking warmth, strength, healing, and sustenance from its lively glow. Only recently has fire been tamed, put in a cage, or with the advent of furnaces, banished from our lives entirely. What a gift we can give to our children by allowing fire into their lives in the form of a candle. Here is a simple bedtime prayer which asks for protection during the darkness of night and also prepares your child for the coming of day:

Guardian Angels whom we love
Shine on us from up above.
Now I lay me down to sleep
I pray the Lord my soul to keep.
In the morning when I wake
Show me the Path of Love to take. Amen

A story can be told, a candle lighted, your favorite bedtime prayer recited and then your child can snuff the candle. This gives him a strong, balanced, safe harbor from which to begin his nightly journey.

If we can take just one idea at a time and slowly work with it, experiment and adapt, we will begin to experience the rewards which are the results of a rich and rhythmic home life.

— Crossroads Waldorf School, Croxet, VA

Creating a seasonal garden

Bringing Nature Inside

CAROL PETRASH

Creating a small Season's Garden or corner in your home or classroom is one way to bring nature indoors and celebrate the rhythms of the seasons of the year. Young children thrive on rhythm – not the rigid holding to a timetable, but the rhythmic flow of one thing into another. It gives them a sense of security and well-being to know that as it was, it shall be again. For many children today, a connection to nature and the passing of the seasons is one of the few constants in their lives. As such it is all the more important to emphasize this connection and provide a space for recognizing and celebrating it.

Where to put it

Set aside a quiet corner somewhere in your classroom (or home) that is out of the way yet accessible to the children. It is nice to have a small table which can be the focus, but you could also use a shelf on a bookcase or an area on a counter top. A large tree stump (about 2-3 feet high) would be especially nice – keep your eyes open for tree work being done in your neighborhood. A small, round table works well, as the roundness is a more natural shape and suggests the circle of the year.

What to include

Once you have decided where the Season's Garden will be, you can begin to create it. One of the first things to consider is color and how you will use it to create the appropriate seasonal mood. Think about the different seasons and which colors they suggest to you. This may be very individual and will certainly be related to the part of the world you're living in. In the mid-Atlantic area with four definite seasons, the following are suggested:

Fall:	Warm colors – soft reds, oranges and golden yellows
Winter:	Cool colors – deep blues, icy blues and violets
Spring:	Pastels – pinks, pale yellows, spring greens
Summer:	Fiery colors – deep intense reds, yellows, oranges

Find or dye small or medium-sized cloths in these various colors and keep them in a special box so you have them when needed. Thrift shops and flea markets are good sources for nice old linens, napkins, etc., that you can use. Dyeing is fun to do with the children. Natural fabric dyes are available from Earth Guild*. If your Season's Garden focal point is a table, you may want to cover it with a white or other neutral color cloth and use smaller, seasonal cloths as color accents.

Another nice touch you can add is a medium blue backdrop cloth to represent the sky. This works especially well if you are setting up your Season's Garden in a corner. Hang the cloth from a point two to three feet above the garden, and drape it gently down and around the edges of the garden, tucking its edges under the seasonal cloths. Light or medium weight cheesecloth works very nicely for the sky cloth. Cheesecloth is available at fabric stores and mail order from Strauss and Company. It sells in wholesale amounts and will send you a sample card of the various weights of cheesecloth on request.

Actually, cheesecloth – particularly the medium weight – is a wonderful, fairly inexpensive material to have in the home or classroom for cloths of all kinds, from those you use in the Season's Garden to play cloths for the children. Get some friends or other teachers together and buy it by the box. It's even cheaper that way.

Now What

Your Season's Garden now has a home and a colorful beginning. What else does it need? Remember that this little place is one in which to celebrate the turning of the seasons and the treasures each season brings. Encourage the children to bring seasonal treasures from nature that they find in their yards or on walks or hikes or even on the way to school. If you live in a more urban area, be sure to take them to places where they have a chance to gather seed pods, nuts, colored leaves, special stones, wildflowers and any other gifts from the Earth that they can find. Going back to the same places at different times of the year allows them to really experience the changes the seasons bring.

Other things that can be part of your Season's Garden are seasonal produce – also a gift from the Earth – and things that you make from natural materials.

Consider including a small garden within your Season's Garden. A plant saucer, suited to the size of your garden, with some kind of protective surface between it and your cloths or table to protect from dampness, works very well as a place for growing things. Place some small rocks or pebbles in the bottom of the saucer for draining and fill it with soil. Then it's ready to accept whatever you'd like to plant, from bulbs (fall) to moss (winter) to seeds (spring). You can also add a nice rock or two, a small piece of bark or an interesting branch or piece of driftwood.

Caring for the Season's Garden means keeping it neat and beautiful. It should not become a junk corner. This will mean sorting through it occasionally, removing some objects when there are too many and organizing the remaining objects so that they are easy to see and appreciate. Water the plants and seeds, put faded flowers in the compost and, generally, just tidy up. Watch for things like milkweed pods which can suddenly surprise you by opening up and sending their silk contents floating around the room. As always, gently remove any little insects to the outdoors.

Natural objects that you remove from the Season's garden can be used elsewhere. Rocks can go into a basket to be used for building; seed pods, etc., can be saved for projects. Especially nice or unusual items can be stored for next year's garden.

Sharing the Season's Garden

Encourage the children to come and play by or in the Season's Garden, exploring its treasures, but a good guideline to follow is that things stay in the garden and don't travel to other areas of the room. The Season's Garden is a special place, and we want to keep it that way.

You can have a special time each day – during circle time might be good – when things that have been brought for the garden can be placed there, perhaps with a brief story about how or where it was found. The idea is not to study things scientifically at this point, but to enjoy and, especially, appreciate them.

Ideas for the Autumn Garden

Objects: Seed pods of all kinds, acorns, nuts, Indian corn, fall flowers, weeds, pressed leaves and fall produce (pumpkins, gourds, squash, apples, pears).

Special Additions: Make a Harvest Wreath with the children to hang over or place near your Season's Garden. Start with a straw wreath form (available at craft shops) and attach sheaves of wheat and pressed leaves to it. Hang apples slices for drying and small bunches of washed seedless grapes from the wreath. If you dip the bunches of grapes in boiling water it will hasten the drying process by breaking the skins and sterilizing them against mold. Hang the wreath up with red ribbon, and add to it as autumn goes along. Don't forget to eat your dried apples and grapes (raisins) for snack one day. This wreath can become a permanent part of your Season's Garden, changing with the seasons. It also represents the circle of the year.

Plantings: If you have an actual indoor garden, plant small bulbs like crocus in it. You could have a little fall festival and let the children do this ceremoniously – tucking them in the Earth to sleep through the winter.

Ideas for the Winter Garden

Special objects: Special rocks and stones; crystals; branches of evergreens, placed in a vase of water as you would flowers; a white candle, even if you can't light it; star-shaped seed pods; tiny brass stars or stars cut from gold paper.

Wreath: Remove the autumn decorations from your wreath. Gather evergreen branches (ask parents to bring in pruned branches) and transform the wreath one day during class. With the children's help, bind the evergreens over the straw base. Use dark colored cord or heavy string to hold the evergreens in place. Using a pretty ribbon to hang the wreath also makes it more festive. Be sure to 'water" the wreath daily with a plant mister to keep it from getting too dry.

Plantings: Carefully gather moss from an outdoor area (a damp area like a creek bed or the ground near the north side of trees) and transplant it in your dish garden (a large clay plant saucer). You don't have to fill the garden, even a small mossy area is nice. Mist it occasionally. Tuck in little stones and pieces of bark or tiny pine cones.

Special Note: Be sure that when you gather things from nature, such as this moss, that you take only a little from any one area, so as not to deplete the "stock" in that area. Also, remove it carefully and refill or tamp down the area so that you don't leave scars. The Native Americans always asked permission of the Earth, tree, etc., before using it. Our rededication to this attitude of reverence towards the natural world will mean a lot to our children, and they will imitate it.

Special Activity: Force paperwhite narcissus bulbs, available at garden or hardware stores. Just two or three of these lovely blooms will perfume your whole room. They are easy to grow in a small dish of pebbles. Nestle the bottoms of the bulbs in the pebbles. Pour in enough water so that the bottoms of the bulbs are always damp, and replenish the water as necessary. I used a dish of bulbs on each of two snack tables – a lively centerpiece. Start the bulbs about two to three weeks before you would like them to bloom.

Ideas for the Spring Garden

Objects: Fresh flowers, small bird nests, dyed eggs (as a symbol of rebirth), polished stones or special rocks, budding branches (in water).

Wreath: Remove the evergreens from your winter wreath. Bind it with wild grasses or weeds, adding flowers here and there for a touch of color. You could also twine ivy around the straw base, again adding flowers for color.

Plants: Just as the children create small dish gardens for a springtime activity, have them help you create a spring class garden in a large clay plant saucer. If you have one that held moss for the winter, transplant the moss to the outdoors or keep the moss in one area of the saucer and place soil in the remaining area, being careful not to disturb any small bulbs you may have planted in fall. Sink a large sea shell, jar lid or tiny clay saucer down into the soil so that its edges are even with the top of the soil. This can become a small pond when filled with water. Lightly dampen the soil with a plant mister, and have the children help you sow grass seed all over the saucer garden. Remember not to sow the seeds too thickly, but make sure all the soil is covered with seed. Sprinkle with a light "blanket" of soil and thoroughly mist again. Remember to have the children mist the seeds or grass each day.

You can add a small blooming branch or flowers either directly into the soil or in a small vase of water, and the children can help you create lots of little beeswax characters to live in the garden. A small white duck or green frog can live in the little pond; perhaps a rabbit or deer in the tall grass; maybe a little red gnome by the rocky, mossy area. A bluebird might build his nest in the budding branch; and there might even be eggs in the nest. The Season's Garden can become a whole story. The possibilities are endless! When the grass grows too long, you can cut using a pair of scissors. We used to send our fresh grass clippings home as a treat for one of the children's pet rabbits, but you could also put them on your window sill for nest-building birds to borrow or, at least, put them in your compost pile.

Ideas for the Summer Garden

Special objects: Shells, sea objects, flowers or weeds that are going to seed, summer produce of all kinds – melons, a bowl or basket of cherries or berries, cherry tomatoes, etc.

Note: Food placed in the Season's Garden should not remain there indefinitely. It can be placed there one day and brought to the children's attention, perhaps with a short story about where it came from or how it grew. Enjoy it for snack or use it in a cooking project before it has a chance to spoil.

Wreath: Your wreath can become a flower wreath in the summertime. Using a base of straw, wild grasses or weeds, you can bind on all kinds of flowers, wild or cultivated. Many flowers actually continue to look quite beautiful even after they've dried and faded, so you don't have to constantly replace them.

It's also nice to add some little bumblebees, as these are familiar summer visitors. Shape them from yellow wool or beeswax, adding a bit of dark color for contrast (even dark blue or purple will do as black is not always available) and, using string, hang them from the wreath.

Plants: It's fun to turn your dish garden into a tiny beach for summer, and it gives you a chance to remove the soil, moss, grass or whatever else you've cultivated during the year so that you an start fresh in the fall. The moss, bulbs or plants can be replanted outdoors in appropriate spots, or, if necessary, put in the compost pile. Add the soil to the compost as well.

Fill your container about 1/2 - 3/4 full with sand. You can add a shell or small saucer of water, if you like. Then place different kinds of sea shells, special stones and other sea objects in the sand. Pieces of beach glass (smooth, weathered pits of broken glass you often find washed up on the beach) are fascinating to the touch. The children will love to come and sift the sand through their fingers and play with the shells.

— *Earthways: Simple Environment Activities for Young Children*

Building a Bridge to Waldorf Fathers

JACK PETRASH

Both parents sit and wait expectantly. In the father's hands is the school brochure, in the mother's a list of questions. They have come to this initial interview with a hopeful sense that this school will allow their young child to flourish.

During the interview they are both attentive and ask perceptive questions. Obviously they have carefully read the school literature and listened well at the information evening. Both are concerned about their child's education, are pleased to have the Waldorf school, and are optimistic about the future. Yet this may be the last time that the relationship of father and mother to the school will be so similar.

Often, though certainly not always, a mother develops a stronger connection to the school than does a father. A mother often finds herself at the school on a regular basis, while a father's contact with the school becomes intermittent with the passage of time. Mothers are more likely to read the newsletter and speak regularly with other parents and with teachers. Hence they become increasingly familiar with the particulars of school life. Words like "developmental", "temperament", and "rhythmic" take on new meaning. Mothers attend advertised talks while fathers, for a variety of reasons, often remain at home with the children. Thus mothers become familiar with the ideas central to Waldorf education.

As mothers develop an understanding of and appreciation for the Waldorf School they begin to bring home life in closer harmony with life in the school. The toys start to change. Plastic is out and natural materials are in. Suddenly there are woven baskets in the home filled with pine cones, nuts, and stones. The child's clothing also changes. "Loose", "layered", and "warm" are the watchwords as the child begins to wear more clothing than ever before. Hats appear for young children throughout the year and woolen undershirts as well.

These changes are healthy and significant. However, the father is often peripheral to the decision to change. This can lead to difficulties. Even more basic than this must be the recognition that for many fathers the questions are different. They are more apt to ask "why?" than "what?". Why must children use only beeswax crayons? Why are competitive sports not promoted? Why are the things that I did as a child so bad? Why is the Waldorf School so particular?

The reluctance of fathers to embrace the school is often seen as a symptom of the debilitating effect of modern life. Fathers are seen as more involved in a materialistic world and hence less able to understand the spiritual principles of the school. Yet fathers of Waldorf children are more nurturing, committed, and involved with their children's lives than fathers have ever been before in our modern times. If we take their response to the school seriously we have an opportunity to explore how to better address our parents. In the book *Awakening to Community*, Rudolf Steiner states:

> It is just in presenting anthroposophy that every attempt should be made to portray what has thus been raised to a clear and conscious level in all its elemental aliveness, to offer it in so living a form that it seems like people's own naive experiencing and feeling. We must make sure to do this (p. 91, 92).

In other words we must explain what we are doing in a way that promotes our "common" sense of the matter. We in the Waldorf school are clearly doing a relatively good job in presenting Waldorf education to mothers so that it makes sense to them, so that it corresponds to their "naive" (i.e., natural) experiencing and feeling. We should assume that this "experiencing and feeling" is different for many, even most, fathers. We need to find an appropriate way to speak to fathers.

The questions which fathers often ask provide the key. One query frequently posed by fathers (and seldom by mothers) is:

> My child is very happy at the Waldorf School. She is interested and creative. She likes her teachers and the children in her class. This is nice. But I have been wondering if the school is preparing her for the "real world".

This question offers an opportunity to explore fundamental assumptions about children and education. The "real world" of the future, which children will meet and about which fathers are concerned, does not yet exist. Its features are at best unclear. We cannot say exactly what we are preparing our children to encounter. The world our parents would have predicted is very different from the world today. Asbestos was the miracle fiber of the 50's, used in ceiling tiles, house siding, steam pipes wrap et. al. Today it is seen as a scourge, its removal from schools and other buildings costing millions. What will be the "asbestos" of tomorrow which our children will inherit?

The future is hard to predict. But the world our children will inherit will certainly have many problems: environmental, social, economic and legal. The solution to these problems will require more than the ability to choose the correct answer on a multiple choice test. And intelligence alone cannot solve these problems. Today's problems remain unsolved by the intelligent men and woman who are in positions of influence. To lead us forward intelligence must be permeated with imagination and vitality. Imagination will help us to view our problems in a new way and to see the full impact of solutions. Vitality will give us the resolve to solve our problems no matter how unpleasant the solutions the resolve to solve our problems no matter how unpleasant the solutions are. Intelligence permeated with imagination and vitality is essential to our children's future. It is just this type of intelligence which Waldorf education seeks to nurture in children.

Yet our children will need more than a lively intelligence. They will also need a depth of feeling and an emotional resilience. It is sad but safe to say that our children's emotional strength will be tested again and again. The stress of modern life will increase. It is likely that our children will have to deal more frequently with traumatic events. We need to help our children become emotionally resilient, yet also flexible and malleable. They will need to be strong enough to withstand and sensitive enough to give way. Also, they will need a sense that they are not alone, that there is an active spiritual world to support them. As Waldorf teachers we have an obligation to convey to our parents how deeply we hold to the belief that the material world is only a partial reality and that we live between two worlds, the material and the spiritual, both equally real.

Our children will also need the strength that arises from the disciplined mastery of essential skills. They should feel at home and capable in the world. They should know how to use a saw, a chisel, and a sewing machine. They should be able to weave, play a musical instrument, change a spark plug, hit a baseball, and wire a lamp. They should feel independent because they can depend on their own capabilities. These practical skills can give them confidence and an unshakable and lasting self-esteem.

Waldorf education nurtures intelligence, emotional strength, and flexibility, and a skill and will in practical matters. It seeks to educate well-rounded individuals who will have the capacity to work effectively regardless of what the future may bring. If we can help fathers to realize this, they will doubtless understand that the school is preparing their children for the "real world" and for the future. We may find then that fathers can be as determined in their involvement and support as mothers tend to be. Then, when we have gained their confidence, we can begin the important work of parent education.

A Fathers' Group

At the Washington (D.C.) Waldorf School, a father's group has met regularly for the past three years. During that time we have read a number of books on Waldorf Education and Anthroposophy. Our study group has served as a forum for questions about our role as parents and specifically as fathers. Yet, it has also enabled us to consider those issues which affect us as individuals. Perhaps even more importantly, it has helped fathers strengthen their connection with the school community by establishing and deepening friendships. Some highlights of our work together have been the building of a large spiral sandbox for our first and second graders as well as hosting a workshop with John Gardner on the role of Anthroposophy in the Waldorf School.

— Renewal, A Journal for Waldorf Education

WARNING: Push-button entertainment may be hazardous
to the health of your soul and the soul of your child.

Push-button Entertainment and the Health of the Soul

CHRISTOPHER BELSKI-SBLENDORIO

We live in an age of electronic entertainment. We are surrounded by radios, televisions, video cassette players, CD and audio cassette players, and computers that run video games and CD-ROM's. At nearly every moment, we can entertain ourselves by the push of a button. And often we do push that button - first thing in the morning, in the car on the way to work, at a lunch break, during dinner, late in the evening before going to bed. We listen to music, the news, the latest weather report; we watch a nature documentary, or a favorite movie. We let ourselves be entertained and informed. It is part of our daily life, and we take it for granted.

The cost of all this push-button entertainment is nominal or seems to be; but, in reality, we and our children may be paying a great price.

For one thing, we may be suffering from "indigestion of the soul." Just as our body consumes food, our soul or psyche consumes sense impressions, experiences, and ideas. And as the body digests food, the soul must digest its food in order to be nourished by it. This is done at night when we sleep and take in no (or very few) further impressions.

The soul-stimulation or food we get from the electronic push-button entertainment is very powerful. If I see a movie, I am very much affected by it for about three days. A jingle I hear on the radio is, if I happen to wake up at night, likely to be still going through my mind. And we receive tremendous amounts of this powerful stimulation, some of which we choose and some of which comes unbidden, when we shop, for example, or are put on hold when making a phone call. The hectic quality of our lives, the undertone of anxiety which permeates the day, our night-time restlessness – are these symptoms of "soul indigestion" caused by too many rock hits, movies, commercials, and news reports?

Also, the entertainment constantly at our fingertips undermines the three essential activities of the soul: thinking, feeling, and willing. It threatens, in effect, the very basis of our humanity.

A person who can create vivid inner mental pictures has, we say, a "good imagination." This good imagination is an important element in creative thinking. It can help us reach a new and original solution to a problem. Also, because it allows us to enter the soul-life of others and to experience what it is like to be another person, it helps us become broad-minded and tolerant. The images of a rich and vibrant imagination, though, can be replaced by images that we receive from outside ourselves. If we are constantly taking in external images and thoughts and struggling to digest them, our imagination, creativity, and capacity for empathy are being dulled.

When we experience something in life and resound with deep and genuine emotion – joy, fear, hope, sorrow, et al. – our soul is enriched, and we are "inspired". With this "wealth of the soul" comes a deep and steadfast satisfaction and an inner peace. If we are immersed in electronic entertainment, much of our emotional life is in response to contrived and imaginary situations. Our emotions are elicited and manipulated (consciously and cleverly) from the outside. We start to lose, therefore, the ability to respond deeply to real people and real-life situations. And we lose that inner peace. So we are never satisfied. We crave more and more stimulation to give us a sense of being "really alive". But vicarious, electronically mediated experience cannot give that.

To enjoy most push-button entertainment, all we have to do is to sit passively and take it in. We do not have to exercise our will, and hence it atrophies. Gradually, we become a "couch potato," an electronic voyeur, a person with little initiative or will. A true couch potato is unlikely to sing a song, practice a musical instrument, draw a picture, tell a story, or carry on an intelligent discussion. He has forgotten what fun it is to "do", rather than merely watch.

Imagination, inspiration, and initiative are of course involved in producing television and radio programs, videos, recorded music, etc. And some of what is proffered does indeed stimulate our imagination, enrich our feeling life, and lead to positive action. Yet if we use the electronic entertainment heedlessly, our own thinking ability, emotional life, and will are threatened.

We can observe the effect of push-button entertainment by going on a media fast. A pleasant and painless way to fast is to go camping. Spend a week or more quietly in nature without access to electronic devices and begin to clear out your soul life. Enjoy the sense of peace that makes a vacation so refreshing. Upon returning to civilization, don't push that button out of habit or just because it is convenient. Deliberately choose some push-button entertainment and carefully observe the effect it has on your inner life of thoughts, emotions, and initiative. You may find that your own self-directed thoughts are replaced by ideas derived from the movie or news broadcast you watched. You may find that your own songs, the folksongs you sang around the campfire, or the tunes that you hum and whistle, are replaced by the songs and tunes you hear on the radio or in commercial jingles. You may find that you have less initiative to prepare a special dish for dinner, or to write a letter, or to go out for a walk.

Our use of push-button entertainment and the resulting "soul indigestion" affect our social interactions as well as our inner soul life. In Goethe's fairy tale, *The Green Snake and the Beautiful Lily,* the Snake is questioned by the Golden King:

"Whence comest thou?"

"From the chasm where the gold dwells," said the Snake.

"What is grander than gold?" inquired the King.

"Light," replied the Snake.

"What is more refreshing than light?" said he.

"Speech," answered she.

Human conversation may be our most precious art, but it has little room in the realm of push-button entertainment. Last Thanksgiving, family and friends gathered at my mother's home. After the meal, we sat around the table, complimenting my mother on her culinary masterpiece and engaging in lively conversation on various interesting topics. The children asked if they could watch the Thanksgiving Day Parade on television in the adjoining room. Thus, after they ate, they went to consume that visual dessert.

The sound of the television was a distraction, but the adults just spoke more loudly and continued their conversation. Pauses in the discussion or a change of subject caused those facing the television to take a peek at the parade. One adult, then another, then another, left the table and stood in the doorway to watch the parade and eventually came to rest on the couch. Soon most of the adults were with the children or had gone home because a program came on which did not interest them. The conversation dwindled to a few comments, during the commercial breaks, on the content of the program. Upon saying good night, I realized that a valuable opportunity to meet and spend time with family and friends had been lost to push-button entertainment. I was sad that again I had been lured from real social interaction by the ever-available push-button.

Some adults today grew up without radio. Many of us grew up without television and stereos or at least were without them during our early childhood. But today's children, from the moment of their birth, are surrounded by a variety of push-button entertainment devices. Their developing imagination and thinking capacity, their equanimity and depth of feeling, their initiative and inner freedom, like our own, are being sacrificed to passive entertainment and to easy, quick information. Will today's children experience their own world of ideas, feel their own emotions, and give themselves direction in life? How much of their soul-content will they be able to call their own? These are crucial questions which every parent and teacher must take seriously.

As a teacher with eighteen years of experience, I can see a change in children in the past ten years that I would definitely attribute to electronic devices. It is not a change for the better. The work of the teacher has become more demanding because a "real life" teacher may not be as entertaining as what is found in the world of CD-ROM's. When they are being entertained electronically, these children are passive and easy to control. But they are easily dissatisfied with real-life situations, relationships, and activities. They prefer to be entertained from outside and have largely lost the ability to play creatively on their own. The negative effects are even more noticeable in teenagers than in younger children. Judgmental attitudes, sentimentality, lethargy and an inclination to addictive behavior are common traits among teenagers of the video era.

For our own sake and for the sake of our children, we need to become acutely aware of the danger that push-button entertainment poses for us. We need to revive the activities and the abilities with which generations of the past amused, entertained and informed themselves.

Doing puzzles, playing parlor games, reading aloud, doing handicrafts, sewing, painting, drawing, singing, playing music, putting on plays and skits, discussing issues and ideas, and many other activities come from and involve the mind, heart, and will. These can and should again become part of the daily life of children and adults.

Every child should be sung to by his mother. Every child should be read or, better yet, told stories by his father. Every child should have her grandparents and other older family members build toys and bake cookies with her and tell her about their own childhood. It is our privilege to tell our children stories, to sing them songs, to make music for and with them. They need to experience these things directly from those who love them. We should not give up our privilege to electronic devices.

Radio, television, CD's, CD-ROM's, et al., are part of our civilization and part of our daily life. But we must use them with consciousness, care and discretion. The health of our souls and the health of our children's souls depend on it.

— *Renewal, A Journal for Waldorf Education*

Who Me,
Make a Doll?

*The Doll is special among toys,
because it is an image of the
human being. With the doll's
help we can seek our own
identity. We can reveal our
innermost thoughts, sorrows,
and joys to our doll-friend.*
— Karin Neuschutz

SHERRY PIMSLER

I have always enjoyed working with my hands, but never felt particularly good at it. I never had the luxury of much encouragement in that regard. When I was first asked to go to a doll-making workshop, my daughter, Ana, was four and had just graduated from the loving embrace of a Waldorf nursery school into kindergarten.

I had so much catching up to do with this new-found time, in addition to my 30 hour a week job at night, that doll making was far down at the bottom of my list. Therefore, it was with a bit of reluctance that I followed my friend to another mother's house on a chilly Berkeley hill one Saturday morning. As the door opened, a flurry of red-headed children shot past. The commotion didn't stop that whole morning, but I remember some surgical stocking and raw wool being thrust into my hands and being told to start stuffing for the head. This was all done with uncritical good humor on my friend's part and when I showed her the over-sized ball I had finally come up with, she patiently laughed, "We'll just make it into a baby doll since the head's so big!"

That was the beginning of one of the most rewarding creative acts of my life! I never gave it that kind of thought at the time; in fact, I'm not one to go to these kinds of "get-togethers", so as soon as I figured out what was needed, I stopped going to the Saturday morning classes and only called my friend, Virginia, once for advice. However, something had taken hold in me. I carried this "head" around everywhere in an old diaper bag, displaying it proudly to friends and relatives.

If it sounds like the "head" took a long time to materialize, you're right. Due to the limits on my time and my slowness, it was a long and sometimes painful process. I had long ago formed my own ideas about not attempting anything unless I was sure I could do it well. However, there was the deadline for the school Faire, and I assumed that every other parent in the school was creating something too – so onward I plunged.

Every flaw looked so huge to me, but I was beginning to fall in love with my little big-headed doll. I loved her more with every sitting, as her face took on an expression of its own and the blond yarn began to curl around her face. Otherwise conditioned or compulsive moments were now being directed into rewarding work on "Rosebud", as Ana later named her. This was a new practice for me, one of letting go of my frantic pace and relaxing into this task.

It was with great pride that I presented Rosebud to the Christmas Faire that year. It wouldn't really have mattered terribly what she looked like. She seemed to be as much a product of my heart as my hands. I see now that with each stage of evolution "Rosebud" went through, I was realizing with my labor a bit of the Waldorf experience. I had been let in on that secret discernible behind the eyes of each Waldorf child. It's a secret of joy in learning and expression fostered by patience and non-judgment.

Rosebud turned out to be a fine doll, and I hope she went on to engender more love yet in some child's heart. If a doll-making group forms at your school or community, say "yes" and create a doll for someone to love.

To tutor or not to tutor

When Your Child Needs Help

ANNE JURIKA

How do you evaluate if your child really needs a tutor? Can you tutor your child yourself? How much time will be needed? How do you find a good tutor? What should you expect? What will it cost you? All of these are important questions to ask if your child seems to be having difficulty learning in school. It often begins when your child's teacher mentions that he is having problems with certain class work, or perhaps you notice that he doesn't seem to have the same knowledge or skills as other children his age. Problems will often appear as early as First or Second Grade, but they may not become major ones until Third or Fourth, when the curriculum has become more complicated and demands more speed, automaticity and integration of skills.

Sometimes children have a slower pace of development and do catch up with their peers by around Third Grade. However, much of the time, in my observation, those who experience difficulty in the First Grade are still experiencing it in the upper grades, where it has become a problem on many levels— academic, social, and emotional. Much of this unnecessary pain can be avoided by taking steps early on to ascertain the nature of the difficulty and to give the child a boost over the rough spots. While it is important not to overreact, it is important also to investigate the problem as soon as possible with the class teacher through close observation and evaluation, with advice from knowledgeable people. The decision to leave the child alone and give him time to grow out of it is a reasonable decision if a careful study of the situation has been thoroughly made. However, this should be a conscious decision, not one based solely upon hope, and should be re-evaluated at close intervals.

If there is enough uncertainty or if it is causing the child social and emotional difficulty, my advise is – **don't wait.** There is nothing to lose by helping the child, and there is a great deal to lose by waiting. For many children it may be enough to support and strengthen the basic concepts that future work will be based on. Some children need to be taught learning skills: how to listen and to organize information, how to see patterns and relationships, how to remember – something quick learners figure out on their own. Often, a little done early on will go a long way and the investment need not be expensive or time-consuming. However, if the foundations for learning are not firmly built, the rest of the structure will be precarious.

Can you help your child yourself? Yes, if you are in the small percentage of parents who are disciplined enough to follow through on a daily commitment to the needed practice, if your child has a teacher who can develop a good, easy-to-follow program, and if you do not get frustrated with your child. However, most children do not want their parents to be their teachers also, and will often resist, and most parents find it too much of a strain on the relationship to try to be teachers as well as parents.

In the early grades, a good solution can be to seek a teacher at the school whom you can pay to tutor your child a couple of days after school. Many regular teachers who are not trained in remediation supplement their income this way, and are perfectly able to help with early skill problems.

There are children whose difficulties with learning go much deeper and who need the skills and services of professionals trained in the emerging field of Educational Therapy. However, these children too will benefit from early work with a tutor or parent, for the problems will be more quickly seen and the child referred to the person who can truly meet his or her needs. These are the children who, in public schools, are referred to an on-site specialist; they must be diagnosed and labeled with a specific "disorder" in order to receive services. If, in a private school, you and your teacher feel that your child may have serious problems of this kind, you are entitled under the law to receive testing services from your local school district. There is no charge if it is done this way. However, the child often receives a more thorough evaluation if it is done by a private learning specialist. No matter who gives the help, there is very little benefit to be derived from once-a-week sessions. If resources are limited, it is far better to do a shorter term of two or three times a week.

Expect a competent tutor to be in good communication with you and your child's teacher to give and receive information. It is helpful if they also assign some short practice work (no more than 10-15 minutes at a time) to be done at home in between sessions to support and further progress.

Most good tutors and educational therapists are found by word-of-mouth; they do not need to advertise. Ask your school, your acquaintances, your doctor, and anyone else you can think of for recommendations. You should phone two or three of these and speak to each one about your child, then compare their responses and your own reactions to decide who seems best for your child. They should be willing to discuss things over the phone or meet in person initially for no charge. Tuition charges often vary depending on the experience of the person; more experienced professionals can do far more in a shorter period of time, and may be more effective, thus they charge higher fees. Some, however, have sliding scales, so it is always wise to ask.

There are many books out on the market these days directed both towards helping parents understand their child's learning difficulties and to helping them tutor their own children. Go to the largest bookstore you can find and enlist their assistance in finding the right titles for you. These can be an invaluable first step in clearing up your confusion and helping you decide what to do.

It takes courage for a parent to face up to the fact that their child may be having a learning "problem". Many parents prefer to hope it will "just go away". Meanwhile, it is the child who suffers, for the child **always** knows that he/she has difficulties. With early intervention, a little difficulty need never develop into a major "problem".

A Birthday Celebration at School

PAMELA JOHNSON FENNER

My daughter entered a Waldorf elementary school beginning in the second grade. We were eager to learn more about the pedagogy, meet other parents and support our daughter as she adjusted to her new setting. Our daughter came home with light feet – singing and reciting little verses complete with all sorts of sweet gestures and telling me stories – day after day!

She had only been in the school for 10 days when her teacher, Rick, asked if my husband and I could join him to celebrate her birthday in the class. With a new birthday list for the year, he had discovered hers was the first and wanted us to be able to attend. Having had two daughters before her with many birthday parties in the local school, I knew the routine – cupcakes, juice, paper plates, cups, and check which students might have allergies. There was one unfamiliar request, to bring some pictures as a baby, toddler, and with the family since she was new to the class. I later learned that parents had shared their photographs during the first grade birthday celebration.

I knew that the school had routines and a rhythm which was different from our other school experiences, but I never dreamed what a soul-enriching celebration was to be created for our daughter and us.

We arrived at the end of the lunch time and were greeted at the door by Rick. The room had already been darkened with the curtains drawn and the lights turned off. We sat toward one side up front and were introduced to the students. The children quieted down as Rick led Francesca out of the classroom. When they returned a minute later, Francesca was wearing an expansive cape and a "golden" crown. This crown was not the usual cardboard nor plastic variety, but was obviously handmade from a shiny, satiny material and stuffed with something soft and tied in the back of the head.

No one in the room moved as they came up the center aisle. Rick lifted her up onto a stool, and very slowly and deliberately lighted a match and then the special birthday candle, large, white, with three molded angels around the perimeter.

A mood of quiet expectancy was created by the candlelight. Opening up his "Birthday Book", Rick opened with the verse:

> *Above my head the stars do shine*
> *Each star is like a flame,*
> *And one is mine, that o'er me shone*
> *When to this earth I came.*
> *Upon this Earth my step is firm,*
> *The stones are 'neath my feet*
> *I see the birds and beasts and flowers,*
> *And loving people greet.*
> *And every year the day returns*
> *When my star shineth bright,*
> *And I receive within my heart*
> *The glory of its light.*

Next, he picked up his hand-colored card and read a poem written just for her. The theme and character were taken from the Waldorf curriculum, in this case *The Story of St. Francis.*

> *May I give*
> *with my left hand*
> *Hold with my right*
>
> *And may love ring*
> *in my voice*
> *Truth in my sight*

> *May the goodness*
> *of Saint Clare*
> *Inspire my thoughts*
> *warm my heart*
> *And kindle deeds*
> *of Love and Light.*

My husband and I sat enthralled as did our daughter. Turning to a stack of hand-made cards from her fellow-students, he lifted up each one thanking each child and mentioning some feature. Then it was her classmates' turn to offer birthday greetings. One by one they told her what they wished – "may you have many friends in this school", "a singing heart", "an animal to take care of", "a smiling face", and "rainbows". The list went on in that mood. Not one child mentioned any material gifts – no Barbie dolls, jewelry, money, nor any of the latest toys being marketed. I was stunned!

Sensing the special mood created in the class, she carefully and gently opened each gift, mostly wrapped in tissue paper. As she opened these gifts from her classmates, my eyes began to glisten. One student gave her a green serpentine stone – "Jade, how lovely", said my daughter. Other gifts included: plain and unusual shells, pieces of found beach glass, shiny stones and crystals.

The final gift was a small glass jar filled with layers of the most delicate peach-colored rose petals, freshly picked that morning. Francesca's eyes widened and she "oohed and aahed". I turned to look at the children at their desks - none were fidgety nor talkative. They watched with interest the scene in the front of the room. My daughter thanked each child without any prompting from her teacher or from us.

Rick then asked us to offer her a birthday wish – I struggled to find the right words. I can't remember today if I wished for her "to find and give love", "to be a dear friend", or " to have a strong heart". We then passed around the pictures we had brought of our daughter when she was little. There was one last wish and a hug from her teacher and then "poof", Francesca blew out the candle. The celebration concluded with carrot cupcakes and lemonade.

As the years went by and the curriculum evolved, so did the birthday celebrations. The cape and crown were left in the drawer, the lights might be on, and my role was just to drop off the cupcakes and juice and leave. Even the gifts changed in character, but they were always handmade gifts or gifts from nature as requested by the teacher. That request alone has transformed her idea of gift-giving more than our own examples for more meaning-filled gifts. The angel candle was used for the entire eight years of birthday celebrations!

A birthday is an appropriate time to make a child feel a special part of one's family, to let her know that our lives have been enhanced by her presence. As we struggle to find ways to nurture our children every day, I reminisce about that first birthday celebration at her Waldorf school. Looking back at the class celebrations over the 30 years of being a parent, this one in her second grade class had not taken any more time than the others – around 12 - 15 minutes. But this experience far surpassed any birthday before or since. Not only did Francesca feel like a "princess" or a "queen-for-a-day", but her soul was nourished by the warmth and love extended to her. And perhaps for her, it created a special welcome, as a new student. As for the rest of us that morning, it was a priceless example of being cherished.

There is no "standard" Waldorf birthday celebration. Other teachers at this and at other Waldorf schools create their own celebrations for each child. But the tradition of a poem (original or not) for the child – and to be learned "by heart" – is part of each child's Waldorf experience.

Francesca framed all her poems, lining them up one-by-one next to her bed year after year. Each one creates a special picture for her, strenghtening her self-esteem, and gently offering a picture of what it means to be a human being.

And yes, Rick, she still knows each one "by heart."

Thoughts on Children's Parties

MIDGE HEATH

When I was a child growing up in the country, birthday parties were virtually unheard of and when they did occur, were heralded long after the event. I personally remember one birthday party in my youth – my sister's – and it was no less exciting because it was not mine – our cousin was the guest. We still remember the glory of this occasion today, 43 years later. The reason for this golden glow around the mere suggestion of a birthday party was: this was a rare treat – a special occasion – not to be taken for granted. One never thought one should have a party, neither did one suspect one could have a birthday and one certainly dared not dream one would have a birthday party.

So, here we are years later with every birthdate heralded brightly and yearly with an event – which is not in itself an unfortunate turn. There are, however, those mis-events; I have seen one-year olds sleeping soundly or trying to close their sleepy eyes while a circle of young mothers bravely sing "Happy Birthday," I have seen two-year olds screaming nonstop as a circle of parents and other two-year olds made an attempt to serenade the birthday boy and make believe this occasion was truly for the child and not the parent; I have seen four and five-year olds who ripped through all the presents without ever looking up to thank the friend or really stop to see what the gifts were.

I have seen six and seven-year olds so bored and blasé about their yearly celebration that it takes a clown, a musician, or maybe a movie to entertain them and take the party into the realm of a "special " event. And, of course, there are the 10 and 12- year olds who have not been properly feted unless they have been driven 40 miles to the closest amusement park. In short, the modern birthday party all too often becomes an occasion for begging and whining on the child's part, with anxiety, annoyance and dread on the parent's part, and no "golden glow" on anyone's part. This type of yearly debacle is not necessary – we can still have Birthday Parties that honor the name – and the child – and are fun for everyone involved.

The best rule of thumb for a young child's party is: never invite more children than the age the child is turning. In two or three-year olds, this would mean one child invited, in order not to have the triangle effect. Invite their one little close friend – an event they can comprehend and deal with on a physical and emotional level. This does not mean an afternoon where there is cake and ice-cream, then just play. There is never a birthday party so successful as one planned by adults and run by adults. The children should not have to wonder how or what to do next – the adults should be there with orderly games and events. This is special, this is different – this is a golden, magic afternoon – and most of all someone calm and relaxed, the parent, is in charge. The child can relax.

This brings us to another very basic issue – if the parent cannot carry the party off in a relaxed and loving way, if the parent is anxious, cross or obviously does not really want to have the party – have a family celebration, with cake and handmade cards from brothers and sisters, and small presents from a loving family.

Remember, the little child is watching you prepare for the party; he watched you shop for the cake, make the cake, put up the decorations, clean the house – all of these things and the attitude with which they are done are stored up in the child. He will reflect them at the party; he will mirror all the parents' pre-party tensions at the party and no amount of your sudden bright smiles when the guests arrive will change the fact that he has seen you these past days and hours and he knows that you have felt angry and tense over this event. He, of course, is going to feel angry and tense too, and there will be no sudden bright smiles from him. So, parents, don't give a party for your child if you are not willing to GIVE a party. Make it the child's, not your own. And don't have it if you can't enjoy the process of giving the party

Preparation

Being shooed away while the parent does all of the exciting preparations is the beginning of frustration and discontent for the child. So, have some preparations that include the child. This not only makes the child extremely happy, but makes him feel that he is "giving" something to his friends. If finger puppets are being made for favors, he can help glue them together. If a cake is being decorated, he can help squeeze the decoration on the icing. Decorating the cake was **the** big event of the week when my children were younger. The cakes were beautiful and the children were so **proud** to be able to present these cakes at their party.

Children are wonderful at decorating the house; if they cannot actually hang the streamers, they can suggest where they should be. There are many ways a child can participate in pre-party fun. The payoff is for both parent and child – the child is happy and the parent finds this is the most fun of any party ever.

Actual activities at parties depend on the season and the child's age. It is not possible here to give age by age and season by season a full list of suggestions, but here are a few.

Summer Parties

The basic thing to remember about a party, particularly one at home, is to plan carefully. Two hours is usually long enough – until age nine or ten, anyway. If the children are old enough to make favors, this should be done first as it relaxes the children, gives them a focal point, and occupies them while you wait on the inevitable late arrivals – plus the children do not get wild and out of control waiting for the party to begin.

After everyone has arrived, play a game or two, then open the presents and eat the treats, then more games. The order is not particularly important as long as YOU guide the party. A total of 4 games is usually enough along with the making of a favor.

Games

Younger children love finding hidden objects – walnuts for example. Give them each a little party basket to collect them in and they take the nuts home with them. Of course any child not having a good "finding luck" will need a helping hand. Summer is a good time for a friend to bring a guitar and sing for games: *Farmer in the Dell, In and Out the Windows*, etc. Live music makes it more fun. Face painting is fun, but should be done at the end of the party as the children get hot, sweaty and messy.

By the age of four or five children love water games. Tell the parents to let the children wear swim suits or shorts. Have four or five water balloons filled for each child before the party, have a nail driven through a board. Line the children up and let them (one at a time) toss the balloon at the nail. It is harder than it sounds – they usually don't get wet and the victorious bursting of the balloon thrills them. This is fun for children from four to eight years. Of course, the board is brought out immediately before the game and removed immediately afterwards. Throwing a water balloon into a box or through a small hoop is fun as the children turn about seven or eight years. If an older sibling wants to stand under the hoop and get wet, that is fun, but it is not advisable to let one of the party children be the "mark."

Water balloon fights are fun for children 10 - 13 years, as long as you have a place outside for them to fill the balloons and not more than eight children are invited to the party. Games like this can turn into a melee if too many children are involved.

Making their own favors is fun for children. Older children are wonderful for these projects as they can help the four to seven-year olds, and the party children are thrilled to have the big brother/sister taking part. For example, my 10-year old son taught his younger brother and friends the intricacies of making paper airplanes. The children colored, folded and flew the airplanes, then took them home. These were six year olds – a good age for paper airplanes. This age can also put together beautiful pinwheels. Use heavy paper of beautiful colors (found at a creative arts store) and have the pieces out beforehand.

Making favors before the party or during the party is a subject in itself and much too lengthy to discuss here. Just remember that homemade favors are to be highly recommended. Through this means, your child realizes consciously that he is giving this party to his friends; he sees the love and care that you put into these gifts – as he becomes older he gets the privilege of helping with the favors. The party takes a turn from being a time when all of his friends come just to give **him** presents. He gives too – this part of the party can become very special for the child.

Winter Parties

When planning a winter party, count on having the children inside. Some good inside games include: sitting on balloons to see who can burst them first; two children holding a long stick or broom while one child goes under, each time the stick is lowered a bit; gossip; and treasure hunts. Dipping candles is a wonderful wintertime favor for the children to make if you have the space for it. (Remember appropriate safety precautions using hot wax.)

A good Christmas past-time for party children is decorating cookies. Have many shapes of fairly large cookies – Christmas trees, Santas, angels, boots, stars, etc. Red, blue, green, yellow and white icing in several bowls should be set so all the children can easily reach, with many toothpicks for detail decoration. I first used this at my nine-year old's party in December. The children spent over an hour decorating their cookies in great detail and took them home for favors.

The list of games and activities for birthday parties is long and varied. If you have time and energy to put into these parties the possibilities are endless. If an adult is good with his hands, a kite-making party is fascinating for the children – an enormous feeling of satisfaction comes from flying your own kite. Making hot air balloons would also be an enjoyable activity.

The best references for children's parties and activities are *The American Girls Handy Book* and *The American Boys Handy Book*, written by Lina and Adelia Beard, and Daniel Carter Beard respectively. Having been out of print for some years, they are now being published by Charles E. Tuttle Co. Check your library or bookstore for more ideas or other books.

— *Chanticleer*

The Unbirthday Party

SANDRA HOLLAND

Midge Heath's down-home wisdom in the foregoing article makes me wish that the idea of small, simple birthday parties had been part of my consciousness when my children were young. The parties I am giving now for my young teenagers, however, are I think just right! They include small family birthday parties and larger, general theme parties. Ideally the party would include the whole class and if it is well-planned and supervised, even the shyest child will feel comfortable and enter into the spirit of the party. Also, if it is a class party and a number of parents are invited to help, then it is not on any one child's shoulders to give a successful party.

Theme parties are a great deal of fun and often party preparations begin in the child's home well before the event with costume- or food-making activities. This usually promotes eager anticipation of the party.

Ideas for games and activities usually come easily if one gives free rein to one's imagination around the party theme. For example a Watermelon Beach Party might have a seed spitting contest, a watermelon eating relay race, a prize for the most seeds in a piece, and a sand castle building contest using rinds and seeds for decorations. (The children will probably think of a few more.) Other summer parties might include a Toga Party, a Softball Game Party, a Scavenger Hunt, and a Teddy Bear Picnic.

Each season has its major festivals and a party planned around one of its themes is sure to generate enthusiasm. Autumn brings to mind hay-rides and square dances. October, of course, could feature Halloween parties. These might take the form of a Pumpkin-carving Party, a Favorite Ghost Story Party, a Build-a-Haunted-House Party, as well as the traditional costume party.

Winter would bring Christmas parties, New Year's Parties and Valentine's Day Parties. In the springtime a Kite-making-and-Flying Party would capture the imagination of every child, and no one is ever too old for an Easter Egg Hunt. Once you enter into the spirit of party giving for this age group, you will find yourself coming up with more ideas. And, what you don't come up with, the children will. Everyone has at least one party idea to share from their childhood or adulthood! Bubble gum relay races (chew, blow a bubble and run) and the Soda Cracker Relay Race (chew, whistle a tune and run) live vividly in my memory.

At one Christmas time, I gave a successful "Christmas Caroling Progressive Dinner Party." The children enjoyed eating their meal in the different, beautifully decorated homes, and they also brought Christmas joy into the neighborhood in which they caroled. At the last home where they ate their dessert each child was sent home with a plate of favorite Christmas cookies which they had all contributed to the party.

Although the youngsters enjoyed this party and were eager to make it an annual event, they enjoyed even more the Valentine's Party which featured more activities and games. The theme of the party was Valentine's Day but the focal point was chocolate. The "Chocolate Dessert Pot-Luck Valentine's Party" was planned to last 3 1/2 hours , from 7 PM to 10:30 PM (3 1/2 to 4 hours is a good length for a party.) The games and activities were listed on a large heart. This gave the children the sense that there was a definite structure and that their participation was expected. As soon as each game was finished, shouts of "What's next?" were heard. The children enjoyed participating in all of the games chosen and it was easy for them to follow the game plan.

I encourage you to try giving parties for this age group. And if you don't provide a little excitement in their lives, you can be sure they will. I have found that if one parent is willing to do all of the planning and be the director, help is forthcoming from other parents. Our children need participatory activities if they are not to go through life merely as spectators.

— *Chanticleer*

Rhythm During the Summer

KAREN RIVERS

June approaches very quickly and suddenly, and after that last assembly and picnic, it's summer. Your children are home now for full days, day after day. The school rhythm is gone. The temptation is there to slip into a somewhat unformed vacation life where most, if not all, regularity has gone.

The daily and weekly rhythm of the school year have a deep significance for children especially up to the age of fourteen. Even high school students need the form and discipline of daily requirements to reach the ultimate goal of setting themselves demanding tasks as adults.

Therefore, we invite you to bring as much form and regularity into your child's summer life as you possibly can. "Regular meal times, regular bed times, regular tasks – this is the backbone of a healthy and happy childhood" as Harwood writes in *The Recovery of Man in Childhood*. Try to install many regular tasks in your child's day. Let them help with all kinds of chores. Allow in-breathing and out-breathing: chores, reading, music practice, should alternate with free time. Ask even more of your child in keeping his or her room neat than you would during the school year.

A daily vacation schedule written out on paper is often an excellent idea for many children. It makes them feel that their contributions are important and that they are taken seriously. If you approach it in the right way, children will love to take part in gardening tasks. Most of them have had gardening experiences at a Waldorf school throughout the seasons. Caring for plants and regularly watering them can be a most joyful summer activity.

Let there be a clear beginning and end to the daily activities, whether these are meals or work tasks. Try to build in a daily story-telling time in the evening. Even middle and upper-elementary school children are not too old for such story sessions. Of course, some activities are woven into a weekly rhythm rather than a daily one.

The weekend brings special opportunities for full family activities. Many families enjoy visiting a particular place each week so that it begins to feel like home. With few adjustments, you will soon have a daily and weekly rhythm that is in harmony with the season and with the family. You may find that there is hardly any time for television.

When your children come back to school after a vacation, or even after a weekend, teachers can immediately notice to what degree they have been nourished and sustained by a wholesome rhythm at home. Such a rhythm is one of the greatest gifts you can give your children.

Celebrations Through the Year

I sincerely believe that for the child, and for the parents seeking to guide him, it is not half so important to "know" as to "feel". If facts are the seeds that later produce knowledge and wisdom, then the emotions and impressions of the senses are the fertile soil in which the seeds must grow.

— Rachel Carson

Festivals, Seeds of Renewal

PHILIP WHARTON

The human being is marked among the creatures of the earth by the capacity to experience him/herself as a self-enclosed being, as an "I." However, this distinction has been purchased at a price. That price is separation. We find ourselves living in a state of separation from nature, from other human beings, even from ourselves. This condition can be felt as painful exile. It begets in us the desire to unite with that from which we are separated. A great longing for wholeness lives in our souls.

Our very separateness has its ground in our deep and original unity with the world. Only a being who has gathered the whole into himself, who is himself an image of the whole, can separate himself from the whole. This is something no mere part can do. It is the spirit of the whole that awakens in us, forgetful of its origin.

Just as the withering of the leaves and the separation of the seed from the mother plant has its place in the continuing life of nature, so the intellectual withering of our soul life and our separation from nature has its place in the total evolution of man. Our separation, grounded in our original unity with the world, is itself the seed of a new unity.

Realizing this, we can begin to see nature in a new way, participate more inwardly in the life of the earth together with the cosmos as it takes its course in the rhythm of the seasons. We look out and see the budding and blossoming, the ripening and withering. We observe the alternation of solstice and equinox, a stately dance of day and night, as now they hold a balance, now bright day dominates, now starry night. We watch the flights of birds and the phases of the moon.

We experience the light in its transformations, the dying light of November, light's fullness in May. We can begin to feel that all this is not merely external to us, but deeply and mysteriously bound up with our inmost soul. We can feel that what streams in the light of the sun is the same that flows from our heart when it is fired with love, that as the moon's pale light is a reflection of the living radiance of the sun, so the pale images of our intellect are reflections of bright, living ideas.

From such a perspective the various festivals, woven into the life of the year, gain a new meaning. These festivals, which have come down to us from the past, had their source in an ancient wisdom, a spiritual knowledge of man and nature. In the modern world they have, to a far reaching extent, lost their substance. They have become matters of tradition, habit, economics, at best of mere sentimentality; but rightly understood, rightly celebrated the festivals can become a source of healing for the individual and society, a harmonizing, community building power.

In the celebration of festivals man and nature can come together in a higher nature, a higher humanity. Individuals can come together, united in a common striving for the truly, the universally, human. Through living with the festivals and seasons we can learn to sense the breath and pulse of the cosmos. We can learn to experience ourselves in the world, the world in us.

The leaves wither and the seeds fall away, bearing rich possibilities of new life. In our separate individualities we bear the seeds of renewal. When individuals come together in freedom to celebrate the festivals with reverence and joy, this renewal begins to grow.

The never-ending seasons
that so lightly come and go
Are miracles of wisdom
no man can ever know.

J. F. Wornal

...We live in a time of hard tests for humanity, of hard tests which must become still harder. We live in a time in which a whole host of old forms of civilization to which men still erroneously cling, are sinking into the abyss, a time in which the claim insistently arises that man must find his way to something new.

— Rudolf Steiner

Michaelmas

KAREN RIVERS

At autumn time, as the life forces of nature recede, turning toward a winter sleep, the inner life of the human soul is awakening. It is a time of conscious selfhood, a time when we celebrate the building and strengthening of our inner life. In many cultures, the autumn time marks the beginning of a new year. The forces of nature are transiting with the autumnal equinox, as the relationship of light and darkness changes in the world around us.

The equinox is for us a turning point, a change in the relation of light and darkness in the world around us. On September 29th the autumn festival traditionally known as Michaelmas is celebrated. This festival is named for the Archangel Michael, conqueror of the powers of darkness, the harvester of the deeds of human souls. It is at this time that the image of Michael with the dragon appears before us as a mighty imagination, challenging us to develop strong, brave, free wills, to overcome love of ease, anxiety and fear. This demands inner activity, a renewal of the soul which is brought to consciousness in the Michaelmas festival, the festival of the will.

Michael is often portrayed as the angel warrior, astride his powerful steed carrying a sword of light. The children hear stories about St. George, a brave knight, who with the help of the Archangel Michael, slays or tames the dragon. Michael is the angel who hurled Lucifer down from heaven for his evil workings against God. St. Michael, warrior of courage, fighter against evil, rules the heavenly spheres; he guides and inspires us to take courage against darkness. St. George symbolizes the human aspect of this conflict; he is the knight who looks to Michael for strength and guidance.

These images truly symbolize the challenge we face in the autumn season. They speak to our deep need to carry an inner light of wisdom and courage at this time when the light is diminishing. Through strength of will, inner activity of selfless consciousness, we bring light to the darkening time. These are very challenging times; the anti-social forces are emerging everywhere. May we gain insight, courage and truth at this Michaelmas time, to bring light to our inner life, our community and the world in these times of darkness.

I rise through the strength of Mi-cha-el

> *Light of Sun*
>> *Radiance of Moon*
>>> *Splendor of Fire*
>>> *Swiftness of Wind*
>>> *Depth of Sea*
>>>> *Stability of Earth*
>>>> *Firmness of Rock.*
>>>> *Mi-cha-el!*

St. Patrick

...or the elemental creatures go
About my table to and fro,
That hurry from unmeasured mind
to rant and rage in flood and wind;
Yet he who treads in measured way
May surely barter gaze for gaze.
Man ever journeys on with them
After the red-rose-bordered hem.
Ah, fairies, dancing under the moon,
A Druid land, a Druid tune!

— William Butler Yeats

All Hallows' Even

RICHARD MOESCHL

Halloween is the one festival with perhaps more ancient beginnings than any other holiday. Few of these origins are known commonly with the result that for many, Halloween has lost any serious meaning. A look at its origins might help us place this festival in perspective both in our hearts and in our calendars.

The celebration that was to become Halloween began with the Druids in Britain and Brittany, France. Two principal feast days for the Druids were the spring festival of Beltane on May 1st and the autumn festival of Samhain on November 1st. The night before Samhain, October 31st, was the most feared evening of the year. On this night beginning at midnight and lasting through the following day, celebrations were held to placate Samhain, the Lord of Death. During the night Samhain allowed the spirits of those who had died within the last 12 months to roam the earth. To frighten the evil spirits away, huge bonfires were lit on hilltops in honor of the sun god.

November 1st marked summer's end and the beginning of a new year. In Ireland, new fires were kindled from fires which had been started by Druid priests rubbing pieces of oak together. The new fires in each hearth would last until next November 1st.

When the Romans conquered Britain they added to the Druid feast of Samhain their own feast, honoring Pomona, the goddess of fruits and the feast of Februalia, the festival of the dead. The month of February was later dedicated to this god. In 900, the Christians moved their celebration of All Saints from May to November 1st. This feast of all the holy ones (All Hallows) was preceded by All Hallows' Even, later to be called Halloween. In the 10th century, the day after All Saints Day was designated as the Feast of All Souls, in which all the dead were remembered. Their close presence was felt at this time. But as many spirits good and bad shared this moment, the people were cautious. "On November Eve there is a bogy on every style" warned a Welsh proverb. For protection from evil spirits, some people carried sprigs of the magic rowan tree. Others kept salt and iron with them, two substances which frightened fairies and evil spirits. Masks kept the ghosts at bay and made it difficult for them to recognize the wearer.

Nuts and apples, tokens of the winter store of fruit were roasted on the great bonfires. Several days beforehand, young boys went around begging for material for the fires. Masked adults often visited homes begging for food. Sometimes the food was meant for the dead as with the soul cakes in Scotland. Great tables were spread both as a celebration for the harvest and to feed the dead.

Charms, spells and predictions were believed to have more power on the eve of Samhain. The usual performers were called witches after the Saxon word "wica" meaning "wise one". Several times a year, witches from all over gathered at a sacred spot. One important date was April 30th, the eve of May, a day sacred to the mating of animals. Halloween was another important date and it recalled the hunting of animals by men. Witches were often depicted with black cats. Stealthy animals whose glowing eyes could see in the night, the cats were considered to be supernatural beings as far back as Egypt. Hecate, the Greek goddess who ruled over witches, wizards and ghosts, had a priestess who was a cat. To the Druids cats were dreaded as human beings who had been changed into animals by evil powers. On Halloween, a number of cats were always thrown into the Samhain fires.

Part of the Samhain fire is recalled in the Jack-O-Lantern. Some say the Jack-O-Lantern originated with a fellow named stingy Jack who broke his pact with the devil. As a consequence the devil forced him to roam the face of the earth carrying a glowing coat from hell in a carved out turnip. Pumpkins later replaced turnips and their orange color became a necessary hue at Halloween along with the black of night and death.

In tracing the origin of Halloween we recognize the source of much that has become the custom at this time of year and why children don masks and costumes, carve pumpkins and go from door to door begging for food. Pranks are played and everyone experiences the eerie quality this festival evokes. We are courting death, that mystery-enshrouded event which continuously reminds us of our dual citizenship; here and in the spiritual worlds. Every religion and every culture sets aside at least one time every year to remember and commune with the dead.

One possible way to relate to Halloween is to compare it with another festival where life and death are the themes. In celebrating Easter we recall that at the death of Christ, tombs were opened and many of the dead appeared to people. Christ, as Lord of Life, visited the abode of the dead having conquered death itself. The nuts and apples of Halloween are replaced at Easter by another symbol of fertility, the egg. One festival occurs at the end of harvest time in gratitude for the plenty before the lean of winter. The other festival arrives at winter's end with the promise of spring and renewed life. Both events celebrate the fullness of life and the necessity of death to enrich it. Both are especially difficult to celebrate meaningfully with young children. Not only is their appreciation of death minimal, but there is little in the outer world to mirror the soul moods of nature at these times of year.

To the teachers and parents is given the task once held by the priests of old; to help create and sustain the proper atmosphere into which an inner experience can come into being. We can prepare ourselves. Then the festivals are truly celebrations.

— *Chanticleer*

Thanksgiving

KAREN RIVERS

For the bountiful gifts the earth bestows upon us, for the golden hues that adorn the land, for the richness of each sunrise and each day's glory in this land of freedom – this is the heartseed of the Thanksgiving Festival. The growing year has come full circle as the harvest comes in. Grains, fruits, vegetables and nuts fill the larders, imbuing man with a sense of completion and gratitude for the miracle of nature.

The harvest season is universal; the harvest festivals are among the most ancient known to mankind. The Egyptians and the Chinese gave thanks for well-filled storehouses. The Hindus held a festival for Gauri, the goddess of the harvest, where the girls wore flowers in their hair. The ancient Greeks honored Demeter, the Goddess of agriculture, while the Romans celebrated the festival of Ceralia, dedicated to Ceres, goddess of vegetation. The Hebrews celebrate the Feast of the Tabernacles, or Sukkoth. American Indians celebrated the harvest by giving thanks to the spirits of the woods for wild game, of the lakes for fish, and of the fields for berries and nuts. At the traditional green corn ceremony, the fires of the old year were put out and new ones kindled. Everywhere on earth the harvest kindles gratitude. During the Middle Ages, England and Europe kept the tradition of the Harvest Festival celebration, known as "Harvest Home." The villagers went to the field and decorated the last load of grain with ribbons and flowers. The people danced around it singing songs of thanks.

Thanksgiving in the United States belongs to the tradition of the harvest festivals but it has another dimension that is unique unto this country. We not only give thanks for the blessings of nature, but for the freedom which marks our heritage. In *The Philosophy of Freedom*, Steiner writes:

> Freedom is based on action, on thinking and feeling that arise from the individual human spirit, that place within that opens out to embrace the eternal truths of existence.

This was the quest of the Pilgrims who came to America in search of religious freedom. When they reached the New World it was autumn.

William Bradford described it as:

> ...a hideous and desolate wilderness, full of wild beasts and wild men... For summer being done, all things stand upon them with a weather-beaten face, and the whole country, full of woods and thickets, represented a wild and savage hue.

There was no harvest for the Pilgrims that year. The winter was harsh and rations scarce. Nearly half of the Pilgrims died the first winter. Although the colony was weak and diseased, spring and summer were beautiful that year. No one chose to return with the ship as it set sail for England that spring.

The Native American tribe that lived in the region was the Wampanoag (also known as the Pokanoket). At the time the Pilgrims arrived, the tribe was under enormous pressure as nearly three quarters of the tribe had been decimated by the diseases introduced by foreign explorers. Those remaining were fending off attacks from a neighboring tribe. With both the Pilgrims and the Indians facing a crisis in survival, the time was propitious for a friendship.

The first contact between the two groups was made by Samoset and Squanto, Indians, who, after being kidnapped and enslaved separately by early English traders, had escaped their captors and returned home. Because they both spoke English, they were able to arrange a treaty between the Pilgrims and Massasoit, chief of the Wampoanoag. Squanto showed them how to plant corn and squash and how to hunt and fish in the unfamiliar territory. When autumn arrived the colony had survived their first year. There was plenty of food. Their crops were harvested inspiring the Pilgrims to hold a three-day harvest festival to celebrate the momentous first year of the colony's survival. The Indians shared in their joyous festival of food, games and songs.

The following year the harvest was small and the winter fierce. Thanksgiving was not celebrated. Winter rations were reduced to five grains of corn daily for each person. Thanksgiving was celebrated with irregularity until the Revolutionary War was over and the thirteen colonies won their freedom from England. At this time President George Washington issued the First National Thanksgiving Proclamation:

> Now therefore I do recommend and assign Thursday the 26th day of November next to be devoted by the People of these States to the service of that great and glorious Being, who is the beneficent Author of all that good that was, that is, or that will be – That we may then all unite in rendering unto Him our sincere and humble thanks – for His kind care and protection of the People of this country previous to their becoming a Nation – for the signal and manifold mercies, and the favorable interpositions of his providence, which we experienced in the course of conclusion of the late war.

We are eternally grateful for the bountiful harvest, the daily miracle of each dawn, the sky's pageantry of rolling mist and the night's brilliant stars; each flower, grain and drop of water, which bedeck our days with beauty and joy. For these we are eternally grateful. Somehow, the greatest of all these, which makes all else magnify in its glory is our freedom. We inherit a great responsibility in this country to open our spirits to Truth so that we may be free.

The Advent Wreath

GERTRUD MUELLER NELSON

Pre-Christian peoples who lived far north and who suffered the archetypal loss of life and light with the disappearance of the sun had a way of wooing back life and hope. Primitives did not separate the natural phenomena from their religious or mystical yearning, so nature and mystery remained combined. As the days grew shorter and colder and the sun threatened to abandon the earth, these ancient people suffered the sort of guilt and separation anxiety which we also know. Their solution was to bring all ordinary action and daily routine to a halt. They gave in to the nature of winter, came away from their carts and wagons, festooned them with greens and lights and brought them indoors to hang in their halls. They brought the wheels indoors as a sign of a different time, a time to stop and turn inward. They engaged the feelings of cold and fear and loss. Slowly, slowly they wooed the sun-god back. And light followed darkness. Morning came earlier. These festivals announced the return of hope after primal darkness.

This kind of success – hauling the very sun back: the recovery of hope – can only be accomplished when we have had the courage to stop and wait and engage fully in the winter of our dark longing. Perhaps the symbolic energy of those wheels made sacred has escaped us and we wish to relegate our Advent wreaths to the realm of quaint custom or pretty decoration. Symbolism, however, has the power to put us directly in touch with a force or an idea by means of an image or an object – a "thing" can do that for us. The symbolic action bridges the gulf between knowing and believing. It integrates mind and heart. As we go about the process of clipping our greens and winding them on a hoop, we use our hands, we smell the pungent smell that fills the room, we think about our action. Our imagination is stirred.

Imagine what would happen if we were to understand that ancient prescription for this season literally and remove – just one – say just the right front tire from our automobiles and use this for our Advent wreath. Indeed, things would stop. Our daily routines would come to a halt and we would have the leisure to incubate. We could attend to our precarious pregnancy and look after ourselves. Having to stay put, we would lose the opportunity to escape or deny our feelings or becomings because our cars could not bring us away to the circus in town.

But to sacrifice our wheel means not so much "to do without" wheels as it means to "make holy" this stopped time. *Sacre ficere* means to make holy, and holy means hale, HEALTHY, whole. And it is not easy to make this time holy. We recognize that the search for the holy is so urgent and real that we are vulnerable to the lure that the commercial world offers in its promise to fill in the gaps that we so painfully feel. Materialism has contaminated the truth that "things" indeed can be carrier of the Divine. We do not want to fall for the ruse or Christmas becomes just another expensive disappointment.

During Advent, we are invited to be vulnerable to our longing and open to our hope. Like the pregnant mother who counts the days till her labor and prepares little things for the child on the way, we count the days and increase the light as we light our candles and prepare our gifts.

We work our way toward Christmas. With quiet excitement, we go about those simple gestures that ratify the mystery about to take place. In ceremonies we deal directly not with thoughts but with actualities. We help ourselves to see again, in the outward sign, the inner truth. If we are awake and if we live the earthly process, we will feel what is inner and hidden. We make the wreath and light the candles, and we gain the courage to stop the wheeling and dealing of our outer life: to sacrifice the wheels that grind away at outward "progress" at the cost of peace and justice in this distraction. The sacrificed wheel of the Advent wreath encourages us to stop and wait. The symbolic life offers us a way to live those feelings which we might otherwise avoid or deny or rationalize away. The symbols speak directly to the heart. Intuitively, we still know that truth; our children know it beyond a doubt. That is why we search for ways to prepare Christmas together and look for the actions and the things that can adequately hold and carry such great mystery.

— *To Dance With God*

The Advent Garden

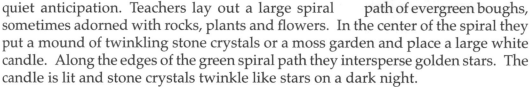

The season of Advent may be marked by the Advent Garden, created for the kindergarten and lower grades. Often held in late afternoon or in the early evening, the room will be dark and filled with a mood of wonder and quiet anticipation. Teachers lay out a large spiral path of evergreen boughs, sometimes adorned with rocks, plants and flowers. In the center of the spiral they put a mound of twinkling stone crystals or a moss garden and place a large white candle. Along the edges of the green spiral path they intersperse golden stars. The candle is lit and stone crystals twinkle like stars on a dark night.

All is quiet. Each child in turn, holding a red apple with a small unlit candle inserted into it, slowly walks along the spiral path and lights the candle from the center light. On the return the child places the apple and candle on one of the golden stars. When all the children have had a turn, the garden path is aglow from all the smaller lights. In many Advent Gardens, lyre playing, where appropriate, helps to create a special mood. Nancy Foster of Acorn Hill Children's Center relates her experience with this special celebration:

> For many years I have told a story in the Advent Garden about Mary's journey seeking threads to weave a robe for the Child soon to be born. More recently, however, the need to penetrate to the very essence of our festivals thus arriving at the universal aspect which can speak to the hearts of all human beings, has become ever more clear and more urgent. The following poem arose as the result of this need. It may be spoken both before and after the spiral is walked.

Deep Mid-winter drawing near,
Darkness in our Garden here –
One small flame yet bravely burns
To show a path which ever turns.

Earth, please bear us as we go,
Seeking Light to send a-glow;
Branches green and moss and fern,
Mark our path to trace each turn.
Brother animals, teach us too
To serve with patience as you do.

We walk with candle toward the Light
While Earth awaits with hope so bright;
In the Light which finds new birth
Love may spread o'er all the Earth.

Deep Mid-winter drawing near –
May Light arise in our Garden here.

Celebrating Advent in One Waldorf Classroom

ANNE JURIKA

Advent time in a Waldorf classroom is always a joyous time of anticipation and excitement. Yet within all the activity there is always a quiet moment each day when wonder and reverence can blossom. The rituals and activities that are woven into the regular classroom work at this time are chosen by the teacher; each class may celebrate in a different way, yet if one really penetrates to the heart of the festival with one's own understanding, one then finds that any little ritual or image one creates will reveal some aspect of the truth.

At least two traditions are kept by all the classes at my school: the Advent Wreath and Advent Calendar. In my classroom each year I decorate with green boughs twisted round with red streamers. I drape red streamers around the windows and tie them in bows. Among the green boughs I place red tissue paper roses easily made by twisting circles of tissue paper and tying the twisted ends. As I make my Advent Wreath I add blossoming sprigs of Rosemary and tie a red tissue paper rose to the base of each red candle. Suspended from the top of the four red ribbons I hang a gold star. I spray all the greens every morning with water to keep them from drying up and becoming too flammable.

Each morning in Advent, after morning verse, the children stand in a circle around the room. We darken the room and when all are quiet, I light a special candle – perhaps a rainbow one – which the children pass carefully from hand to hand as we say this verse:

> *The gift of the light we shall thankfully take*
> *But it shall not be alone for our sake,*
> *The more we give light, the one to the other*
> *It grows and gives light, and shines even farther*
> *Until every heart, by love set aflame*
> *In every place great joy shall proclaim:*
> *Not long shall continue the darkness of year*
> *The light draws near.*

The last child lights the Advent wreath candle with it. Then we break into song: *Rise Up O Flame*, followed by *People Look East* while we walk around the classroom to the Advent Calendar.

The Advent Calendar has been placed on the window sill so that light will shine through the pictures behind the windows. Pine boughs have been arranged around it. *People Look East* mentions all four kingdoms of earth – the rose (plant), the star (mineral), the bird (animal), and Mankind. Each week one of these appears in our nature table by the Calendar: first crystals, then a fresh rose, then a bird's nest, and finally the children's handmade gifts to one another.

I usually try to relate the Advent Calendar to important aspects of the curriculum for that year. In Third Grade – Old Testament – I drew Noah's Ark, and behind each window was an animal, including fish in the water and a dove with an olive branch in the sky. The large window, for December 25, opened to reveal the child in the manger with the rainbow arching over him.

In Fifth Grade when we studied Ancient Civilizations, I arranged each circular window in a large spiral on a piece of dark blue poster board. In gold I painted the symbols for the 12 signs of the Zodiac upon twelve of them and stars upon the other 13. Beginning with the signs of Aries the windows were removed to reveal gods and spiritual teachers from India, Persia, and Mesopotamia through Egypt, Greece, and the Hebrew culture, culminating in the birth of Christ under the sign of Pisces. Some teachers have made tissue paper pictures behind their windows, and some have let the children make the calendars. One need not be a great artist – the children notice not this, but the feeling with which something has been done.

After the Calendar window has been opened, we sing our way back to the Advent wreath where we "take the light into ourselves" before putting out the candle(s).

Another tradition during Advent is that of "Kris Kringle". Each child has his or her secret friend who does nice things for him or her and makes a gift to be given at the class holiday party.

Ritual and ceremony help to find one's way to the meaning that is hidden in the most common everyday occurrences. I do not explain any of it to the children, but allow them to take these things quietly into their hearts. It matters not which songs, poems and rituals the teachers choose – what is behind them all is the same feeling of wonder and reverence for a great mystery.

—The Marin Waldorf School Parent Handbook

The Festival of Lights

Hanukkah

KAREN RIVERS

Near the time of the winter solstice, the people of the Jewish faith celebrate Hanukkah, or the Feast of Lights, in remembrance of a miracle that took place in Judea over 2100 years ago. This festival is a rededication of the Jewish people to the ideals of religious freedom and political liberty under God.

The primary source for the history of Hanukkah is in the First and Second Books of the Maccabees, which were written in 142 B.C., shortly after the events they describe. The Syrian king, Antiochus, prohibited the practice of the Jewish religion in Judea. He captured the great temple in Jerusalem, ordered the burning of all Jewish holy books, and condemned to death all the scholars who studied them. The temple was desecrated, swine flesh was offered, and idols were set up. Scrolls of the Torah were burned. The Maccabees were the first to fight for the right of religious freedom.

When King Antiochus sent his soldiers to the village of Modin to force the Jews to sacrifice to his gods, a man named Mattathias and his five sons refused to obey the order; they killed the soldiers and fled to the hills. Under the name of the Maccabees they raided the king's men for three years, until their victories enabled them to return to Jerusalem.

On entering the city, Judah, one of the sons, who was now the leader of the Maccabees, vowed to cleanse and rededicate the temple. According to Talmudic tradition, a small quantity of consecrated oil was found to relight the "Eternal Light" of the temple. This light was not to be left unlit, but it appeared that the holy oil would last for only one night. It would take a week to get more. To the Maccabees' great surprise, the oil kept burning for eight days.

The Hanukkah Festival celebrates the bravery of the Maccabees and the miracle of the oil. It starts on the 25th day of the Jewish month of Kislev which is usually in December and lasts for eight days. The principal ceremony is lighting of the special nine-branched menorah each night of the holiday. The practice is essentially a home ceremony. On the menorah there is space for eight separate candles (or oil lamps) – one for each night the oil burned – and a space for the helper candle called the *shammash*.

On the first night of Hanukkah, one candle is placed on the far right space. The *shammash* is used to light the candle. Each night a new candle is added until on the last day of the festival all eight candles are burning. They should burn each night for at least one half hour.

Before the lights are kindled, the following blessings are said (traditionally in Hebrew):

> Blessed are Thou, O Lord our God, King of the Universe, who sanctified us with Your commandments and commanded us to kindle the Hanukkah light.

> Blessed art Thou, O Lord our God, King of the Universe, who performed wondrous deeds in ancient days and today.

On the first night, this prayer is included:

> Blessed art Thou, O Lord our God, King of the Universe, who kept us in life, sustained us, and enabled us to reach this season.

Children eagerly look forward to the special foods and games of this holiday. Songs are sung which recall the wondrous triumphs and victories wrought by their forefathers in ancient times. One tradition has been to give a gift of money (Hanukkah *gelt*) to the children.Today they receive toys and chocolate coins as gifts. Another tradition is playing the game of *dreidel*. A dreidel is a 4-sided top with a Hebrew letter on each side – *nun, gimmel, hay, shin* – which stand for "a great miracle happened there."

— *The Marin Waldorf School Parent Handbook*

The Christmas Festival

A Token of the Victory of the Sun

RUDOLF STEINER

Christmas is not a festival of Christendom only. In ancient Egypt, in the regions we ourselves inhabit, and in Asia, thousands and thousands of years before the Christian era we find that a festival was celebrated on the days now dedicated to the celebration of the birth of Christ.

Wonderful fire festivals in the northern and central regions of Europe in ancient times were celebrated among the Celts in Scandinavia, Scotland and England by their priests, the Druids. What were they celebrating? They were celebrating the time when winter draws to its close and spring begins.

It is quite true that Christmas falls while it is still winter, but Nature is already heralding a victory which can be a token of hope in anticipation of the victory that will come in spring – a token of confidence, of hope, of faith – to use words which are connected in nearly every language with the Festival of Christmas. There is confidence that the sun, again in the ascendant, will be victorious over the opposing powers of Nature. The days draw in and draw in, and this shortening of the days seems to us to be an expression of the dying or rather of the falling asleep of the Nature-forces. The days grow shorter and shorter up to the time when we celebrate the Christmas festival and when our forefathers also celebrated it, in another form. Then the days begin to draw out again, and the light of the sun celebrates its victory over the darkness.

In all religions this Christmas festival has been one of confidence, of trust and of hope, because on this day it was felt that the light needs must prevail; out of the seed planted in the Earth something will spring forth which seeks the light and will thrive in the light of the coming year. Just as the seed of the plant is cradled in the Earth and matures in the light of the Sun, so the divine truth, the divine Soul itself is immersed in the depths of the life of passion and instinct and there in the darkness this divine Sun-Soul must grow to maturity. Just as the ripening of the seed in the Earth is made possible by the victory of the light over the darkness, so is victory assured for the soul inasmuch as ever and again the light prevails over the darkness. And as truly as strife can only exist in the darkness and peace in the light, so with an understanding of the harmony in the universe there will come Peace upon Earth.

> "Glory on this day, revelation of the Divine Powers in the heavenly heights on this day, and peace to those who are of goodwill."

The regularity with which the Sun moves through the seasons, the regularity manifested in the growth of plants and in the life of animals – this regularity was once chaos. Harmony has been attained at the cost of great travail. Humanity stands today within the same kind of chaos, but out of the chaos, there will arise a harmony modeled in the likeness of the harmony in the universe.

If the glory, the revelation of the divine harmony in the heavenly heights is a real experience with us, and if we know that this harmony will one day resound from our own souls, then we can also feel what will be brought about in humanity itself by this harmony: peace among men of good-will. When with this great vista of the divine ordering of the world, of the revelation, the glory of the heavens, we think of the future lying before mankind, we have a premonition even now of that harmony which in the future will reign in those who know that the more abundantly the harmony of the Cosmos fills the soul, the more peace and concord there will be upon the Earth. The great ideal of Peace stands there before us when at Christmas we contemplate the course of the Sun. And when we think about the victory of the Sun over the darkness during these days of Festival there is born in us an unshakable conviction which makes our own evolving soul akin to the harmony of the Cosmos – a conviction that this harmony will not flow into our soul in vain.

And then the seed which brings to the Earth that peace of which the religions speak takes root in the soul. The 'men of goodwill' are those who feel this peace. It is a peace which will spread over the Earth, when in our life of feeling and in our soul that harmony reigns which has been achieved today in the realm of reason alone. Strife and discord will have given way to the all-pervading love of which Goethe speaks in his Hymn to Nature: "A single draught from this cup of love will render us invulnerable to a life of toil and stress."

— *Festivals and Their Meaning*, Christmas 1923

The day of the Holy Kings

Epiphany

KAREN RIVERS

January 6 is an ancient celebration often referred to as the Twelfth Night, the night the Three Wise Men reached Bethlehem, twelve nights after the birth of Jesus. The church calls this day "Epiphany" – a Greek word derived from *epi* and *phainein,* meaning to show or shine upon.

The Feast of the Epiphany is more ancient than that of Christmas. It commemorates the manifestation of the Son of God to man. The realization of the divine event of the birth of the Christ child, and the journey to find him, symbolize the essence of this festival. Epiphany celebrates man's role in the divine drama of Christmas. One version of this story is told by Mala Powers in "The Gifts of the Three Wise Men" from *Follow the Year:*

> The Three Wise Men were royal personages and followers of an ancient Persian teacher. They knew the prophecies which foretold the birth of God's own Son on earth and they were wise in understanding what the stars foretold about happenings on earth. The Magi were Melchior, old Balthazar and young Caspar (who came from Africa) – a king, a priest, and a doctor. In short, they were masters of all the wisdom that men and women had gained on earth since earliest times.

> They were the first of the heathen world to do homage to Christ. One by one, in the name of all mankind, they presented their gifts to the sleeping child.

> Melchior presented his gift of gold, symbolic of wisdom, intelligence and a testimony of his nobility and royalty. "Oh, Holy Child, you who will bring the golden light of heavenly wisdom into the thoughts of men and women – accept my offering of gold!"

The great power of intuition was symbolized by the gift of Balthazar. "Oh, Holy Child, you who will bring to earth the true power to love unselfishly – accept the gift of frankincense."

Caspar's gift foreshadowed the suffering and death of the Son of God. "Oh, Holy Child, you who will someday save mankind from the forces of death and grant to men of goodwill your power to heal – accept the gift of myrrh."

In Christian churches today Epiphany celebrates three events in the life of Christ as told in *John 2: 1-11:* the visit of the wise men to Bethlehem; Jesus' baptism by John the Baptist; and the first miracle of turning water into wine at the marriage feast in Cana of Galilee.

There are many customs surrounding this festival. In many countries it is a day of gifts. Before going to bed, the children place water, a box of grass, or some grain under their beds (or in their shoes by the door) for the weary camels to enjoy. In the morning when the children awake, they find a gift from the kings in place of the greens.

In England it marks the end of the Christmas holidays. In the Eastern Church, the waters are blessed on this day. In some countries on the Vigil of Epiphany, the eve before the feast, a special Epiphany cake is served in which three beans are hidden (two white ones and one black one). The children (or adults) who got the beans in their cake may dress as Holy Kings and are the guests of honor at the table. Before the evening is over, the three majesties offer their gifts of gold, incense, and myrrh.

Festivals of Spring

LUCILLE CLEMM

Long before the birth of Jesus Christ in Bethlehem, ancient peoples celebrated festivals of death and rebirth and the return of spring each year. The Anglo-Saxons held a celebration in April in honor of Eastre, the goddess of spring and light.

The Greeks had several myths and mysteries which remind us of our Easter mood. In the festival for Adonis (originally held in the autumn but later moved to the springtime) a statue of the god was lowered into the water for three days while everyone remained in earnest mourning. When the image was raised, hymns of joy were sung to the resurrected god.

The story of Demeter tells how the earth was denied her blessing while she mourned the loss of lovely Persephone, her beloved daughter, to the Lord of the Underworld. Persephone did return and spring came and everything blossomed and was fruitful; however, because she had eaten three pomegranate seeds, Persephone was fated to return to the Underworld each year for three months while all nature mourned.

In the mysteries of Dionysus or Bacchus, there was also a death and resurrection. Of course, Dionysus was also the god of the vine. Nothing looks more dead than a pruned grape vine in the winter; yet, it seemingly comes back to life and produces the grapes which give the juice or wine used as a symbol in the religious rituals in Christian churches and as a part of the Seder at the time of Passover.

The Norse Mythology also has stories which are relevant:

> *"Nine whole nights on a wind-rocked tree,*
> *Wounded with a spear,*
> *I was offered to Odin, myself to myself,*
> *On that tree of which no man knows."*[1]

Odin gained wisdom because of his sacrifices which included giving up one eye. Baldur the Beautiful was slain by a brother through the treachery of Loki. Then, just before his funeral ship was about to be fired and sent to sea, Odin whispered in Baldur's ear that Baldur would return after Ragnorok.

As a Waldorf teacher approaches the time before Easter, he or she varies the images given to the children. With little children it is lovely to plant bulbs in the autumn and then enjoy sharing the children's delight when crocuses, daffodils and lilies bloom in the spring. Colored eggs are wonderful to make or find. They give a picture of the secret of life within something outwardly hard and cold.

In the Third Grade the wonderful stories of Moses and the Passover and wandering in the wilderness before coming to the promised land are lived through in pictures, paintings ,and sometimes in drama. The Fourth Graders learn of Baldur and Odin and the myths of Greece are brought to the Fifth Grade.

It is not until the Sixth Grade that the life of Jesus Christ is told in connection with the study of Roman History. Some beautiful masterpieces of the Renaissance, such as Michaelangelo's "Pieta," are enjoyed in the seventh grade.

When the long winter begins to show signs of retreating and purple and yellow crocuses miraculously peep out from lingering snow banks, one's heart responds. Fruit trees put on their wonderful blossoms and the sunshine brings warmth of our bodies and souls. There is a feeling of having been through a dark time and having survived; one experiences a rebirth of energy and health and a longing to sing "Alleluia."

Spiritual Threads of Passover and Easter

KAREN RIVERS

For more than three thousand years Jews have celebrated the Feast of Passover. One asks, "Why is this night different from any other night?". As with the two other Pilgrim Festivals (*Shavu'ot* and *Sukkot*), Passover has both agricultural and historical elements, and it celebrates both the themes of creation and redemption. Yet, the inner meaning of this festival offers a message to all mankind.

The ancient origin is the Hebrew nomadic festival, celebrated in the spring, when a lamb was sacrificed. Historically, Passover commemorates the Exodus of the Children of Israel from Egyptian bondage and their emergence as a free nation.

During the reign of the Pharaoh Merneptah, approximately 1200 BCE, the Hebrew people were living in slavery. According to tradition, God sent two messengers, Moses and his brother Aaron, to the Egyptian Pharaoh to free them. He refused, and as punishment, God sent ten plagues down upon the Egyptians: water turned to blood; frogs; lice; wild beast; cattle disease; skin disease; hail; locusts; and darkness. Though Egyptians suffered throughout these nine plagues, the Pharaoh would not soften. The tenth plague was the death of the firstborn child in every Egyptian family. God commanded the Hebrews to smear newly-sacrificed lamb's blood on the doorposts of their homes. Because of this sign, the Angel of Death "passed over" every Hebrew home, killing only the Egyptian children, including the Pharaoh's own son and heir. The Pharaoh became frightened and called for Moses and Aaron and ordered them to lead the Hebrews out of Egypt.

On the fifteenth day of Nisan, they left in great haste, taking their bread dough without waiting for it to rise. Later, during their flight, they baked the unleavened bread in the hot desert sun. The Hebrews were still afraid that the Pharaoh might change his mind, which in fact he did. They soon found themselves trapped between the advancing Egyptian soldiers and the Red Sea. It was then that God divided the waters, allowing Moses and his people to cross the sea on dry land, then closed the sea to drown the pursuing Egyptian army.

After the Exodus, the historical events were combined with a spring agricultural festival. On the second day of this festival, a measure of the new barley crop, called an *omer*, was harvested and taken to the Temple and presented to God as an offering. These rituals of spring, rebirth and revival, celebrate the forces of creation.

The name, Passover, derives from *Pesach*, which in Hebrew literally meant "skipping over" and refers to the "passing over" of Jewish homes by the Angel of Death. The Passover festival calls for extensive preparation based on strict rules and begins with a special feast called a *seder*.

This story of the quest for human freedom bears a relationship to the inner significance of the Easter Festival. This festival, too, has its origins in ancient traditions. The Anglo-Saxons held a festival in April in honor of Eastre, the goddess of spring and light. The Greeks celebrated the rebirth of nature with the return of Persephone from the Underworld. In a festival to Adonis, the Greeks lowered a statue of the god into the water for three days while everyone remained in earnest mourning. When the image was raised, hymns of joy were sung to the resurrected god.

The cosmic forces of the spiritual worlds upon humankind become visible in the myths and symbols of the ancient mystery religions. These ancient festivals prefigure the Christian Easter story. Not unlike the Hebrew story of Passover, at the time of Jesus of Nazareth, the Jewish people were oppressed by the reign of King Herod. The crucifixion of Christ was an effort to rid Israel from the threat of one who was not fearful of the rulers. As was the case with Moses, Jesus wished to lead the people of Israel to a condition of freedom.

Both of these spiritual leaders were taking a step in the evolution of human consciousness. After crossing the Red Sea, Moses wandered in the wilderness for 40 years before reaching the land of "milk and honey". After his death on the cross, Jesus descended into hell before His resurrection. With the festivals of Passover and Easter come the victory of good over evil, of light over darkness, of life over death.

As Steiner writes in "Spiritual Bells of Easter, I":

> Festivals are meant to link the human soul with all that lives and weaves in the great universe. We feel our souls expanding in a new way during these days at the beginning of spring. . . . It is at this time of year, the time of Passover and Easter, that human souls can find that there lives. . . in the innermost core of their being, a fount of eternal, divine existence.

If we can begin to penetrate the cosmic significance of the mystery of this season, the rebirth of nature, the freeing of the Israelites, and the death and resurrection of Christ, we begin to understand that Easter is as A. P. Shepherd writes, "... the Festival of the spiritual future of humanity, the Festival of Hope and the Festival of Warning."

— With adaptations from Rudolf Steiner, *Festivals and Their Meaning*, 'Easter'

Easter Symbols

The Cross

The vertical stroke represents the one-ness of God, or the Godhead in general; it also symbolizes power descending upon mankind from above, or, in the opposite direction, the yearning of mankind towards higher things. In the horizontal stroke, on the other hand, we see the Earth, in which life flows evenly and everything moves on the same plane. In the sign of the Cross, God and Earth are combined and are in harmony. From two simple lines a complete sign has been evolved. The Cross is by far the earliest of all signs, and is found everywhere, quite apart from the conception of Christianity.

The Easter Egg Tree

The Easter Tree can be a simple tree branch or a constructed cross design entwined with greenery and decorated with Easter Eggs, flowers and other symbols of life. With its three branches it brings a message of "three-foldness" and becomes a real "tree of life" bearing the yolk of light and hope. The "tree of life" can be placed in the Easter Garden and secured within a flower pot with green shoots or moss growing in it. Fresh spring flowers brighten the display and decorated eggs are hung from the cross pieces.

The Easter Hare

Themes of resurrection and new life are popular symbols of the Easter season. The Easter Hare, one of the favorites of Easter, is of European descent. The hare is not found upon the North American continent and so in this country we substitute its cousin, the Easter Rabbit.

Because there are distinctive differences in temperament between these two creatures, much of the original symbolism is lost. The rabbit lives in clans, but the hare is a wandering solitary being whose home shifts from place to place. The hare's inherent sense of "brotherhood" impels it to thump on the ground to warn other hares of the pursuit of a predator; it will risk its own life to save its fellows, and thus it has become an earthly symbol of "resurrection" and "sacrifice."

The hare was also a favorite symbol in Ancient Egyptian culture. It was a reminder of the fertility of nature in spring and was also connected with the influence of the sun and moon upon the earth. Folklore tells us that the Easter Hare is invisible, magical and belongs to the moon. This wondrous being comes especially for children, hides brightly colored, beautifully decorated eggs and special treats of all kinds, and always just escapes being seen.

— *The Marin Waldorf Parent Handbook*

May Day

KATHRYN HALL

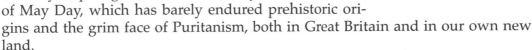

It is fascinating to delve into the histories of holidays that persist after so many centuries of celebrations. It is particularly inspiring to look at the history of May Day, which has barely endured prehistoric origins and the grim face of Puritanism, both in Great Britain and in our own new land.

In 1644 the Puritan Long Parliament issued a decree that all such "devilish instruments" as May poles be abolished and appealed to the "Constables… Tything men, petty Constables and Church Wardens" to take down any existing structures and ensure that none be erected in the future. The tradition subsided until the return of the Stuarts.

It appears that the earliest May Day Celebrations were to honor the changing of the seasons, from darkness into light, and that a tree, the symbol of the "tree of life" and of the great strength and vitality of Nature, was used in the ritual. One could draw a connection between early May Day trees brought in from the woods by peasant youths of old Europe and the sacred pine tree representing the god Attis used in a procession to the temple of Cybele in Rome, a spring ritual.

Most commmonly May Day is associated with Flora, the Roman goddess of flowers and spring. Garlands of flowers were gathered and carried to her temple by exuberant, brightly dressed youths who wound their sweet blossoms round the huge marble column inside the temple. They then danced round the column, singing their praises to Flora. This celebration was known as Floralia, and lasted from April 28 until May 3.

For the Druids of the British Isles, May 1 was the festival of Beltane, the midway point of the year, again reflecting the turning of the seasons. A huge bonfire was built, thought even to lend life to the incoming spring.

Eventually the celebrations were emancipated from their "pagan" origins and large May poles, cut from the tallest trees which could be found, were erected in England's public squares or occasionally before churches, to ward off evil spirits that might abound at this time, during the transition between darkness to light.

For years it was the custom for women on May 1st to rise before dawn and walk deep into the woods seeking the Maydew of hawthorn branches to bathe their faces to ensure lasting beautiful complexions.

May Day is a joyful, colorful festival of spring. Unlike Halloween its polar opposite (the festival of death), May Day brings with it the promise of rebirth – the renewed life of the soul.

The May pole Dance

Music: *The Rakes of Mallow* or *Piper's Fancy*

Step: Skipping 2/4 time

In May pole dances the girls stand on the right of the boys.

All dances begin by honoring the May pole with the boys bowing and the girls gesturing with a curtsey. Then each honors one's partner.

It is best to hold the ribbon with both hands, so that one can "play it out" or pull it in easily. For a simple dance, the boys and girls weave the ribbons in a simple over and under pattern.

Girls may begin by turning to the right and going around the circle, moving first inside towards the pole (with a boy passing them on the right) and then outside (away from the pole).

Boys begin by turning left and moving towards the outside and lifting their ribbons over that of the approaching girl.

To unwind, turn and face the other direction and undo the plait or braid. All dances end by honoring first one's partner and then the May pole as one did at the outset of the dance.

— *Chanticleer*

Whitsun or Pentecost

KAREN MORTENSON

Seven weeks after Passover is a celebration with ancient roots, differing names and rites. It has both an historical basis and deep seasonal meaning. *Shavu'ot* celebrates the spring harvest of wheat and the first fruits. It also marks the day upon which the Torah was given to the Israelites on Mt. Sinai. Freedom was given to them at Passover, but Shavu'ot gave them rules to live by as a free people. *Pentecost* is the Greek name for "50th" and thus was adapted by Greek-speaking Jews of the first century. For Christians, Pentecost falls 50 days after the Resurrection of Jesus, celebrated on Easter. Whitsun or "White Sunday" is the first English name for the Festival of Pentecost and is a time for Baptism (and the traditional white garments).

With the multiple characterizations of this festival – the first fruits of the earth and the first fruits of the spirit, the festival of awakening, of free individuality, of baptism – how may we find the thread that binds them together?

Christmas is a "fixed feast;" i.e.,, it occurs each year on the same day. Christ is born. Easter, however, is a "movable feast," set by the relation of sun and moon in the spring of the year. Friedrich Benesch[1] speaks of this as an equally true setting, as the Easter experience comes to each man in his own time. Whitsun/Pentecost is both moveable and fixed, in that it follows fifty days after Easter; that is to say, the experience of death and resurrection leads in due course to the experience of understanding oneself as a spiritual being.

A traditional Easter song provides the picture of Easter:

> *Now the green blade riseth from the buried grain;*
> *Wheat that in dark earth many days hath lain.*
> *Love lives again, that with the dead has been:*
> *Love is come again, like wheat that springeth green.*

As the sprouting grain is a picture of resurrection, so the blossom is the image of the flowering of the spirit at Whitsun:

> The heart of man as it opens may be symbolized by the flower opening itself to the sun; and what pours down from the sun, giving the flower the fertilizing power it needs, may be symbolized by the tongues of fire descending upon the heads of the disciples.[2]

As there are many blossoms but one sun, so there are many languages of the Spirit, but one Spirit. The second chapter of Acts describes the scene. (Words in parentheses are in Greek.)[3] We read that, according to custom, the Jews had made the Shavuot-Pentecost pilgrimage to Jerusalem. Here too, Mary and the disciples are gathering in one accord together. They hear "a sound (*echo*) from heaven as of a rushing, mighty wind," and a cloven tongue (*glossa*) of flame rests upon the head of each. They speak in other tongues (*glossa*), and the devout Jews hear each "in the language (*dialektos*) in which he was born."

Note that the disciples speak *glossa*, and the devout hear *dialektos*. In Greek, *glossa* (literally tongue) refers more to the archetypal language, and *dialektos* (literally "speaking through") is more the body of differentiated speech. Each man hears the Spirit in his own individual language. Many blossoms, one sun. We have in this story the teleological summation of the Genesis story of Babel. There it is written that:

> the whole world had one language (**cheilos**, lips) and a common speech (**phoni**, sound, void). " They "decide to build a city with a tower that reaches to heaven, so that we may make a name for ourselves and not be scattered over the face of the whole earth.

On seeing this, the Lord said,

> Behold, the people is one, and they all have one language (cheilos); and this they begin to do: and now nothing will be restrained from them, which they have imagined to do. Go to, let us go down, and there confound their language (glossa) that they may not understand one another's speech (phoni). So the Lord scattered them over the face of the whole earth

Here we can see that when the people had **one** voice and **one** form of expression; they had not their freed individualities. "Behold, the people is one." They wanted already to return to heaven, and not to live individually scattered on the earth. Lest they do this, the Lord confuses their *glossa*, meaning that not only the form of expression is individuated, but also the expression itself. Thus, they cannot understand each other's *phoni* (sound voice).

At Pentecost, the festival of the free individuality, the *glossa*, confused at Babel to allow the development of that free individuality, is now rightly transformed into new unity. Awakened individuals meet each other in the higher spirit and form the first Christian community. This is the Baptism of the Spirit; the First Fruits of the Spirit.

In *Shavu'ot*, the Jewish festival of Moses receiving the Ten Commandments on Mount Sinai, we can see the prototype of individuation – truly an Old Testament Pentecost. The Mountain is swathed in cloud, flame, and rushing wind. Moses is called to ascend, but the people must remain below – they "must not break through to the Lord to gaze, lest many of them perish." But they hear the voice *(phoni)* of the Lord and tell Moses, "You speak to us and we will obey, but not let God speak to us, lest we die."

Rabbinical tradition tells us that the Law was offered to all people, but that none would accept it save the Hebrews. The Ten Commandments are addressed to them individually, saying, "Thou shalt... Thou shalt not... At this time the Hebrews are, with many failures, going about the world-evolutionary task of developing individuality and personal responsibility. When Moses returns, the people tell him, "We have heard His voice *(phoni)* out of the fire; we have seen this day that man may live though God has spoken to him."

On Sinai, the mountain is clothed with flame; only Moses may ascend. God speaks *"I AM"*. His words are to the Hebrews, and are graven in stone. At Pentecost the flame rests on the heads of men. All men may ascend to the Spirit; those that do, speak the divine "I AM" from their own higher ego, and these words are graven in the hearts of all devout men. The apostles go out to bring this message to all people.

This is Whitsun or Pentecost, the festival of the awakening of man to the divine Spirit in himself and others, an awakening permeated with consciousness and understanding. This awakening is most beautifully painted in this hymn:

"Sleepers, wake!" a voice is sounding,
From watch to watch the call rebounding:
"Awake, Jerusalem, awake!"
Midnight past, the hour is nearing
When in the East, the darkness clearing,
A new and brighter dawn will break.
The Bridegroom to receive,
Arise! your couches leave,
Your torches light,
And mount the light
Of Zion's wall
To greet His coming, one and all.

— Johann Sebastian Bach

St. John's Tide

KAREN RIVERS

High summer has been celebrated with fire since ancient times. Huge bonfires were lit on the Summer Solstice to help the sun continue to increase rather than to diminish in the light it brings. An old custom required that people should jump over the fire to burn away their woes and weaknesses.

Just after the Summer Solstice is the Festival of St. John, celebrated on June 24. Some hold the belief that Elizabeth, John's mother, built a large bonfire to notify her cousin, Mary, of the birth of her child, that she might come to share in her joy. Since many customs of the Summer Solstice festivals blended with aspects of St. John's life, the two festivals have become interwoven in many regions of the world. From now until the Winter Solstice in December, the sunlight will be diminishing. "He must increase but I must decrease" *(John III, 30).*

In the book, *Blessed Among Women,* Author Michael Arnold imagines Elizabeth speaking the following words to her son, John:

> The sages of the ages called you harbinger. The prophets shall look at you and say, "He is Elijah come again!" Your mission is to prepare the hearts and minds of men for the coming of their Savior. Only through purity can they understand the words and the purpose of Christ.
>
> To teach men to be pure in heart you must yourself be pure in heart, word and deed. By being the example, the pattern, you provide men with that which they can follow. It is not enough to stand where the paths part and point the way; you must lead the way, so that those who follow do so with the assurance that their teacher leads them over a path which to him is familiar.
>
> Men grow to know the unseen, inner life by outer symbols which they can see and understand. It is your work to wash men's bodies free of the lower nature and the fumes of anger, greed and lust, so that they can see and comprehend the truth.
>
> Water is to be the symbol of this cleansing rite. Through this outer symbol man will grow to know its inner meaning. You shall baptize men with water, preparing them for him who shall baptize with the fires of holy love.

John the Baptist represents man at the center of history, devoted to what is beyond himself, to the revelation of the spirit brought by Christ. His summons was to turn inward, to search within toward a confrontation with oneself. What must we do to prepare the way for him who comes? John's reply was:

> Practice helpfulness to all mankind; spend not all you have upon yourselves... Be honest in your work... Do not increase for selfish gain... Do violence to no one...

Summer is the time in which the blossoms bring forth seeds. John's task was to make fertile the soil in our hearts that the seeds of summer might grow and become fruitful in the inner life of mankind. Our task is to bring to life within ourselves the power of conscience, the reflection of our divine origin, and to develop purity of heart, word, and deed.

As parents we may prepare the way for our children. On this day, when the sun is at its height, we may turn our eye inward with the conviction that in times of abundance, the need for inner strength is just as great as in times of little or darkness.

Children's Prayer

The golden sun so great and bright
Warms the world with all its might,
It makes the dark earth green and fair
And tends each thing with cesaseless care
It shines on blossom stone and tree,
On bird and beast, on you and me!
Oh may each deed throughout the day,
May ev'ry thing we do and say
Be bright and strong and true,
Oh golden sun like you.

Author unknown

The Waldorf School is not an "alternative" school like so many others founded in the belief that they will correct all the errors of one kind or another in education. It is founded on the idea that the best principles and the best will in this field can come into effect only if the teacher understands human nature. However, this understanding is not possible without developing an active interest in all of human social life. The heart thus opened to human nature accepts all human sorrow and all human joy as its own experience. Through a teacher who understands the soul, who understands people, the totality of social life affects the new generation struggling into life. People will emerge from this school fully prepared for life.

— Rudolf Steiner, *The Spirit of the Waldorf School,*
lectures surrounding the founding of
the First Waldorf School
Stuttgart - 1919

Appendix

Acknowledgements
Authors and Sources
Recommended Reading
Anthroposophical Resources

The secret of education lies in respecting the pupil.

— Ralph Waldo Emerson

Acknowledgements

      My father taught me how to sail with the wind against the tide. Reaching one's destination can take a long time

      My journey in publishing has taken me seven years and literally 3000 miles from the Pacific Ocean in Marin County, California to the mouth of the Merrimac River along the Atlantic seaboard in Massachusetts. As with most adventures of this length, this was not a solo journey. Along the way many people taught me new skills, offered me their wisdom along with fresh "provisions", and I would like to acknowledge their contributions.

The Waldorf Community

Karen Rivers and the Marin Waldorf School Community:

You wholeheartedly endorsed and supported my vision of the *Marin Waldorf School Parent Handbook* in 1988 and my new venture, this book.

I am especially grateful to you, Karen, for offering the fruits of your own creativity and experience as co-editor of *Chanticleer.* The beautiful and sensitive articles you wrote or edited comprise major sections for this book – "Moving Through the Grades" and "Celebrations Through the Year". Above all, I treasure the many years we spent together as parents and colleagues.

David Mitchell:

Your enthusiastic words, "Why not publish it yourself?", set me off on this marvelous odyssey!

David and Marianne Alsop:

Thank you for believing in the merits of this initiative and in my capacity to carry it. You and the AWSNA staff generously answered my questions and offered important commentary.

René Querido:

Your inspiring words led me to Rudolf Steiner College and back into the classroom.

Denise Torres:

Your objective sharp eyes and keen intellect helped shape this book into its final form. I always could trust your natural instincts for knowing what articles to include or eliminate. Thank you for writing the "Foreword" and being my friend.

The Authors:

This book, of course, would not have been created without your generous contributions and well-wishes for this project. You translated your knowledge and experience into well-crafted words offering not only vital information, but also much-needed inspiration to the reader. Your message of hope for the future extends far beyond your respective individual Waldorf communities.

Friends and Family:

Old and New:

I have been blessed to have had my youngest daughter, Francesca, as a dedicated and patient Waldorf crew member. Claude Julien, Dale Hushbeck and members of the Marin Small Publishers Association, especially Malcolm Barker, offered valuable publishing expertise. I am grateful for my friends – especially Karl Andrek, Karen Andrews, Carlin Diamond, Mary Echlin, Lynn Jericho – who helped me ride through the inevitable obstacles along the course.

Tuckerman Moss:

Thank you for being such a long-term and stalwart friend. I could always count on you to rescue me from computer crashes, suggest design layouts, or just to say, "Do it!"

Leonard and Helen Johnson:

How could I venture out without having had the necessary preparation during my childhood? Being a parent seemed to come so naturally to you both. Your gifts were immeasurable. Most importantly, you taught the four of us children to never be afraid to strive for the truth, to act on our beliefs, to find the goodness in oneself and the world, and to give thanks by giving back to others.

Paul Fenner:

I have been accompanied on many a voyage for the past 30+ years by my loving husband, Paul. Though truly my "First Mate", you have often dubbed yourself "chief cook and bottle washer" for our three daughters and me, particularly during this odyssey. But you offered far more – trimming the sails, following me eastward into ports-of-call, and always providing time, love, and stability when I needed it most. And you always believed I would complete the journey with fair winds and an incoming tide!

With love and hugs to you all,

Pamela Johnson Fenner – All Saints' Day, November 1, 1995

Authors and Sources

Editors

Pamela Johnson Fenner

Born and raised (with a fraternal twin sister and twin siblings) in a small New England manufacturing town and attended local public schools. She received a Master of Arts in Teaching (Natural Science) from Harvard University following a BS in biology from Chatham College. She has taught science classes in both elementary and secondary public schools. As a childbirth educator, Pam not only taught couples, but also created a course for children who would be attending a sibling's home birth. After becoming a Waldorf parent, she inaugurated a Parent Association, served as a trustee for five years, and worked as a staff member coordinating enrollment and community relations. She originated the concept for the *Marin Waldorf School Parent Handbook* and established Michaelmas Press to publish it in a new form. Her first publication, *Waldorf Student Reading List*, edited with Karen, is in its third edition. Following her Waldorf Teacher Training (Rudolf Steiner College), Pam was the Director of Community Development at the Waldorf School of Princeton (NJ). She currently resides in northeastern Massachusetts along the Merrimac River with her husband and youngest daughter.

Karen L. Rivers

Karen has lived in northern California all her life. She received a BA from the University of California at Berkeley in World Literature and Comparative Religion and a secondary education credential from Dominican College. Following five years of teaching in public high schools, Karen received her Waldorf teacher training. She created and was co-editor with Mary Beth Lugrin Rapisardo of 'Chanticleer', a seasonal publication produced by the Marin Waldorf School. Karen recently completed 10 years as a member of their faculty. During that tenure, she served as Faculty Chair, Administrator, Trustee and College Chair. She compiled and edited the first edition of *Waldorf Student Reading List* published by Pam in 1992. Karen lives on a forest hilltop in northern California with her husband and daughter and currently is writing and directing dramas and festivals.

Design Work

Mary Beth Lugrin Rapisardo, illustrator, received a BFA in photography and fibre art from Kansas City Art Institute. Formerly the art, handwork, and gardening teacher at the Marin Waldorf School, her artistic talents graced posters, brochures, lazured walls and the school's publication, Chanticleer and The Marin Waldorf Parent Handbook. A mother of two sons living in Mill Valley, CA, Mary Beth is currently completing a master's degree.

Illustrations for "Fifth Grade", "Creating, a Balance of Thinking, Feeling, and "Home Life" were drawn by Manette Teitelbaum, faculty member at Marin Waldorf School.

Cover logo, and calligraphy by Dale Hushbeck, Chestnut Ridge, New York.

Cover art: crayon drawing by Magda Yunque, a student at the Waldorf School of Princeton. Watercolor of flowers – artist unknown – Green Meadow Waldorf School. Truth and Beauty Exhibit, Phoenix Art Group, Inc., Metuchen, NJ. Exhibit photography by Kathy Perlett.

Typography, page design, and digital scanning and enhancement of illustrations by Robert Severn and Adam Brodsky, Severn Associates. Inc., Ivyland, PA.

Cover design execution: Karen Merk and Phoenix Offset Printing, Portsmouth, NH.

Foreword

Denise Torres

Received a BA degree in Social Change from California State University, Sacramento. She has 21 years of experience working with non-profit organizations, including the Marin Waldorf School in San Rafael, CA. While at the Marin School, Denise became President of the Board of Trustees, and conceived and published *Main Lesson*, a periodical for the larger community describing Waldorf Education. Currently, Director of Religious Education for All Souls Unitarian Church in Colorado Springs, CO.

SECTION I — *An Overview of Waldorf Education*

Joan Almon
Chair of the Waldorf Kindergarten Association of North America and a board member of the International Waldorf Kindergarten Association. She is also a part-time teacher in Waldorf teacher training centers and a consultant to Waldorf kindergartens in North America and abroad.

Footnotes
1. The July 1993 issue of the Readers Digest contains an article describing the program.

2. For more information about such programs, contact Gary Lamb, Threefold Review, PO Box 6, Philmont, NY 12565

Henry Barnes
For 35 years class teacher, history teacher and chairman of the faculty at the Rudolf Steiner School, N.Y.C.; co-founder of the Rudolf Steiner Educational and Farming Association, Harlemville, N.Y.; advisor for many Waldorf schools; former General Secretary of the Anthroposophical Society in America; lecturer and author.

John Davy
British scientist, journalist, lecturer
Author of *Hope, Evolution and Change.*

Footnotes
1. *The Philosophy of Freedom* by Rudolf Steiner; Rudolf Steiner Press, 1979.
2. *The Story of My Life* by Rudolf Steiner; Rudolf Steiner Press, chapters 29 and 30.
3. *Ibid.* chapter 29.
4. *Ibid.* chapter 30.
5. See, for example, *Modern Architecture and Expressionism* by Dennis Sharp; Longmans, 1966.

6. *Anthroposophy:* Steiner's preferred term, which he once said should be understood to mean, quite simply, 'awareness of one's humanity'.
7. *Op. cit.* chapters 1 and 2.
8. *Op. cit.* chapter 26.
9. See especially various lectures given in 1910.
Reprinted with permission of Gudrun Davy, widow of John Davy

SECTION II — *Moving Through the Grades*

Grades, classes, and ages of students in the US and Britain from *Between Form and Freedom* by Betty K. Staley, Hawthorn Press

Age	USA Grade	Britain
6-7	1	Top infant
7-8	2	1st year junior
8-9	3	2nd year junior
9-10	4	3rd year junior
10-11	5	4th year junior
11-12	6	1st year
12-13	7	2nd year
13-14	8	3rd year
14-15	9	4th year
15-16	10	5th year
16-17	11	Lower 6th
17-18	12	Upper 6th

The curriculum pages were reviewed by Mary Echlin, Kimberton Waldorf School (PA), Ekkehard Heyder, Waldorf School of Princeton (NJ), and Penelope Smyth, Marin Waldorf School (CA).

Deborah Meyer
Former faculty member, Marin Waldorf School (San Rafael, CA).

Footnote:
1. Henry Barnes and Nick Lyons, *Education as an Art: The Rudolf Steiner Method*

Barbara Jacquette and Alan Greene
Former faculty members, Marin Waldorf School.

Manette Teitelbaum
Long-time faculty member, Marin Waldorf School. She has completed three cycles of grades 1-4.

Daniel Bittleston
Former faculty member, Marin Waldorf School.

Fifth and Sixth Grade Curriculum
The material for Grades Five and Six was taken from a variety of sources including *Teaching as a Lively Art* by Marjorie Spock and *The Recovery of Man In Childhood* by A. C. Harwood. These descriptions were prepared for admissions' packets and parent education by Mary Echlin. Formerly with the East Bay Waldorf School (El Sobrante, CA), Mary teaches English and is the high school chair at Kimberton Waldorf School, (PA).

Lucille Clemm
Former faculty member, Marin Waldorf School. Currently associated with the Lukas Foundation.

Betty K. Staley
For more than 25 years, a member of the faculty of the Sacramento Waldorf School (Fair Oaks, CA). Currently chair of the High School Teacher Training Program, Rudolf Steiner College (Fair Oaks, CA). Author and lecturer. This section was from her book, *Between Form and Freedom*, p. 146-152

SECTION III — *Understanding the Waldorf Curriculum*

René Querido
A Waldorf educator for more than four decades. Established teacher training and adult education at Rudolf Steiner College (Fair Oaks, CA). Former General Secretary of the Anthroposophical Society in America. He lectures and consults worldwide in four languages. He is the author of numerous articles and books including: *Creativity in Education, The Golden Age of Chartres, The Mystery of the Holy Grail,* and *Questions and Answers on Reincarnation and Karma.*

The Role of Temperament was originally a lecture delivered with the customary added emphasis by tone of voice, phrasing, special facial expressions and gestures well-known and appreciated by René's audiences. To enhance readability, the portions of dialogue have been italicized as well as set off with quotations.

Nancy Foster
Has been a teacher for more than 21 years. Former kindergarten teacher at Acorn Hill Children's Center, Silver Spring, MD, and author of many articles for the *Waldorf Kindergarten Association Newsletter.*

Eugene Schwartz
An educational consultant, a member of the faculty of Sunbridge College in Chestnut Ridge, NY. He was formerly a class teacher at the Green Meadow Waldorf School. This article is adapted from his forthcoming book, *Millennial Child* (Anthroposophical Press).

Eurythmy in Education
Author unknown. Article was obtained from the Steiner Centre, England by Mary Echlin.

Richard Leviton
From "The ABCs of Movement", the *Yoga Journal.* August 1993. Remarks were made after having seen a performance by the members of Eurythmy Spring Valley.

Arthur M. Pittis

A class teacher at Waldorf School of Baltimore, MD. He is presently in his second 8-year teaching cycle. In addition, he is currently completing a Masters of Drama Studies at Johns Hopkins University and working on a book dealing with pedagogical dramaturgy and performance theory.

Grace Broussard and Richard Lindley

Parents and former part-time drama teachers at the Austin Waldorf School (Austin, TX) Ms. Broussard currently teaches drama at the Whole Earth Builders and also guides a performing group "The Gateway Players". Mr. Lindley is a Spanish teacher, writer, historian, musician and playwright. Both artists are involved in writing and producing dramas for festivals and celebrations.

Clifford Skoog

Graduate of Waldorf teacher training program, Emerson College, England. Part-time faculty member at Marin Waldorf School.

Joseph Chilton Pearce

Child development specialist and author of five best selling books including: *Evolution's End; The Crack In The Cosmic Egg, The Magical Child,* and *The Magical Child Matures.*

SECTION IV — What About...?

Robert Schiappacasse

Administrator and member of the faculty, Shining Mountain Waldorf School (CO). Formerly with the Portland (OR) and East Bay (Emeryville, CA) Waldorf Schools.

Jeffrey Kane, Ph.D.

Dean of School of Education, Adelphi University. Author and lecturer. Former class teacher and presently editor of *Holistic Education Review.*

Barbara Shell

Has been an educator for nearly 30 years. After many years of teaching elementary grades in public schools, she began to do consulting work and for the past 12 years has been a founder, class teacher, former director of development and rising 7th grade teacher at the Emerson Waldorf School (Chapel Hill, NC).

Bibliography—

Waldorf

Grunelius, Elizabeth M., *Early Childhood Education and the Waldorf School Plan.* Spring Valley, NY: Waldorf School Monographs, 1983.

Piening, Ekkehard and Nick Lyons, ed., *Educating as an Art.* New York: The Rudolf Steiner School Press, 1979.

Richards, M.C., *Towards Wholeness: Rudolf Steiner Education in America.* Wesleyan University Press, Middletown, CN, 1980.

Montessori

Gitter, Lena L., *The Montessori Way.* Seattle: Special Child Publications, Inc., 1970;

Lillard, Paula Polk, *Montessori: A Modern Approach.* New York: Schocken Books, 1973.

Montessori, Maria, *The Absorbent Mind.* New York: Hold, Rinehart & Winston, 1979.

Others

Pearce, Joseph Chilton, *Magical Child.* New York: Bantam Books, 1977.

Piaget, Jean, *Play, Dreams & Imitation in Childhood.* New York: W. W. Norton & Co., 1962.

Herbert Saperstein

Artist and member of the faculty, Waldorf School of Princeton (NJ). Completed his first 8-year cycle in 1994.

Richard Betz

Member of the faculty, Marin Waldorf School. Completed his first 8-year cycle in 1992 and, after a year's sabbatical, is in his second cycle.

James Shipman

Member of the faculty at Marin Academy, San Rafael (CA).

SECTION V — Family Life and Waldorf Education

Sharifa Oppenheimer
Member of the faculty at Crossroads Waldorf School (Crozet, VA). Contributes articles to the *Waldorf Kindergarten Association Newsletter*

Carol Petrash
Waldorf kindergarten teacher for more than 10 years. Currently registrar of Rudolf Steiner Institute (Waterville, ME). Reprinted with permission from Earthways, By Carol Petrash, (C) 1992; Gryphon House, Inc. Box 207, Beltsville MD 20704-0207; pages 22-24.

Resources mentioned in text:
Earth Guild, 37 Haywood Street, Asheville, NC 28801
Strauss and Company, 1701 Inverness Avenue, Baltimore, MD 21230

Jack Petrash
Waldorf teacher for more than 20 years at the Washington Waldorf School (MD). As a parent, he formed the Fathers' Group at that school. Faculty member, Rudolf Steiner Institute. A member of Editorial Board of the *Holistic Education Review.*

Christopher Belski-Sblendorio
Waldorf teacher, who has taken two classes through the eight-year cycle. He is totally involved in push-button entertainment—playing the accordion for country dancing at the Rudolf Steiner School (MA). Since Christopher spent his childhood with his Italian maternal grandparents on Long Island in the 1950's, pushing accordion buttons was inevitable. He has three teenage children who have successfully survived growing up without a radio, a television, or a VCR.

Sherry Pimsler
Office manager, Marin Waldorf School and longtime Waldorf parent.

Anne Jurika
Former Marin Waldorf School faculty member, has 11 years experience in class teaching and two years consulting with Waldorf schools. Since then, she has received a Master's Degree in Special Education and a Certificate in Educational Therapy. Currently in private practice as an Educational Therapist, working closely with local private schools, doing diagnostic evaluations and ongoing tutoring sessions.

Midge Heath
A founding parent and trustee Marin Waldorf School, and an active volunteer in the school for more than 18 years.

Sandra Holland
A founding parent, Marin Waldorf School, co-founder and mentor to Huckleberry Preschool, Point Reyes Station (CA). Lecturer and workshop leader.

Rhythm During the Summer
The illustration was taken from the cover of *Chanticleer* seasonal periodical during the mid-1980s edited by Karen Rivers and Mary Beth Lugrin Rapisardo of the Marin Waldorf School

SECTION VI — Celebrations Through the Year

Philip Wharton
Former faculty member Marin Waldorf School and a member of the administrative staff at the Waldorf School of San Francisco (CA).

Richard Moeschl
Former member of the faculty, Marin Waldorf School. Author of *Exploring the Sky* (Chicago Review Press) and director of Star Resources, an astronomy education service.

Advent
Begins on the Sunday nearest the Feast of St. Andrew (November 30), and includes the four Sundays prior to Christmas, and ends Christmas Eve.

Gertrud Mueller Nelson

Reprinted from *To Dance with God* © 1986 by Gertrud Mueller Nelson p. 63-65. Used with permission by Paulist Press, Mahwah (NJ).

Rudolf Steiner,

"The Christmas Festival", from *Festivals and their Meaning,* used with permission by Rudolf Steiner Press, London.

Epiphany

Footnote
1. Mala Powers, *Follow the Year: A Family Celebration of Christian Holidays.*
    p. 45-46
2. *Ibid.*

Spiritual Threads of Passover and Easter

With adaptations from *Festivals and Their Meaning* , Rudolf Steiner. Used with permission of Rudolf Steiner Press, London.

Kathryn Hall

Former faculty member, Marin Waldorf School.

Karen Mortenson

Former faculty member, Marin Waldorf School. Easter hymn taken from Anglican hymnal.

Footnote
1. F. Benesh, *Whitsun, the Festival of the Free Individuality.*
2. R. Steiner, *The Whitsun Mystery and its Connection with Ascension*
3. The Greek translation on Genesis in the following paragraphs are from the Septuagint, a translation from Hebrew made in Alexandria in the third century BC, and so accurate as to be universally acknowledged by the Hellenistic Jews as divinely inspired.

St. Johns Tide

Footnote
1. Dialogue was taken from *Blessed Among Women* by Michael Arnold

SECTION VII — *Appendix*

Recommended Reading

This list is only a beginning, and readers are encouraged to request a catalogue from the leading Waldorf/ Anthroposphical publishers and bookstores.

What is Anthroposophy?

From *Toward a More Human Future: Anthroposophy at Work,* and the Directory of the Anthroposophical Society in America, published by the Anthroposophical Society in America.

Waldorf Education Resources

From AWSNA and the Waldorf Teacher Training Institutes.

Recommended Reading

There are many excellent books for those interested in knowing more about Waldorf education, Rudolf Steiner, Anthroposophy, child development, and seasonal celebrations.

If these books are not available in a local library or bookstore, they can be ordered from the bookstores at Rudolf Steiner College, Waldorf Institute at Sunbridge College or through the Anthroposophical Press. (Please see Anthroposophical Resources for addresses).

Books & Lectures About Waldorf Education by Rudolf Steiner

An Introduction to Waldorf Education

The Education of the Child in the Light of Anthroposophy

The Kingdom of Childhood

The Child's Changing Consciousness

The Four Temperaments

Education as a Social Problem

Education and Modern Spiritual Life (Also known as *A Modern Art of Education)*

Human Values in Education

The Roots of Education

The Renewal of Education

Soul Economy and Waldorf Education

Deeper Insights into Education

Self-Education; Autobiographical Reflections

Balance in Teaching

Study of Man

Practical Advice for Teachers

Discussions with Teachers

Waldorf Education for Adolescence

The Genius of Language

Waldorf Education and Anthroposophy

The Foundations of Waldorf Education Series

This forthcoming series from Anthroposophical Press will contain all of Rudolf Steiner's lectures and writings on Waldorf Education, some of which have never been published in English before. The first in the series is *The Spirit of the Waldorf School, lectures surrounding the opening of the first Waldorf School.*

Education and Parenting

Aeppli, Willi : *Rudolf Steiner Education and the Developing Child*
Writing out of practical experience as a Waldorf teacher, the author brings us into his class-room to remember what it was like as a child, thereby gaining insights to guide teachers and all adults.

AWSNA: *Multiculturalism in Waldorf Education. Volumes I, II, III*
The Association also publishes other titles. Please write them for current list.

Baldwin, Rahima: *You Are Your Child's First Teacher*
Out of her research and her experience as a Waldorf early childhood teacher, Baldwin answers the question: "What can parents do with and for their children from birth to age six that will enhance their development without having negative effects at a later age?"

Barnes, Henry, Alan Howard and John Davy: *An Introduction to Waldorf Education*
This is an excellent beginning book for parents new or unfamiliar with Waldorf education.

Bettelheim, Bruno: *The Uses of Enchantment: The Meaning and Importance of Fairy Tales*
The renown child psychologist gives us a moving revelation of the enormous and irreplaceable value of fairy tales — how they educate, support, and liberate the emotions of children.

Britz-Crecelius, Heidi: *Children at Play: Preparation for Life*

Carlgren, Frans: *Education Towards Freedom: Rudolf Steiner Education*
A comprehensive, detailed overview of the work of Waldorf schools throughout the world. It is filled with extraordinarily beautiful colored photographs of the work of Waldorf students throughout the grades.

Childs, Gilbert: *Steiner Education in Theory and Practice*
A clear exposition of Steiner's view of the child as a developing personality based on body, soul, and spirit. It describes the stages of the child's development and gives a detailed account of the Waldorf school curriculum and teaching methods. Useful both to those already in-volved with Waldorf schools and also to anyone who wants to learn more about this alterna-tive.

Coplen, Dotty Turner: *Parenting: A Path Through Childhood*
Combining her experience as a mother and a grandmother with her studies in psychology and social work, the author presents a warm and human way of understanding the nature and needs of children. Parents and professionals working with children will find this a helpful book.

Cusick, Linda: *Waldorf Parenting Handbook*
This handbook was developed originally to meet the needs of young parents and teachers interested in Waldorf child psychology and curriculum. This handbook traces the growth of the child from conception through adolescence, and explains how Waldorf education nurtures the developing individuality at each stage along the way.

Darian, Shea: *Seven Times the Sun: Guiding your Child Through the Rhythms of the Day*
Practical and playful. A fresh view of daily life at home. The author shows how to bring joy to such daily events as mealtimes, bedtimes, chores, and naps.

Davy, Gudrun and Bons Voors: *Lifeways: Working with Family Questions*
Lifeways is about children, about family life and about being a parent. But most of all it is about freedom — and how the tension between personal fulfillment and family life may be resolved. It is a resource book for parents, those involved in kindergartens and play groups and for women's support groups.

Edelman, Marion Wright: *The Measure of our Success: A Letter to my Children and Yours*
A compassionate message for parents trying to raise moral children, and a message of hope and purpose for everyone.

Edmunds, Francis: *Rudolf Steiner Education*
A most respected figure in English speaking Waldorf schools authoritatively answers the question, 'What is a Waldorf school?'

Renewing Education

Elium, Don and Jeanne: *Raising a Daughter; Raising a Son*
Changing cultural and social attitudes affect how we treat our daughters and sons. The authors help parents unravel and make sense of all the conflicting information, going step by step through each stage of development–infancy through the teens and into early adulthood.

Elkind, David: *Growing Up Too Fast Too Soon*
Makes a detailed examination of the world of today's children to see where the hurrying occurs and why. He gives parents and teachers insight and hope for encouraging healthy development while protecting the joy and freedom of childhood.

The Hurried Child
The Ties That Stress, The New Family Imbalance

Fenner, Pamela and Karen Rivers: *Waldorf Student Reading List,* **revised 3rd edition, 1995**
Comprehensive reading list to help parents, teachers, librarians, and home schools select quality books for children. Sections include: Books to Read Aloud from Preschool to Grade 8; Anthologies of Verse, Rhymes, and Stories; Music for Families; Celebrations, Crafts and Games, American History, Science (for Grades 7 - 12) and Newberry Award List .

Finser, Torin M: *School as a Journey: The Eight-Year Odyssey of a Waldorf Teacher and his Class*
A lively, colorful and absorbing account of one class teacher's journey from Grade 1 - 8 in a Waldorf School. Filled with pedagogical gems, tips and resources, it will also be invaluable to current class teachers.

Gabert, Erich: *Educating the Adolescent: Discipline or Freedom*
Based on Waldorf pedagogy, Gabert provides clear explanations of the underlying spiritual development taking place within the young person and manifesting outwardly in sometimes difficult behavior. Through a sensitive and insightful discussion, readers are led not to take the young person as he or she is here and now, but to work with "what has future in itself and what will some day develop."

Gardner, John F: *What is a Waldorf School*
A distinguished Waldorf teacher, John Gardner inspires the reader to explore the deeper aspects of Waldorf education.This was originally published in *The Journal of Anthroposophy,*

Gatto, John Taylor: *Dumbing Us Down: The Hidden Curriculum of Compulsory Schooling*
In his 26 years of award-winning teaching in New York City's public schools, Gatto has found that independent study, community service, large doses of solitude, and a thousand different apprenticeships with adults of all walks of life are the keys to helping children break the thrall of our conforming society.

Glöckler, Michaela and Wolfgang Goebel
A Guide to Child Health
This is a medical and educational handbook written out of many years' experience in the consulting rooms at the large anthroposophical hospital in Herdecke, W. Germany. With medical, psychological, and educational insights, it presents a practical yet profound work.

Grunelius, Elisabeth: *Early Childhood Education*
This pioneering work describes the organization and purposes of the Waldorf kindergarten, including the layout of a kindergarten, indoor and outdoor equipment, and the rhythms of the day.

Haller, Ingeborg: *How Children Play*
Imaginative play is a vital element in the growth of the preschool child. A child's freedom to play lies at the root of a happy and well-balanced attitude to work and responsibilities in later life.

Harwood, A. C: *The Recovery of Man in Childhood: A Study of the Educational Work of Rudolf Steiner*
A lucid presentation of the Waldorf approach from preschool through 12th grade. Highly recommended for in-depth description of theoretical and practical aspects of this education.

The Way of a Child
This is one of the most popular introductions to child development and Waldorf education.

Healy MD, Jane: *Endangered Minds; Why Children Don't Think and What We Can Do About It*
Explores the relationship between language, learning, and brain development. She explains how present-day lifestyles sabotage language acquisition and thinking. Proving that the basic intelligence of children is not an issue, she then shows how parents and teachers can make a positive difference in children's development.

Howard, Alan: *You Wanted to Know. . . .What a Waldorf School is. . . and What It is Not*
Written by a leading Waldorf educator, this small book is designed in a question-and-answer format. It answers basic questions concerning the history of Waldorf education, the learning experience, and school/community relationships.

Kane, Franklin: *Parents as People*
This book is both an inspirational and excellent child development resource for all parents of young children, whether or not they are attending a Waldorf school. The author, a veteran Waldorf teacher, describes the life of the young growing child and the importance of rhythm in a child's life. His interpretation of Waldorf education and Steiner's philosophy is presented in an easy-to-read style with little jargon.

Leist, Manfred: *Parent Participation in the Life of a Waldorf School*
This small pamphlet describes the areas of concern of parents and teachers in a Waldorf/Steiner school. Although it has been written in 1980 out of German Waldorf School experience, this booklet provides a good point of departure for parent-teacher discussions.

Lievegoed, Bernard: *Phases of Childhood*
Explores the cycles of child development in the light of Anthroposophy. One of the most read and re-read books for many Waldorf parents and teachers.

Meyer, Rudolf: *The Wisdom of Fairy Tales*
Observations on the Grimm's fairy tales for teachers and parents. Meyer rediscovers the lost meaning of these stories and shows how they can have a profound positive influence on the developing mind of the child.

Mitchell, David, Editor: *The Art of Administration*
An important handbook for Waldorf schools produced by AWSNA. Included are chapters on: the Faculty meeting, College (Council) of Teachers, Communication, Committee structure, the Role of Administrator, Business Manager and Development Director, Admissions and Parent Education, Communications and Public Outreach, Evaluation, Working Together and Board of Trustees.

Mitchell, David and David Alsop, editors: *Economic Explorations*
An economic handbook for Waldorf schools dealing with such issues as budget, tuition, tuition aid, salaries, and fundraising. A practical manual including many examples drawn from schools across the continent.

Pearce, Joseph Chilton: *Evolution's End: Claiming the Potential of our Intelligence*
Employs both the results of academic research and personal experience to develop his thesis on the evolution of human intelligence. He offers some far-reaching insights into the challenges and obstacles to human development created by our culture.

The Magical Child
The Magical Child Returns

Pusch, Ruth, editor: *Waldorf Schools, Volume I and II*
A collection of articles on every aspect of Waldorf education written by teachers round the world, even by several of the early teachers in the first Waldorf School in Stuttgart. These were published over almost 40 years of *Education as an Art,* the bulletin from the Rudolf Steiner School of New York City. These two books are of benefit to parents and teachers alike.

Querido, René M: *Creativity in Education: The Waldorf Approach*
Seven lectures given at the San Francisco Waldorf School wherein the author, director of Rudolf Steiner College, describes an Waldorf educational approach that has as its goal the balanced development of the whole child.

The Wonders of Childhood: Stepping Into Life.
Describes the first three years in the life of the child.

Richards, M. C : *Towards Wholeness: Rudolf Steiner Education in America*
Celebrated author, teacher and artist brings her unique style to a discussion of Steiner's holistic approach to education — that life and learning can be experienced in the same way as art, as a union of inner experience and outer sensory life.

Rudel, Joan and Siegfried: *Education Towards Freedom,* English edition
This survey of the work of Waldorf Schools throughout the world is an extraordinary book. One's view is flooded with color leaping from the page. This book not only describes in detail the philosophy as well as the details of a Waldorf curriculum, both elementary and the high school, it has chosen examples of children's art from Waldorf schools around the globe.

Salter, Joan: *The Incarnating Child*
Even in today's modern technological world the mystery and miracle of conception, pregnancy and birth stir within many people a sense of wonder. A specialist in maternal and child care, Salter examines pregnancy, birth, and childhood on up to adolescence, addressing both physical and spiritual development, health, environment, and learning. This book is filled with practical advice for parents and caregivers.

Schwartz, Eugene: *Rhythms and Turning Points in the Life of the Child*
Examines the importance of rhythms in the child's life, and describes the developmental signposts from ages 9 through 14.

Adolescence: The Search for the Self **and** *Weaving the Social Fabric of the Class*
Two lectures on Waldorf Education.

The Waldorf Teacher's Survival Guide
Seven conversations between a new teacher and his older and wiser mentor, offering a wealth of practical advice.

Millennial Child (to be published late 1996)
A study of the hindrances to the unfolding of the forces of thinking, feeling and willing in the 20th century that have led to the present crisis in the lives of children. Thoughts are shared for parents and children concerning what is needed so that the child of the next century—the Millennial Child—can awaken with the fullness of his/her powers.

Sleigh, Julian: *Thirteen to Nineteen: Discovering the Light - Conversations with Parents*
Writing directly to the parents, Sleigh sheds light on the familiar adolescent problems of loneliness, meeting with others and relating to them, difficulties with parents, awakening of sexuality, drinking and drugs.

Smit, Jurgen: *The Child, the Teachers, and the Community*
Four lectures given in Garden City, NY in 1989 by the late J. Smit, Waldorf educator for more than 50 years and leader of the Pedagogical and youth Sections of the Anthroposophical Society. In a lively and personable way, Smit addresses the spiritual impulse of Waldorf education, the faculty meeting as the heart organ of the school, the general and the individual stream of evolution of the child, and the school community and the society of the present time.

Solter, Ph.D., Aletha J: *The Aware Baby*
The author questions most of the traditional beliefs about childrearing and describes a new theory that is useful and practical as well as far-reaching in its implications. She provides new answers for age-old questions.

Helping Young Children Flourish
Continuing the same approach to parenting described in earlier book, the author presents her insights into young children's emotions, and describes effective alternatives to both punishments and rewards.

Spock, Marjorie: *Teaching as a Lively Art*
Written by an experienced Waldorf teacher and eurythmist, this book describes in detail the curriculum of the eight elementary years, showing how the needs of the developing child are met with sensitivity, insight and appropriate timing.

Staley, Betty K: *Between Form and Freedom*

This book offers a wealth of insights about adolescents. There are sections on the nature of adolescence, the search for the self, the birth of intellect, the release of feeling, male-female differences and character. This is a very significant book for all parents whether one's children are in a Waldorf or non-Waldorf school, She has taught literature and history at the Sacramento Waldorf High school for many years and also leads workshops and serves on the faculty of the Rudolf Steiner College.

Thomson, John: (general editor): *Natural Childhood: The first practical and holistic guide for parents of the developing child*

Contributors include: Rahima Baldwin (consultant), Tim Kahn, Mildren Masheder, Lynne Oldfield, Dr. Michaela Glockler, and Roland Meighan.

One of the most significant contributions to an understanding of the child in this decade. The ideas of enlightened thinkers such as Rudolf Steiner, John Holt, and Carl Rogers provide new insights into the internal development of the child. By weaving together the work of leading psychologists, educators, counselors, and doctors, *Natural Childhood* explores a wealth of new ideas as well as the more traditional aspects of relationships, education, health, creativity, and play.

Wilkinson, Roy: *Commonsense Schooling*

A practical introduction to Rudolf Steiner's educational thought and methodology. It examines such topics as the purpose of education, the nature of the child, and the structure and organization of the school.

Questions and Answers on Rudolf Steiner Education

An overview of: English and English Literature, Mathematics, History, Geography, Nature Study and Science, Foreign Languages, Religion Classes, Handwork, Gardening, Art, Music, Eurythmy, Gymnastics, and Sports.

Rudolf Steiner on Education: A Compendium

Gives a comprehensive survey of Steiner's educational thinking, along with a helpful overview of his life and educational work.

Winn, Marie: *The Plug-In Drug: Television, Children and the Family*

Examines the effects of passive watching of TV, video games, and computers on the developing child.

von Heydebrand, Caroline: *Childhood: A Study of the Growing Child*

A wealth of observations and insights on human growth and development from a teacher of the first Waldorf School. A classic work on the Waldorf kindergarten.

The Curriculum of the First Waldorf School

Festivals, Music and Crafts

Barz, Brigitte: *Festivals with Children*
Offers a description of the nature and character of each Christian festival, its symbols and customs, and gives practical suggestions for celebrating these festivals in the family.

Berger, Petra: *Feltcraft: Making Dolls, Gifts and Toys*
Feltcraft, an old creative art, is being revived in many schools and homes. Felt is durable, flexible, does not fray and is ideal for children to work with. Traditionally it is used for making small dolls, finger and glove puppets, animals, wristbands, little gifts and even wall tapestries. Detailed instructions, patterns and bright colorful photographs help the beginner and advanced crafter.

Berger, Thomas: *The Christmas Craft Book, The Easter Craft Book, The Harvest Craft Book*
This series of books offers a wealth of ideas for seasonal decorations with easy to follow directions and accompanying bright colorful pictures. Teachers and parents will refer to these for years.

Capel, Evelyn Francis: *Celebrating Festivals Around the World*
The purpose of this book is to explore the question of what it means in real life to celebrate festivals in different parts of the globe – particularly the southern hemisphere. The author delves into what lies behind the rhythms of the natural year. Look for other titles from this prolific author.

Carey, Diana and Judy Large: *Festivals, Family and Food*
This is a resource book for exploring the festivals – those 'feast days' scattered round the year which children love celebrating. There are over 650 songs to sing, games for fun, food to make, stories, poems and things to do. The festivals are grouped into the four main seasons with sections on Birthdays, Hungry Teatimes, Rainy Days, etc. It will be a book the whole family will enjoy.

Cooper, Stephanie , Christine Fynes-Clinton and Mary Rowling: *The Children's Year*
Here is a book relating the making-of-things to the seasons; taking the reader through Spring, Summer, Autumn, and Winter with appropriate toys and gifts to create, with full, clear instructions and illustrations. You need not be an experienced craftsperson to create something lovely, and the illustrations make it a joy to page through while choosing what to make first.

Druitt, Ann and Christine Fynes-Clinton and Marije Rowling: *All Year Round*
A new book to carry parents, teachers and children through the seasons with verse, rhymes, stories, songs, and creative activities. The authors believe that observing a round of festivals is an enjoyable way of bringing rhythm into children's lives. Another marvelous resource from Hawthorn Press.

Fitzjohn, Sue and Minda Weston and Judy Large: *Festivals Together: A Guide to Multi-Cultural Celebration*
This resource guide seeks to enrich and widen our celebrations experience and to reflect the 'global village' nature of modern society. It brings together the experience, sharing and activities of individuals from a multi-faith community – Buddhist, Christian, Hindu, Jewish, Muslim and Sikh.

Green Marian: *A Calendar of Festivals: Traditional Celebrations, Songs, Seasonal Recipes & Things to Make*
From holy days to holidays, high days to hey days, every month is a festival. This book explores the fascinating details of seasonal customs – what they are, what they represent, their original meaning, where they are continued and their relevance to us today. Many not celebrated in the United States. Recipes, songs and activities for us all to enjoy are included.

Jaffke, Christophe and Magda Maier: *Early One Morning: Folk Songs, Rounds, Ballads, Shanties, Spirituals and Plantations Songs and Madrigals*
A book which has a diverse selection of music for parents, teachers and children. Another important resource.

Jaffke, Freya: *Making Soft Toys*
Tells how to make simple children's toys (puppets, dolls, and special surprises) with very little cost and using only natural materials. In an era of mechanical toys and television, this book helps to satisfy the young child's great need for unsophisticated toys which cultivate the imagination. A best seller in Germany, this book has been translated into many other languages.

Toy making with Children
This is an excellent handbook abounding with ideas for parents of young children.

Johanson, Irene: *Stories for the Festivals of the Year*
Told for children. The author has retold some of the major events in the life of Christ in a pictorial way appropriate for young children. Although the stories in this collection are meant for children, even adults can find new perspectives from them. They should be read aloud — or better still, retold – to the child or the family together.

Klocek, Dennis: *Drawing from the Book of Nature*
Mention drawing to a group of elementary school teachers, and the pained looks on most faces attest to the presence of psychic scars in the adult's attitude toward the arts. In order to develop skills in drawing from the book of nature, it is necessary to develop the science of observation in such a way that our observing stays "warm" and does not degenerate into a cold "onlooker consciousness." Those adults who have experienced the death of the imagination will benefit from Dennis' gentle approach. Many teachers and non-teachers have found this book indispensable.

Kraul, Walter: *Earth, Water, Fire, and Air*
This craft book for children shows how to make a waterwheel, paddle-steamer, propeller plane, parachute, windmill, spinning tops, a little hot-air carousel, a hot-air balloon, and lots more. Some suggestions are simple enough for six-year olds, others challenging enough for a skillful twelve-year old.

Leeuven, M.V. and J. Moeskops: *The Nature Corner*
Seasonal nature tables are an invaluable way of making young children aware of the changing cycle of the year. Gives simple and effective directions for creating simple and effective tableaux for depicting the seasons and major festivals at home or school.

Meyerbroker, Helga: *Rose Windows and How to Make Them*
One of the glories of the medieval cathedrals was the rich display of color and light in their great rose windows. Following the same principles but using simple materials, the reader can make decorative transparencies to hang in a window at home or in school. Step-by-step directions for simple and more complex transparencies.

Müller, Brunhild: *Painting with Children*
Müller suggests ideas for encouraging and stimulating active imaginations and creativity in children through watercolor painting.

Muller, Christa: *Seasonal Songs, Book 1*
Another resource for teachers, parents and those working with children and music.

Nelson, Gudrud Mueller: *To Dance With God: Family Ritual and Community Celebration*
Makes relevant for the modern reader the importance of ritual for connecting us to the meaning and flow of life.

Neuschutz, Karin: *The Doll Book: Soft Dolls and Creative Free Play*
This has been a successful book in Europe. It has a special charm that comes from the simple, childlike style with which the author expresses many valuable insights she gained through experiences as a child psychologist, teacher, mother and a sympathetic observer of Waldorf education methods in Sweden. This books not only gives instructions on making soft cloth dolls, but also discusses how children play at different ages.

Petrash, Carol*: Earthways, Simple Environmental Activities for Young Children*
Filled with hands-on nature crafts and seasonal activities carefully described and beautifully illustrated. Activities are graded in difficulty so that children will learn how to play safely with the elements of earth, air, fire and water. The activities will help children develop a respect for nature and all living creatures and experience the world with awe and wonder. Includes seasonal suggestions for creating a more earth friendly home and classroom. This book will be used – not left on the shelf – in homes, public, private and home schools, libraries and day care centers. It is already being used in England (with the title *Earthways)* and it has also been translated into Dutch.

Powers, Mala: *Follow the Year*: *A Family Celebration of Christian Holidays*
This beautiful book helps today's family, whatever the denomination, to understand and follow the rhythm of the Christian festivals through the course of the entire year. It concentrates on those more meaningful and interesting celebrations which fall near the solstices and equinoxes; those great pillars of the year which usher in our four seasons.

Reinckens, Sunnhild: *Making Dolls*
This little book with its many color photographs and simple diagrams gives clear instructions on how to make seventeen different kinds of dolls.

Russ, Johanne: *Clump-a-Dump Snickle-Snack: Pentatonic Children's Songs*
These songs are published for the many children who love them already, having learned them from their teachers in Waldorf Kindergartens in USA. The fairy-tale content and holiday mood of the texts have made them particularly useful in rhythmic games and plays.

Anthroposophical Resources

What is Anthroposophy?

Echoing the ancient Greek axiom, "Man, know thyself," Rudolf Steiner, the founder of Anthroposophy, described it as "awareness of one's humanity." Nowhere is the need for such awareness greater than in relation to our fellow human beings, and to the life and work we share with them. It is this awareness that lies at the heart of the practical work described in this section. The number and breadth of these initiatives, fostered by the Anthroposophical Society that Steiner founded in 1923, reflect Anthroposophy's progressive, healing influence on cultural life in North America.

Anthroposophy embraces a spiritual view of the human being and the cosmos, but its emphasis is on knowing, not faith. It is a path in which the human heart and hand, and especially our capacity for thinking, are essential. It leads, in Steiner's words, "from the spirit in the human being to the spirit in the universe." Humanity (*anthropos*) has the inherent wisdom (*sophia*) to transform both itself and the world.

Today, when many aspects of our culture are in crisis and people are easily drawn into cynicism and despair, Anthroposophy's vision of human potential is a source of hope and renewal.

> *Anthroposophy intends to be a living presence; it wants to use words, concepts and ideas so that something living may shine down from the spiritual world into the physical. Anthroposophy does not only want to impart knowledge, it seeks to awaken life.*

— Rudolf Steiner

— *Toward a More Human Future,* Anthroposophical Society in America

Books on Anthroposophy

Frequently those new to Waldorf education may be unsure about which book or lecture of Rudolf Steiner to read first - whether it's about Waldorf education or Anthroposophy. If you are a member of a Waldorf school community, there are teachers and parents who can direct you to particular books depending upon your interests and questions. Often there are study groups arising out of the interest of parents at a Waldorf school.

The following books — by Rudolf Steiner and other interpreters of Steiner and Anthroposophy—can help the reader get started.

Rudolf Steiner saw four of his books as fundamental to the recovery of human dignity, freedom, and wisdom. Although Steiner wrote other books and more than 6,000 lectures, he again and again returned to the essential nature of these four:

The Philosophy of Spiritual Activity

Theosophy

Occult Science

How to Know Higher Worlds
(formerly called *Knowledge of the Higher Worlds and Its Attainment*)

Easton, Stewart C: *The Way of Anthroposophy — Answers to Modern Questions*
This small book serves as an introduction to Anthroposophy by one of the most noted interpreters of Rudolf Steiner. This book will be of great help to the growing number of people concerned about the disturbing trends in the life today, who really feel the need to seek for a solution, and who are, as the author says, "looking for something that goes beyond the traditional religious teachings, and who do not think modern science has all the answers."

Man and World in the Light of Anthroposophy
This book outlines the teachings of the many areas in which Steiner made his contributions, providing the reader with an appreciation of the enormous wealth of richness of what Steiner gave to mankind.

Kühlewind, Georg: *Working with Anthroposophy — The Practice of Thinking*
The goal of this study is not any particular content, but a process, a method, an event — the cultivation of the experience of living, intuitive thinking such as we experience it with every new understanding. This unique contribution to the practice of Anthroposophy will be of interest to beginning and longtime students who wish to revitalize their approach to the path opened up by Steiner.

McDermott, Robert: *The Essential Steiner*
Anyone coming to the teachings or writings of Rudolf Steiner for the first time cannot help but be bewildered in the face of several hundred volumes. Where to start? How to proceed? With introductory essays by McDermott, 17 selections from Steiner's books and lectures, this book is an accessible introduction to Steiner's thought and work. Unique to this book is a comprehensive 90-page Reading Guide and Bibliography. This work is one many students of Anthroposophy find indispensable!

Seddon, Richard editor: *Understanding the Human Being*
This carefully selected anthology of works by Rudolf Steiner gives a panoramic view of his fundamental ideas in a wide range of topics, including: The Nature of the Human Being, Coming Events, Reordering of Society, Philosophical Foundations, Natural Science and Spiritual Science, Renewal of the Arts, The Path of Development, and In Daily Life.

Waldorf Education Resources

There are now over 600 Waldorf (Steiner) schools worldwide, with over 100 in the United States and Canada. These include: 1087 Preschool/kindergartens; 640 schools; 300 Curative Centers, and 60 Teacher Education institutes.

Argentina
Australia Austria Belgium
Brazil Canada Chile Colombia
Croatia Czech Republic Denmark Ecuador Egypt Estonia Finland France
Georgia Germany Great Britain Greece Hungary India Ireland Iceland
Israel Italy Japan Kenya Kirgiziya Latvia Lichtenstein Lithuania
Mexico Nambibia Netherlands New Zealand Norway
Peru Philippines Poland Portugal Romania Russia
Slovakia Republic of Slovenia South Africa
Spain Sweden Switzerland Thailand
Ukraine United States of America
Uruguay

**Association of Waldorf Schools
In North America**
3911 Bannister Road
Fair Oaks, California 95628

Telephone   916-961-0927
Fax   916-961-0715

The Waldorf Schools in the United States are privately funded. The Association of Waldorf Schools of North America is a not-for-profit organization whose purpose is to support and encourage the work of all Waldorf Schools in North America. Toward that end, four stages of member have been instituted: full-member, sponsored-member, developing school, and new initiative.

Full Membership indicates that a school has fulfilled the requirements of the Association as outlined in the booklet "Steps to Membership." As a full member, a school takes part in delegates' meetings in which common concerns are discussed, responsibility for the school movement is undertaken, and Association business transacted. There are currently 44 full member Waldorf schools.

Prior to full membership, a school assumes **sponsored member** status. Ordinarily, this is a three-year period in which a member school acts as advisor and consultant to the school it sponsors. It is on the recommendation of the sponsoring school that the sponsored school is admitted to full membership. There are currently 13 sponsored Waldorf schools.
Developing school membership (previously Federated membership) is for those schools which are not yet ready to assume the responsibilities of sponsored schools because of their youth and size, yet have a grade school program and wish to establish and strengthen their ties with the

mainstream of Waldorf Education through their ongoing relationship with the regional committees. There are currently 42 developing Waldorf schools.

New Initiative membership is for those new initiatives which have the intention to begin a Waldorf school, but that have not yet begun their grade school program. Currently, 21 such initiatives have affiliated with AWSNA.

Teacher training centers may be full member, sponsored or developing status. Currently there are four full member, one sponsored, and three developing teacher training institutes.

AWSNA also serves as a center for the gathering and distribution of information about Waldorf education. Through surveys, questionnaires and other means, the association gathers information about the Waldorf movement as it is developing in North America. AWSNA makes this information available to all interested parties through its newsletter, through Renewal: A Journal for Waldorf Education, and through other publications.

In 1991, the Association instituted a new Individual Membership category. To enable individuals to support the work of AWSNA and to maintain a direct connection with the Waldorf School Movement at large. For further information, please contact the Association.

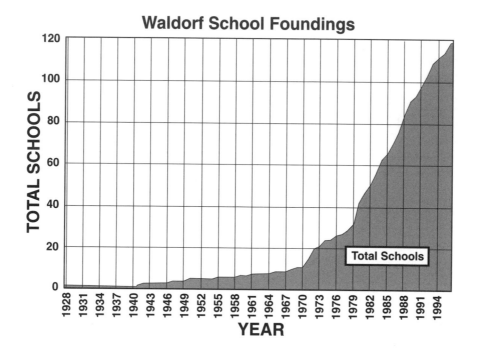

Membership in the Waldorf Kindergarten Association is open to any individual wishing to support the development of Waldorf early childhood education. For information about Waldorf preschools and kindergartens, new schools which do not yet have grades, membership or subscriptions to the newsletter, please contact:

Waldorf Kindergarten Association of North America

1359 Alderton Lane, Silver Spring, Maryland 20906 • 301-460-6287 phone/fax

International Waldorf Kindergarten Association
11 Heubergstrasse, D-70188, Stuttgart, Germany

Waldorf Education – A Family Guide

Waldorf Teacher Training and Adult Education

North America

Adult education centers provide learning and practice for those interested in renewing their private, professional and social lives from a spiritual perspective. The programs balance study with inner development and artistic work, stressing the potential for change and creativity. The Rudolf Steiner Institute [P. O.. Box 207,Kensington, MD 20895, Telephone/Fax 301-946-2099] offers 3-week intensive seminars each summer in Thomasville, Maine. Many of the larger Waldorf schools also have teacher in-service and adult education programs.

The following teacher training programs are affiliated with the Association of Waldorf Schools of North American in three categories. Since each institute varies in the offerings of certificate or degree programs as well as classes, workshops and seminars, those persons interested in receiving specific information should contact the individual school.

Antioch Waldorf Teacher Training Program
40 Avon Street
Keene, NH 03431
603-357-3122

Rudolf Steiner College
9200 Fair Oaks Boulevard
Fair Oaks, California 95628
916-961-8727

Sunbridge College
260 Hungry Hollow Road
Chestnut Ridge, New York 10977
914-425-0055

Waldorf Institute of Southern California
Northridge, California 91325
17100 Superior Street
818-349-6272

Rudolf Steiner Institute
P. O.. Box 207
Kensington, MD 20895
Phone/Fax 301-946-2099

Rudolf Steiner Centre, Toronto
9100 Bathurst Street, #4
Thornhill, Ontario L4JC7
905-764-7570

Arcturus Rudolf Steiner Education Program
1300 West Loyola Avenue
Chigago, IL 60626
312-761-3026

Waldorf Teacher Development Association
PO Box 2678
Ann Arbor, MI 48106-2678
313-741-4808

Outside of North America

Those persons interested in having a complete list of all training programs in Europe or other continents or for information about Waldorf/Steiner schools outside of North America, please contact:

Padagogische am Goetheanum
Postfach 81
ch-4143 Dornach (Switzerland)
From USA, telephone: 011-41-61-706-4314
From USA, fax: 011-41-61-706-4314

Rudolf Steiner Schools Fellowship
Kidbrooke, Park, Forest Row,
Sussex, RH18 5JB UK
From USA, telephone: 011-44-1342-822115
From USA, fax: 011-44-1342-826004

ANTHROPOSOPHICAL SOCIETY

The Anthroposophical Society in America is the national organ of the General Anthroposophical Society, founded by Rudolf Steiner in 1923 as "an association of people who would foster the life of the soul, both in the individual and in human society, on the basis of a true knowledge of the spiritual world."

Steiner's writings, lectures, and artistic and practical activities offered a wealth of insights in the spiritual dimensions of our world. Since his death in 1925, many people have sought to continue his research through study, reflection and meditation, and to apply it in many areas of human endeavor.

The international center for this work is the School for Spiritual Science at the Goetheanum in Dornach, Switzerland. Membership in the organization is open to everyone regardless of nationality, social standing, scientific or artistic conviction, or religion. It is entirely non-sectarian and non-political. The sole criterion for membership is "to consider as justified the existence of an institution such as the Goetheanum in Dornach, in its capacity as a School for Spiritual Science."

Activities of the Society
For information regarding membership, resources, services conferences, study groups, programs and newsletter

Anthroposophical Society in America

1923 Geddes Avenue
Ann Arbor, MI 48104

313-662-9355 phone
313-662-1727 fax
Toll-free 1-888-757-2742

Journal for Anthroposophy: Through its twenty five year history, this publication has carried quality articles, interviews, poetry, historic correspondence and book review, all documenting the many insights from within and around the edges of the Anthroposophical perspective on subjects old and new. It is published twice yearly. For subscription information, write to:

Journal for Anthroposophy
3700 South Ranch Road 12
Dripping Springs, TX 788620
Telephone: 512-894-0746

The Rudolf Steiner Lending Library is located at Harlemville. It holds a collection of nearly 13,5000 volumes, consisting of Rudolf Steiner's works in German and in English translation as well as many secondary works and periodicals. *(Send for brochure, and lists of books)*

Rudolf Steiner Library
RD 2 Box 215
Ghent, NY 12075
518-672-7690

Many of the larger Anthroposophic centers in the United States also have libraries on Anthroposophical subjects

Anthroposophic Societies Outside the United States
Anthroposophical Society of Canada
P.O. Box 38162
Eglinton Ave., W.
Toronto Ontario M5N 3A8 Canada
416-488-2886

Anthroposophical Society in Great Britain
Rudolf Steiner House
35 Park Road
London NW1 6XT
England

General Anthroposophical Society
Postfach 134
CH-4143 Dornach, Switzerland
011 41 61 701 42 42

BIODYNAMIC AGRICULTURE

Healing the Earth

The principles and practice of biodynamic agriculture relate to the earth as a living organism, within which each farm has its own identity. This approach builds upon established methods of sustainable agriculture — compost, manures, soil and plants are treated with specially fermented herbal preparations that enhance the earth's organic processes and produce healthy, poison-free foods. At present, there are 30,000 acres under biodynamic management in the U.S.A.

The Biodynamic Farming and Gardening Association founded in 1938, holds conferences, publishes and distributes literature, and consults with farmers and gardeners.

Biodynamic Farming and Gardening Association
PO Box 550
Kimberton, PA 19442
610-935-7797

The Demeter Association is an independent agency that certifies biodynamic farms in the United States and abroad.

Demeter Association, Inc. for the Certification of Biodynamic Agriculture
1090 Rock Creek Canyon Road
Colorado Springs, CO 80920
719-579-8082

Michael Fields Agricultural Institute is a public, non-profit foundation committed to revitalizing agriculture through education, research and advisory support to current and future farmers.

Michael Fields Agricultural Institute
W. 2493 County Road ES
East Troy, WI 53120
414-642-4028

CURATIVE WORK

Soul Care for Those in Need

Anthroposophical work in curative education and social therapy is based on the assumption that every individual, regardless of ability, is an independent spiritual being. Developmental disabilities and mental retardation are treated not as illnesses, but as part of the fabric of human experience, and are cared for in the context of a healthy home and community life.

In the United States there are special schools, therapeutic centers, training centers for young adults, a children's village, and a number of residential villages and communities for adults.

Camphill Villages are the largest and oldest Anthroposophically-inspired organizations in this field in North America. For information about a number of smaller initiatives addressing the needs of individuals considered "at risk" through mental illness, family crisis, homelessness or unemployment, contact:

Camphill Foundation
Pughtown Road
PO. Box 290
Kimberton, PA 19442
610-935-0300

Lifesharing Foundation, Inc.
207 North Plain Road
Great Barrington, MA 01230
413-528-0705

Waldorf Education Remedial Training Program
Box 300A RD#1
Glenmoore, PA 19343

MEDICAL PRACTICE

Treating Patients, Not Symptoms

Anthroposophically extended medicine does not regard illness as a chance occurrence or mechanical breakdown, but rather as something intimately connected to the biography of a human being.

Anthroposophic medical care emphasizes the prevention of illness through strengthening the person's own healing forces, and reestablishing balance and rhythm in life processes: metabolism, breathing, waking and sleeping.

The patient is seen and treated holistically, as a being of body, soul and spirit. This approach integrates conventional practices with new and alternative remedies, dietary and nutritional therapy, rhythmical massage, hydrotherapy, art therapy and counseling.'

Physicians' Association for Anthroposophical Medicine
5909 SE Division
Portland, OR 97206
503-234-1531

Medical Section
7953 California Ave
Fair Oaks, CA 95628
916-967-8250

Anthroposophical Therapy and Hygiene Association
241 Hungry Hollow Road
Chestnut Ridge, NY 10977
914-356-8499

Anthroposophic Nurses' Association of America
215 E. Main St
Elkton, MD 21921
516-921-3548

Rhythmical Massage Therapy Association
457 Harlemville Road
Hillsdale, NY 12529
518-672-4476

American Hearing Services
104 North Main Street
Spring City, PA 19475
610-948—0992

Artemisia
Association for the Anthroposophical Renewal of Healing
7953 California Avenue
Fair Oaks, CA 95628

Lilipoh (newsletter dedicated to natural medicine, see under Publishing)

HEALTH AND HYGIENE
Products for Sound Living

Weleda (USA) produces prescription and non-prescription medicines and a full range of body care products. The medicines are formulated to stimulate the individual's own healing capacity.

Weleda uses plants that are biodynamically grown or harvested from nature, with no artificial coloring agents or synthetic preservatives, and no animal testing.

The company was founded in Switzerland in 1920 and now operates in 26 countries. All Weleda products are available directly from the manufacturer. The body care products are available nationwide at health food stores.

Weleda, Inc.
175 N. Route 9W
P. O. Box 249
Congers, NY 10920
914-356-4134

Wala is another medicine/body care company whose product line - including *Hauschka, Lindos,* and *Phytokosma* - are sold in North America.

COMMUNITY

Living and Working Together

In many areas of North America, people have formed "communities of work", drawing together by their interest in anthroposophy and a common concern for answering human needs.

In Kimberton, outside Philadelphia, for example, there are now three villages with the handicapped, a Waldorf School, a medical practice, a biodynamic farm and store, and several smaller enterprises. Similar communities, each with its own character, can be found in the following:

Boston, MA , Boulder, CO, Chicago, IL, Detroit, MI, Los Angeles, CA, Milwaukee, WI, Washington, DC, Fair Oaks, CA, Wilton, NH, Harlemville, NY, & Chestnut Ridge, NY

For a listing of activities by region, please write

Anthroposophical Society in America
1923 Geddes Avenue
Ann Arbor, MI 48104

313-662-9355 phone
313-662-1727 fax
Toll-free 1-888-757-2742`

FOR THE ELDERLY

An Active Retirement

The Fellowship Community is an inter-generation community focusing on care for the aging. A farm, craft shops for weaving, pottery and candlemaking, workshops for printing, woodwork and metalwork, a gift shop, a medical practice, study groups and an active cultural life ensure that growing old does not mean growing apart from the nurturing rhythms of day-to-day life.

Because co-workers and their families live in the community, both young and old have the opportunity to learn from and to nurture each other.

Fellowship Community
241 Hungry Hollow road
Chestnut Ridge, NY 10977
914-256-8499

Hesperus Community
Toronto, Canada

Iona Residential Fellowship
(a retirement home at Rudolf Steiner College)
c/o Dr. Uwe Stave
8481 Menke Way
Citrus Heights,CA 95610
916-722-4610

Simeon Center
715 Wolf Hill Road
Hillsdale, NY 12529

THE ARTS

Color, Form and Movement

Eurythmy translates the sounds, phrases and rhythms of speech, or the dynamic elements of music, into movement and gesture. The result is what Steiner called "visible speech" and "visible song." All that is sounded audibly is brought from our inner life; thus eurythmy could be called the movement language of the soul.

Eurythmy is performed on stages across the world; but it also has applications in pedagogy – including an integral role in the Waldorf school curriculum – and as an art therapy.

Eurythmy Association of North America
84 Suffolk Lane
Garden City, NY 11530
516-741-7167

School of Eurythmy
285 Hungry Hollow Road
Chestnut Ridge, NY 10977
914-352-5071

Section for Speech, Eurythmy and Music
P. O. Box 639
Kimberton, PA 19442
215-935-2524

Speech and Drama

The art of speech formation draws on the creative and curative forces inherent in language. The rhythms, sounds and gestures of speech become tools of expression for the poetic imagination. The actor who delves into this realm of language and gesture can bring an inner world of soul and spirit to the stage. There are several speech and acting programs in the English-speaking world.

Association for the Arts of Speech and Drama
c/o Camphill Special Schools
R. D. 1, Glenmore, PA 19343
610-469-9236

Speech and Drama Program of Sunbridge College
100 La Salle Street, #12C
New York, NY 10027
212-678-4471 or 212-580-8115

Association of Speech and Drama
169 Castle Street
Great Barrington, MA 02130
413-528-2932

Music

Much work is being done to revive the musicality of the human being. Sophisticated instrumentation, electronics and amplification, even as they have stretched the boundaries of sonic imagination, have also estranged us from our inner experience of tone.

The popularity of concerts and recorded music reflects our enduring fascination with musical sound, but we also need to *make* music. Workshops and conferences emphasizing this need, and drawing on the fundamental sounds of acoustic instruments and the human voice, help people reconnect with the "harmony of the spheres."

Lyre Association of North America
P. O. Box 504
Kimberton, PA 19442
610-933-3635

Stephan Rasch
Camphill Village
Copake, NY 12516
518-329-3119
Fax 518-329-3215
(Lyre distributor)

Music Studies Program
Norma Lindenberg
1784 Fairview Road
Glenmoore, PA 19343
610-469-2583
(Anthroposophic 3-year music training)

Rose Harmony Association, Inc.
Arnold and Joanne Logan
171 Water Street
Chatham, NY 12037
518-392-7815
518-392-3415 fax
A not-for-profit corporation dedicated to social renewal through the arts. Windrose is the publishing and educational services of the Association. Brochure available.

Catharsis
4625 Minnesota Avenue
Fair Oaks, CA
916-967-7846

IDRIART USA
825 Chestnut Ridge Road
Chestnut Ridge, NY 10977

Painting
The laws of color and form are not bound by matter. As laws of the spirit they play no less a role in the creative process than the brush, the canvas, or the painter's conscious intent.

The painter who allows these laws to work, who lets the colors themselves 'speak', opens the doors to art that can do more than reproduce the visible world: it can embody something of the world of spirit. There are many artists and programs, here and abroad, working out of this understanding of visual art.

Atelier House School of Painting
R. D. 2, Box 233, Harlemville
Ghent, New York 12075
518-672-7222

Arteum School of Painting in America
RD#2, Box 233A
Harlemville-Ghent, NY 12075
518-672-7222

Phoenix Art Group
247 Main Street
Metuchen, NJ 08840
908-906-1999

Architecture

It is not enough that a home, office building, school or factory blend beauty and function. It should also be ecologically sound, and reflect the character of its region or culture.

Rudolf Steiner's architectural vision balanced these and other parameters in search of environments that could enhance the physical, psychological and spiritual well-being of the people who live and work in them.

Structures that echo the organic forms found in nature are a distinctive element in many such buildings. The Goetheanum in Dornach, Switzerland, designed by Steiner himself, is a prominent example of this 'style' of architecture.

Center for Architectural and Design Research
David Adams
15654 Rattlesnake Road
Grass Valley, CA 95949
Brochure and information about architects, artists, lazuring services

Form - Color - Design
Jorge Sanz-Cardona
PO Box 722
Westwood, NJ 07675-0722
201-664-6007

Color in Architecture

Charles Andrade
1113 Kingwood Drive
Takoma Park, MD 20912
301-445-5918
Lazure custom interiors

ColorSpace
Robert Logsdon
PO Box 581
Great Barrington, MA 01230
413-528-3524
Furniture, interior design, decorative painting, stained glass

John Stalfo
3405 N. Hamlin
Chicago, IL 60618

Terry Mullen
PO Box 272
Great Barrington, MA 01230
413-528-4319
US distributor of organic lazure products

Sculpture

Steiner spoke of the spiritual qualities inherent in sculptural forms and how they influence the human being, both as sculptor and as viewer. He also related the spatial arts to time, through the laws that govern the metamorphosis of one form into another. This approach to the plastic arts can also shed new light on the principles of human development.

Sculpture Studio
32 Mansfield Road
Hillsdale, NY 12529
518-325-4782
Atelier House 518-672-7222

Goethean Studies

Offers students a profoundly spiritual yet practical approach to the study of nature. Based on Goethe's scientific method — starting with the phenomena and integrating science and art — this course focuses on developing powers of perception as awakeners of the inner life.

Dennis Klocek
Goethean Studies Program
Rudolf Steiner College
9200 Fair Oaks Boulevard
Fair Oaks, CA 95628
916-961-8727

FINANCE AND CONSULTANCY

Learning to Cooperate

In a community of human beings working together, the well-being of the community will be the greater, the less the individual claims for himself the proceeds of the work he has himself done; i.e., the more of these proceeds he makes over to his fellow workers, and the more his own requirements are satisfied, not out of his own work done, but out of work done by the others.

– Rudolf Steiner

The Rudolf Steiner Foundation is linked to a network of banks and financial institutions in other countries that are seeking new ways of working with money. The Foundation is set up to facilitate transactions between donors, lenders and receivers. Interest-bearing loan accounts are available to individuals and organization who wish to participate in the growth of Anthroposophical initiatives.

The Rudolf Steiner Foundation
RD. 1, Box 147A
Chatham, NY 12037
518-672-4414

The **Shared Gifting Group of the Mid-States** is a foundation promoting financial awareness and mutual support through giving. Grants go primarily to anthroposophically inspired initiatives in the Mid-West. Encouraging shared giving among Waldorf schools is a particular concern.

**The Shared Gifting Group
of the Mid-States**
1555 N. Sandburg Terrace, #402K
Chicago, IL 60610

Envision Associates is an organization and community development consultancy group working in the non-profit and profit sectors. Areas of focus include team building, long-term planning, and conflict resolution. It is connected with similar consulting organizations working with anthroposophy in other countries, whose members form the Association for Social Development.

Envision Associates
285 Hungry Hollow Road
Chestnut Ridge, NY 10977
914-425-3334

PUBLISHING

Alternative Presses

The Anthroposophic Press has been publishing English translations of Rudolf Steiner's writings and lectures, and the work of other related authors, since 1929. There are currently almost 300 titles in print. The press distributes its books, and those of many other Anthroposophical publishers, throughout North America.

Anthroposophic Press & Lindisfarne Press
R. R. 4, Box 94 A-1
Hudson, NY 12534
Phone 518-851-2054
Fax 518-851-2047
Toll-free fax 1-800-925-1795

Mercury Press is a small publishing house owned and operated by the Fellowship Community.

Mercury Press
241 Hungry Hollow Road
Chestnut Ridge, NY 10977
914-425-9357

Rudolf Steiner College Press publishes books on Waldorf education, lectures and essays by Steiner and other authors, available at its store or by mail order.

Rudolf Steiner College Press
St. George Press
9200 Fair Oaks Boulevard
Fair Oaks, CA 95628
916-961-8729

Journal for Anthroposophy
3700 South Ranch Road 12
Dripping Springs, TX 78620
518-894-0746

Anthroposophical Translators and Editors Association
136 Neck Road
Old Lyme, CT 06371
203-434-7442

Margaret Fuller Corporation publishes the *Threefold Review*, a journal devoted to questions of social, cultural and economic renewal.

Margaret Fuller Corporation
P. O Box 6
Philmont, NY 12565
518-392-5728

Adonis Press is devoted primarily to the arts.

Adonis Press
315 Rodman Road
Hillsdale, NY 12529
518-325-7182

Michaelmas Press publishes resources on topics related to Waldorf education: *A Waldorf Student Reading List* and *Resources for Parent Associations.*

Michaelmas Press
P.O. Box 702
Amesbury, MA 01913-0016
508-388-7066
508-388-1450

Octavo Editions produced *Physics is Fun* by Roberto Trostli

Octavo Editions
Thomasina Webb
160 Varick Street
New York, NY 10013
212-229-2266

Lilipoh is a new newspaper dedicated to natural medicine (4 x a year)

Lilipoh
228 Hungry Hollow Road
Chestnut Ridge, NY 10977

Studio Editions publishes plays for use in Waldorf communities

Studio Editions
Martha Keltz 410-467-8561
3303 Guilford Ave. #3
Baltimore, MD 21218

AWSNA Publications
Chairman, David Mitchell
3911 Bannister Road,
Fair Oaks, CA 95628

Publishers in The United Kingdom

Steiner Education is a journal for Rudolf Steiner Waldorf Education (2 copies per year).

Steiner Education
The Sprig,
Ashdown Road, Forest Row,
East Sussex RH18 5HP, England
(0342)-82- 2115

Anthroposophy Today
36 Church Walk
Leatherhead
Surrey KT22 8HH
United Kingdom

Hawthorn Press
Hawthorn House
1 Lansdown Lane
Stroud GL5 1BJ, England
043-75-7040

Robinswood Press
30 South Avenue
Stourbridge
West Midlands, DY8 3XY, England
0384 -39-7475

Rudolf Steiner Press
35 Park Road
London, NW1 6XT, England

Temple Lodge Press
51 Queen Caroline Street
London, W5 9QL , England
081-748-0571

THE CHRISTIAN COMMUNITY

Movement for Religious Renewal

The Christian Community is a world-wide movement for religious renewal founded in 1922 with the help of Rudolf Steiner. The Christian Community, as organized, has no formulated doctrine and neither the priests nor the members are required to believe in any "official" doctrine; there is complete freedom of thought and belief.

In North America there are twelve centers with resident priests who also visit areas without established congregations. The priests provide pastoral counseling and religious education for children and adults, as well as celebrating the renewed seven sacraments which accompany and bless all stages of life from birth to death. The Service for Children is held for school-age children and their parents. All events are open to everyone.

For information and to locate the nearest center or inquire about priest's training, contact:

The Christian Community
1545 West Pratt Boulevard
Chicago, IL 60626
312-465-3375